THE SECRET WAR BETWEEN HITLER AND STALIN

THE SECRET WAR BETWEEN HITLER AND STALIN

INTELLIGENCE AND COUNTERINTELLIGENCE ON THE EASTERN FRONT

NORMAN RIDLEY

FRONTLINE
BOOKS

THE SECRET WAR BETWEEN HITLER AND STALIN
Intelligence and Counterintelligence on the Eastern Front

First published in Great Britain in 2025
by Frontline Books
An imprint of
Pen & Sword Books Ltd
Yorkshire - Philadelphia
Copyright © Norman Ridley
ISBN 978 1 036122102

Typeset by Lapiz Digital
Printed and bound in the UK by CPI Group (UK) Ltd,
Croydon, CR0 4YY.

Printed on paper from a sustainable source by
CPI Group (UK) Ltd, Croydon, CR0 4YY

The Publisher's authorised representative in the EU for product safety is
Authorised Rep Compliance Ltd., Ground Floor, 71 Lower Baggot Street,
Dublin D02 P593, Ireland.
www.arccompliance.com

For a complete list of Pen & Sword titles please contact
PEN & SWORD BOOKS LTD
47 Church Street, Barnsley, South Yorkshire, S70 2AS, England
E-mail: enquiries@pen-and-sword.co.uk
Website: www.pen-and-sword.co.uk
or
PEN & SWORD BOOKS
1950 Lawrence Rd, Havertown, PA 19083, USA
E-mail: uspen-and-sword@casematepublishers.com

CONTENTS

Chapter 1

INTELLIGENCE AND COUNTERINTELLIGENCE

'The question of how policy makers gauge their
adversaries' intentions remains fundamental to
international relations... and world affairs.'[1]

Intelligence has been called the 'eyes, ears and nose' of a state and its armed forces filtering the sensual input for signs of danger, while counterintelligence, adhering to the analogy, might be described as its 'immune system', which identifies and seeks to eliminate threats.[2] The threat might then evolve to outwit such defences and so the battle goes on. In time of war, the adaptability and resilience of the 'immune system' will ultimately determine whether or not the host can survive. By comparing the performance of the intelligence and counterintelligence agencies of Germany and the Soviet Union during the course of the war on the Eastern Front between 1941 and 1945, it will be shown that they had a profound effect on the ultimate outcome. Good intelligence, used correctly, helps a combatant to magnify such advantages as they may have and minimise the debilitating effects of their weaknesses. In this way intelligence acts as a 'force multiplier', but faulty intelligence, or good intelligence misapplied, has the opposite effect of misdirecting operations as a 'force diluter', squandering material and strategic advantages.[3]

Intelligence is inherently complicated, muddled and difficult to interpret. It hardly ever provides an unambiguous picture of the enemy's capabilities, and even less so of its intentions. When trying to predict the future policy and behaviour of potential or extant adversaries, political decision makers are constantly required to cut through the 'noise' of intelligence feeds and home in on those aspects that provide the best chance of determining what the most advantageous position might be for their own forces. Analysing an adversary's intentions is often a complex process involving differentiating the credible from the spurious. What often amounts to an overload of information clouding the issues derives from a number of difficulties. Not least is the probability that some intelligence has been manipulated by an adversary to deceive. Then there is the likelihood of contradictory intelligence emanating from various agencies who, although on the same side, are often in competition with each other for funding and influence and their own champions in the decision making hierarchy do not have a strong incentive to compromise. Often these differences, especially regarding interpretation of the intelligence are not so much a personal matter for individuals but reflect an entrenched philosophy within each department.

Each decision maker has their own background and cognitive capabilities, alongside what may be deep-rooted beliefs and prejudices, and it is against this that they evaluate information. In this case there may be some divergence of opinion if decisions are made by a group. The response to intelligence is a process that does not always free itself from conceptual bias and does not necessarily result in rational action. Some decision makers are influenced more by intelligence that appeals to their emotional sense by virtue of their ability to understand it and visualise its context within their world view. In others, a personal impression acquired from direct interaction with leaders about whom intelligence has been gathered can have an overriding influence on how they evaluate information especially if it conflicts with their pre-existing theories and stated position. If intelligence demands a re-evaluation of a personality or situation, to avoid embarrassment, the decision maker may choose not to embark upon what for them might be a psychologically costly and destabilising journey. It may become a question of rank or authority within the decision making group as to which opinions are given greater consideration.

The level of perceived threat resulting from a reading and assessment of the intelligence will determine what course of action a state might take. An assessment of an adversary's military intentions is often made on the basis of the investment assigned to a particular action. Where intelligence reveals enemy activity that involves expenditure of significant resources it might be afforded greater credibility whereas 'cheap talk' backed up by little or no factual evidence is often ignored. Sometimes a state will deliberately send signals to indicate that it is taking a particular course of action while at others it will be at great pains to disguise it and, of course, there will be times when it wishes to suggest that it is taking an action when, in fact it is not or may be doing the opposite of what it appears to be doing. States might, for instance, undertake significant expenditure in the manufacture of armaments in order to send signals of intent, or at least capabilities, to influence political negotiations or gain psychological advantage in a dispute.

There might well be a difference in response to intelligence based on whether it relates to short or long-term issues. During crises and wartime, there is considerable pressure to arrive at quick decisions whereas less time constrained evaluation might be delayed pending further investigation. If a state is perceived to have expansionist intentions to increase its power and influence beyond its own borders, then intelligence about its preparations becomes of paramount importance. There are two issues involved here. Firstly, it is vital for a potential adversary to ascertain the level of credibility of any intentions about hostile actions and secondly, they will want to find out the extent to which any response they make affects the ongoing plans of the aggressor.

During the 1930s and 1940s, strategic intelligence gathered by countries mostly came through normal diplomatic channels as part of the everyday activities of embassies but the gathering and reporting from countries under totalitarian regimes was fraught with particular difficulties. In the Soviet Union, for instance, most foreign diplomats lived in conditions more appropriate to an open prison. In such heavily controlled societies, the secret acquisition of intelligence was often the only recourse and, for that reason, was clearly more important. By its nature, however, this intelligence lacked effective means of verification. It was what historian Richard Overy called 'a jigsaw puzzle full of missing pieces'.[4]

Where intelligence was gathered, either through diplomatic channels or through a variety of other agencies, some of which were part of the armed forces, there were often issues surrounding the compilation, analysis and integration of information not to mention its application free of political distortion and interference. Such manipulation of intelligence was in evidence particularly in both Germany and the Soviet Union where it was often tailored to conform with preconceptions and established prejudices of Adolf Hitler and Joseph Stalin. Hermann Göring, for instance, remarked that 'when [Hitler] had a certain purpose in mind, he only reasoned according to that purpose'.[5]

While both of these countries made the acquisition of useful intelligence difficult there were distinct differences when it came to analysing strategic intentions against which the intelligence was to be assessed. However much Hitler claimed that he had no warlike intentions towards the end of the 1930s, the overriding mood in Europe was that such assurances in no way reflected his true ambitions but no country could claim to have similar confidence about understanding the real intentions of the Soviet leadership.

During the Second World War, in terms of intelligence and counterintelligence, the roles of aggressor and resister; of occupier and liberator, were quite different. One was operating in a hostile, alien landscape while the other had more awareness and understanding of the environment and its populations. At the outset, Hitler and the German High Command scorned their intelligence services as quite superfluous to the requirements for victory, which left them very much in the dark concerning Soviet capabilities beyond their own deeply arrogant and prejudiced misconceptions. In a short time, however, they were forced to revisit that assessment time and time again as Soviet counterintelligence and military deception strategies combined to thwart their ambitions.

Intelligence and counterintelligence had been a concept deeply embedded in the Soviet state since its inception in 1917 as it battled against enemies, real and imagined, beyond its border and was well placed to adapt to its wartime role. The three foundations underpinning its operations were:

- The recruitment of large numbers of informants to the point of redundancy.
- The use of security forces to man extensive checkpoints on roads and railways and carry out incessant document checks.
- The use of terror and deportation to deter collaboration with the enemy.

For the Soviets, the security of the state depended upon its counterintelligence services. One German *Fremde Heere Ost* (Foreign Armies East, FHO) report noted that there was little distinction between 'police spying for the protection of the regime and [combatting] foreign activities'. Every Soviet citizen they said was 'encouraged to be on guard' to the point where 'security and counterintelligence work [went] hand-in-hand, and a great amount of energy [was] devoted to both'.[6] The Germans, however, had been obsessed with identifying and eliminating enemies within the Reich and had much less experience of operating beyond its own borders.

The application of deception as a device to achieve military advantage is fundamental to the narrative of German-Soviet intelligence and counterintelligence operations on the Eastern Front and much of this book will examine the ways in which both sides used it. On the German side, their most effective use of deception was during Operation Kremlin but as the tide of war turned against the Wehrmacht it was the Soviets who applied the strategy to spectacular advantage during a number of operations from Stalingrad to Kursk and beyond.

Chapter 2

THE EARLY YEARS OF SOVIET INTELLIGENCE

'We stand for organized terror –
this should be frankly admitted.'

Feliks Dzerzhinsky,
Head of the VCheKa secret police, 1918

Ever since 1917, Soviet counterintelligence had earned a reputation as a force to be reckoned with by being ruthlessly efficient at combatting clandestine operations on its territory by foreign countries. They had elevated their operations to a fine art underpinned by terror and brute force. Despite the leader of the Bolshevik Revolution in Russia Vladimir Lenin having publicly insisted, even before the start of the revolution, that a proletarian dictatorship would have no need for an internal security service, he had already laid the foundations of a coercive organisation to ensure the success of the revolution and bring about the eliminate of any political opposition. Numerous peasant revolts had erupted throughout Bolshevik-controlled territory and Lenin's response was to unleash terror to quash them. The *Ministerstvo Vnutrennikh Del* (Ministry of Internal Affairs – MVD), which had been created to implement this was renamed some months later as the *Naródny Komissariát Vnútrennih del* (People's Commissariat of Internal Affairs – NKVD). When it was clear that the largely inexperienced and unqualified NKVD staff were unable to carry out all functions allocated to it, a secret political police, the *Vserossijskaya Chrezvychajnaya Komissiya* (All-Russian Extraordinary Commission for Combating Counter-Revolution, Sabotage and Speculation – abbreviated to VCheKa) was established on 20 December 1917. It basically took over the duties of the dissolved *Ochranka* secret police force of the repressive Tsarist regime. Seeing no necessity to 'reinvent the wheel', the VCheKa made liberal use of *Ochranka* methods and in some cases its personnel, as well. The head of this new organisation was a Polish aristocrat turned communist, Feliks 'Iron Felix' Edmundovich Dzerzhinsky, who had spent years in Tsarist prisons or exile, for his pre-revolutionary activities with Polish and Lithuanian Social Democrats between 1895 and 1912. Described by the historian Richard Deacon as 'ruthless, cold, clear-headed, gifted with organisational talents', he insisted from the start that he must have full powers and not be subject to any supervision, a demand that the founding head and leader of the Bolshevik government Vladimir Lenin was quick to concede with the comment that 'The important thing for us to remember is that the VCheKas are directly carrying out the dictatorship of the proletariat, and in this respect their role is invaluable'. The diplomat Robert Bruce Lockhart described Dzerzhinsky as 'A man of correct manners and quiet speech, but without a ray of humour in his character. The most remarkable thing about him was his eyes. Deeply sunk, they blazed with a steady fire of fanaticism. They never twitched. His eyelids seemed paralysed.'[1]

Theoretically subordinated to the *Sovnarkom* (Council of People's Commissars), the VCheKa's function was to

liquidate counter-revolution and sabotage, to hand over counterrevolutionaries and saboteurs to the revolutionary tribunals, and to apply such measures of repression as confiscation, deprivation of ration cards, publication of lists of enemies of the people etc.[2]

Then, having been designed initially to focus on internal opposition, in September 1918 the VCheKa, now operating as a militarised agency, launched a six-week campaign of mass arrests, rape, torture and extra-judicial executions in response to a failed assassination attempt on Lenin. This 'Red Terror' as it became known, was a strategy designed to eliminate entire social groups of the former ruling elites and anyone acting or conspiring against the government.

In this they were assisted by elements of the *Glavnoye Razvedyvatel'noye Upravleniye* (Bolshevik military intelligence – GRU). They rounded up First World War deserters and also played a leading role in the suppression of the anti-Soviet Kronstadt rebellion, a 1921 insurrection of Soviet sailors and civilians from various ships and garrisons. These insurrectionists had passed resolutions demanding immediate new elections to the Soviet by secret ballot, freedom of speech and the press for all left-wing Socialist parties, freedom of assembly for trade unions and peasant organisations, abolition of communist political agencies in the army and navy, immediate withdrawal of all grain requisitioning squads, and re-establishment of a free market for the peasants. Overall estimates of the number of people murdered by the Chekists vary widely but scholars are confident that it is in the region of 250,000. The Bolshevik leadership showed little enthusiasm to curb the VCheKa excesses and actually seemed to encourage them as a means of consolidating their control of the Russian state and its population.

On 28 January 1918, the Red Army was created and the first military counterintelligence organization, the *Voennyi Otdel* (Military Department – VO), was established within the VCheKa. It included counterintelligence organisations that had previously existed in the armies in the field. On 1 January 1919, the VO was renamed *Osobykh Otdel* (Special Department of the Main State Security Department – OO/NKVD) whose responsibilities were defined as 'fighting counterrevolution and espionage within the army and fleet' but their role went far beyond the purely military.[3] Counterintelligence within the Red Army itself was deemed essential given that non-communist specialists were recruited to create the new Bolshevik economy. The OO kept these men under constant surveillance for security reasons. Special sections were stablished in military units under VCheKa control. For the first time in modern history, a military intelligence agency was established that was independent of the military it sought to monitor.

With a mandate to fight against the counterrevolutionaries, the first OO chief, Mikhail S. Kedrov, executed many civilians, including children, during the Russian Civil War. Kedrov was also expected to deal with corruption, desertions and criminality within the armed forces especially activity that was seen as anti-Soviet. The Bolsheviks had no choice but to retain former Tsarist army officers during the Civil War (1918–1922) that had followed the October Revolution but their loyalty was always questioned, however, and many were suspected of disloyalty to the new regime and were purged from the ranks, imprisoned and in some cases executed.

On 20 December 1920, the foreign intelligence, part of the OO, became a separate department, the *Sluzhba Vneshnei Razvedki*, (Foreign Intelligence Service – SVR) later becoming the all-powerful First Directorate. Then, on 7 July 1922, the OO was split. One half retained the OO acronym (counterintelligence in the armed forces) and the other was the *Kontrrazvedyvatel'nyi Otdel* (Counterintelligence Department; later the 2nd Directorate – KRO) in charge of internal counterintelligence and run by Artur Artuzov. From a mere 25 employees at its inauguration, the VCheKa, at the end of 1919, boasted a staggering 37,000.

The threat of invasion by foreign powers to crush Bolshevism and prevent it spreading demanded that the VCheKa also quickly develop a strategy to warn of such an eventuality. The lack of diplomatic relations with other countries meant that they had to work outside the normal political structures and infiltrate agents into neighbouring states to report on military activity there. A special foreign section was created in spring 1920 to recruit agents locally and then in September, a special commission chaired by Dzerzhinsky issued a decree that required it to

- Organise and control agents abroad.
- Combat foreign intelligence agencies working within Russia.[4]

In particular, it was to collect information about the Menshevik counterrevolutionaries.

Then, on 6 February 1922, the VCheKa was abolished and replaced by the *Gosudarstvennoe Politicheskoe Upravlenie* (State Political Administration – GPU), which was effectively the intelligence service and secret police of the Russian Soviet Federative Socialist Republics and as such it became a section of the NKVD. Later, with the creation of the Soviet Union in December 1922, all state security was unified under the *Ob'edinennoe Gosudarstvennoe Politicheskoe Upravlenie* (Joint State Political Directorate – OGPU) with extra responsibility for political control to do the following:

- Identify counterrevolutionary terrorist organisations in neighbouring countries.
- Develop an intelligence and counterintelligence capability.
- Process and analyse intelligence.
- Implement measures against the Mensheviks.[5]

On 11 January 1923, a Special Bureau for Disinformation was created within the GPU to confront counterrevolutionary elements both within and beyond the borders of the Soviet Union. Its methodology included the creation of bogus opposition movements in order to attract anti-Soviet elements and probe their links to Western intelligence services and émigré organisations.

For most of the 1920s, the Fifth (foreign intelligence) Department of the *Glavnoe Upravlenie Gosudarstvennoi Bezopastnosti* (NKVD's Chief Directorate for State Security – GUGB) focused on foreign threats to the young Bolshevik state ranging from Russian émigrés to the followers of Leon Trotsky. Gradually it broadened its coverage to include the acquisition of foreign technical secrets. After the VCheKa excesses of the Red Terror, the GPU was expected to act with more restraint and, rather than be allowed to execute suspected counterrevolutionaries at will, was obliged to bring them to a court of law.

The GPU continued to run the Gulag system of VCheKa forced labour camps that Dzerzhinsky had set up but, in a foretaste of deception as a tool of counterintelligence, which was to play such a crucial part in the Second World War, also created The Trust, a fabricated anti-Bolshevik underground used as a deception against White Russian émigrés and foreign intelligence services, which operated from 1921 until 1926.[6]

As well as striving to discover the military plans and intentions of adversaries such as Britain, France, Germany, the United States and Japan, Soviet spies set out to obtain Western industrial and economic secrets to take forward their plans for industrialisation of the Soviet economy. To do this, they employed a number of different types of spy. Along with other countries they used *'legal'nye rezidenty* ('legal' diplomatic cover) in their consulates and embassies and also *nelegal'nye rezidenty* ('illegal' agents) posing as Soviet press and trade delegates, as well others who infiltrated workers' unions, defence industries, and merchant marine crews. Some served a dual purpose by fomenting labour disputes and strikes in vulnerable industries. When he came to power in 1924, after Lenin's death, Josef Stalin authorised his intelligence agencies to hunt down and murder opponents of the regime living in exile. Little pretence was made to indicate that state security was anything other than under the direct control of the Soviet Politburo.

The Soviet state, insecure to the point of paranoia, invested much in its intelligence agencies right from the start. Even in 1917, it already had years of experience in conspiracy, sabotage and intelligence activities against the Tsar's *Okhrana* secret police. By the mid-1920s, counterintelligence was the living essence of an administration obsessed with rooting out and destroying its enemies, real and imagined, both within and without. The question was whether political control and manipulation of the state's intelligence and counterintelligence agencies would allow them to meet the challenges from a resurgent Nazi German state or whether they would be devoured by the demons, again real and imagined, that stalked the Kremlin.

Chapter 3

THE ABWEHR

'[The Abwehr] functioned as an intelligence service, provided the
OKW with information about the nation's enemies, while under the
directorship of a man who by 1936, and perhaps earlier, had become
more than simply a passive anti-Nazi.'[1]

American historian Robin Winks says that the Abwehr was 'an abysmal
failure, failing to forecast Operation Toch, or Operation Husky, or
Operation Overlord'.[2] British historian Hugh Trevor-Roper says it was
'rotten with corruption, notoriously inefficient and politically suspect'.
He adds that it was under the 'negligent rule' of Admiral Canaris,
who was 'more interested in anti-Nazi intrigue than in his official
duties'.[3] Historian Norman Davies agrees with this observation and
avows that Canaris 'was anything but a Nazi enthusiast'.[4] According
to Trevor-Roper, for the first two years of the war the Abwehr was a
'happy parasite' that was 'borne along ... on the success of the German
army'.[5] When the tide turned against the Nazi's and the Abwehr was
unable to produce the intelligence the leadership demanded, it was
merged into the SS in 1944. Numerous intelligence failures and general
incompetence led to catastrophic disasters in both the eastern and
western campaigns for the German military.

Two months after the end of the First World War, the Paris Peace
Conference was formally opened on 18 January 1919 where the
victorious Allies discussed peace terms to be imposed upon the
defeated Axis Powers. These were formalised into the Treaty of
Versailles, signed on 28 June 1919, the terms of which included the
dissolution of the German *Abteilung Fremde Heere* (Foreign Armies
Department), which had been established during the war to deal with
enemy reconnaissance and military-political issues. The size of the
Reichswehr (German defence force) was to be no more than 100,000
men but the Germans found ways and means of circumventing the

restrictions by creating a *Truppenamt* (General Staff Headquarters), the third department of which was *Heeres Statistische Abteilung* (Army Statistics Department) tasked with 'collection and processing of statistical material on foreign armies'.[6] This was essentially a military intelligence and counterintelligence organisation and an illicit reincarnation of the *Abteilung Fremde Heere*. It became commonly known as the *Amt Auslands und Abwehr* (Abwehr) with Lieutenant Colonel Friedrich Gempp as its first chief. At first it had little relevance within Germany's humiliated military establishment consisting, as it did, of only ten officers with a small clerical staff. It would face an uphill battle to assert itself after Field Marshal Paul von Hindenburg's had called its predecessor unreliable and little more than an annoyance. Condemnation from such a luminary was a poor foundation on which to build.

The Allies had initially prohibited any reformation of a German intelligence service and frowned on it but they compromised by allowing the Abwehr to operate on a severely restricted basis acting only as a defence against foreign espionage. The Abwehr took advantage and set up their *Abwehrstellen* (stations – ASTs) at the headquarters of each of the *Wehrkreise*) (military districts), all located in major urban centres throughout the country. ASTs were staffed by officers who had some knowledge of the Russian language. Over time, as restrictions eased, the number of military districts increased and some of the bigger ASTs acquired *Abwehrnebenstellen* (substations – NESTs). It was organised into three sections:

- Reconnaissance
- Cipher and radio monitoring
- Counterespionage

The Abwehr was independent of the three service commands – army, navy and air force – each of which had its own intelligence staff who were essentially devoid of intelligence gathering capabilities and restricted to analysis, evaluation and dissemination of information rather conducting their own secret intelligence gathering activities themselves. Under Gempp, the Abwehr was mostly occupied monitoring the activities of trade unionists and communists as well as embryonic nationalist organisations such as the NSDAP.

In June 1927, Gempp was promoted to general, which made him far too high ranking to be left in the Abwehr so he was replaced by Major Günther Schwantes, a weak administrator who quickly fell prey to the unscrupulously ambitious Kurt von Schleicher. Before long, von

Schleicher had inveigled a new German defence minister to centralise all intelligence agencies under a single independent command, separated from the General Staff, with him at its head. Within a few years, von Schleicher, himself, had been appointed as German Minister of Defence and, on 7 June 1932, resurrected the old title of *Abteilung Fremde Heere* and brought in a naval officer, Captain Konrad Patzig, to reorganise it, but it still remained a backwater, and not a place where ambitious and capable military officers would choose to go advance their careers. Resources were thin on the ground and only manipulative politicians like von Schleicher were attracted to it as a stepping stone to higher office.

During peacetime there were no facilities for ground and aerial reconnaissance, radio and wireless intercepts and, of course, no prisoner interrogation opportunities. Patzig, however, made good use of open intelligence sources such as technical magazines and daily press reports, which proved invaluable for not only their editorials and news but for intelligence gleaned from classified advertising sections such as job advertisements and scientific articles. This was much more difficult when analysing the Soviet press, which was under total political control and heavily propagandised.

Under Patzig, the Abwehr established lines of communication with all three services – navy, army and air force. He proceeded to divide the service into three *Abteilung* (groups):

- *Abt I* was charged with offensive intelligence, including espionage.
- *Abt II* was given sabotage and subversion.
- *Abt III* dealt with counterintelligence and security.

Abt I had sections for army, naval, air and economic intelligence, which were further broken down into geographical subsections, dealing with particular countries or areas. In neutral countries, the Abwehr frequently disguised its organisation by attaching its personnel to the German Embassy or to trade missions. Such postings were referred to as *Kriegsorganisationen* (War Organisations – KOs) and usually operated under cover of the diplomatic mission.

Patzig, who had never been a supporter of the NSDAP, made few friends in the High Command and found himself exposed to scrutiny when the Nazis came to power. He was soon dismissed from post by Reichminister of War, Werner von Blomberg ostensibly for authorising illegal aerial surveillance of Poland and France and, on 1 January 1935, another navy man, Admiral Wilhelm Canaris, replaced him. Patzig warned Canaris that he would have to settle in quickly to defend the service against the constant plotting of Heinrich Himmler and Reinhard Heydrich who conspired endlessly to have the Abwehr taken under the wing of the *Sicherheitsdienst* (intelligence agency – SD – of the *Schutzstaffel* (Nazi paramilitary organisation – SS). The SD existed independently of the German military as an organ of the NSDAP, a subsidiary division of Himmler's powerful *Reichssicherheitshauptamt* (Reich Security Main Office – RSHA) whose focus was on rigorous pursuit of real and imagines enemies of the state. While the Abwehr was limited to military intelligence, the SD was free to focus on political and ideological intelligence both inside and outside Germany. Himmler had founded the SS in 1931 to counter what he saw as the threat posed by subversive elements within the Nazi Party and under Heydrich's ruthless leadership this had been built up into a formidable surveillance and intelligence gathering agency adept at employing all the dark arts in the interminable power struggles within the Nazi Party. In practice, there was no clear delineation of responsibility between the Abwehr and the SD who often invaded each other's sphere of interest, leading to constant conflict and rivalry. They did, however, reach an understanding on 'ten principles' to coordinate action, which included an agreement that military intelligence and counterintelligence were the exclusive prerogative of the Abwehr and political intelligence under the control of the SD.

The Abwehr and SD were not the only intelligence services, however. All Nazi leaders of consequence had their own private intelligence agencies to varying degrees, which they employed primarily to further their own personal ambitions. Naturally, intelligence gathered by such as Göring's *Forschungsamt* was jealously hoarded and not shared with other agencies but, in any case, none apart from the Abwehr had the capacity, or indeed the inclination, to operate beyond Germany's borders. It is a reflection of the stresses within the political sphere that most of the others were preoccupied with spying on each other, and the armed forces, to gain advantage and preferment within the Nazi political structure.

At the time of Canaris's arrival, the Abwehr was still a small department that was mainly preoccupied with reporting intelligence about Poland but the new man was determined to build up the service through his many foreign contacts. In 1936, Canaris visited Estonia for secret negotiations with the Chief of the General Staff of the Estonian army and an agreement was reached on the exchange of intelligence information on the Soviet Union. An Estonian intelligence centre, called Group 6513 was established under Baron Andrey von Uexkul.

Under the authority of the Estonian government, the Abwehr now set up sabotage and reconnaissance bases on Estonian territory and equipped the Estonian special services with cameras with telescopic lenses and radio interception equipment to organise covert surveillance of the territory of a potential enemy. Photographic equipment was also installed on the lighthouses of the Gulf of Finland to photograph warships of the Soviet navy.

Even the Abwehr was described as Canaris's own private intelligence agency. Working out of his tiny, cramped office on the Tirpitzufer by the Landwehr Canal next to the OKW complex, he was able to follow the established pattern by running his agency virtually as a personal fiefdom, which would later attract the approbation of Reich Propaganda Miniter Joseph Goebbels in particular. The internal layout of these central offices was a maze of chaotically interconnected rooms and halls, winding corridors, and stairs that went up and down in no discernible pattern. It was easy for visitors to get lost in the building. Left very much to his own devices, Canaris prioritised making best use of his resources, which meant that he set about stripping the Abwehr of its non-espionage functions such as aerial reconnaissance, suggesting that Canaris did not fully realise the value of serial photographs as a source of intelligence in the planning of tactical operations.

His own lukewarm enthusiasm for the Nazi regime ensured that many of those he recruited for higher staff roles, as his department slowly grew, exhibit a political scepticism and more often than not, an independent frame of mind. Avid Nazis were posted to outstations. Then, after Hitler's removal of his Minister of Defence, Field Marshal Werner von Blomberg, on trumped up charges in January 1938, Canaris reorganised the Abwehr by subdividing it into three *Abteilungs* (main sections) after which it increased its importance and became an *Amstgruppe* within the OKW (Supreme Command of the German Armed Forces).

Abteilung Zentralabteilung (Central Division, Department Z) was the control and coordinating section under General Major Hans Oster. *Amtsgruppe Ausland* (Foreign Branch and later known as Foreign Intelligence Group) liaised with the OKW and the general staffs of the services and coordinated with the German *Auswärtiges Amt* (Foreign Office) on military matters, including evaluation of captured documents, and evaluation of foreign press and radio broadcasts. This was run by Captain Bürkner.

A third section was subdivided into *Abwehr I, II* and *III* (also called *Abteilung I, II, III*). *Abwehr I* (Abt I) was commanded by Canaris's friend the 'bluff, hearty, keenly intelligent' Colonel Hans 'Piki' Piekenbrock and was responsible for the collection and evaluation of foreign intelligence.[7] Its main customer was the OKW since most of the information collected was of a purely military nature. It recruited *Vertrauensmannen* (V-men, informants) and engaged in espionage, counterespionage and information gathering. In the west, V-men were generally high calibre Abwehr agents, but in the east the term was used much more loosely and usually used to describe Soviet and other non-German nationals often recruited from exile or émigré groups. Agents were active all across northern European countries and even Britain. This section proved to be the least successful of the three Abteilungs due in no small part to Canaris's indulgence. Trevor-Roper said of him that he was 'a poor organiser and an even worse judge of men as he gave worthless officers considerable independence'.[8] Many on his staff were appointed on the basis of his personal friendship with them. He turned a blind eye to the many instances of operational staff taking advantage of opportunities for self-indulgence in cities such as Paris, Athens and Estoril and as long as the required quota of reports flowed in, they were rarely held to account. It is certain that had OKW seen the Abwehr as a vital component of the German military, it would never have tolerated such a state of affairs. There is little evidence to show that Canaris ever did much to change that opinion or that he ever wanted to take the Abwehr any closer to the heart of the German military machine.

Such a situation within the Abwehr was allowed to continue essentially only because there was no centralised control of the many scattered stations across the globe each with its own priorities, methods and practices according to the physical and social environment in which they operated not to mention the quirks and preferences of station bosses. The inevitable result of allowing such a degree of independence was a shockingly high failure rate of Abwehr operations all throughout the Second World War. It was impossible in many cases to separate truth from fiction and the agencies abroad had little incentive to spend time and effort trying to do so. While Hitler was getting his own way through belligerent diplomacy this hardly made much difference and even after the conquest of Poland, France and the Low Countries few people took much notice of intelligence. 'Who needs it?' seemed to be the attitude, 'look how well we're doing without it'.

It was a different matter altogether putting agents into unconquered enemy territory, however. Here intelligence took on a whole different significance and agents operated in a much more hostile environment. For instance, all known agents who were infiltrated into Britain after 1939, who were, to say the least, inadequately trained and resourced, were rounded up by British counterintelligence in double quick time.

Abwehr II (Abt II) commanded by the aristocratic ex-Austrian army officer, Colonel Erwin von Lahousen-Vivremont, was tasked with subversive activities and sabotage in enemy territory, which it called 'special duties'. It made contact with discontented minority groups in foreign countries for intelligence purposes and included the Brandenburg Regiment. It would become the largest and most active of all German intelligence agencies. Abt II had three major centres for the training of saboteurs and agents in Tegele, near Berlin, in Kwinzsee (Quenzsee), near Brandenburg, and in Himsee, all of which were carefully camouflaged and hidden from prying eyes. Training practice of sabotage techniques was conducted in conditions as close to actual combat as possible.

The Brandenburgers were a special regiment created as part of *Abwehr II* to carry out subversive activities in western Ukraine and the Baltics. Its genesis went back to the First World War in East Africa when Captain Theodore von Hippel had successfully used scouts to penetrate into the rear of the enemy disguised as local residents or dressed up in enemy uniforms. When Canaris took up his post with the Abwehr, he had come across von Hippel's reports and drafted him into his department to form a small detachment of professional intelligence saboteurs called the *Ebbinghaus* Battalion. Prior to the German invasion of Poland, von Hippel recruited Polish-speaking Germans from either side of the border, Poles resident in Germany and Freikorps veterans, as well as a fair number of petty criminals. Unfortunately, they did not cover themselves in glory. A raid on a factory complex at Slask ended in failure with half the attackers killed, was fairly typical of their performance. When Poland capitulated, the *Ebbinghaus* Battalion was disbanded.

Undaunted, von Hippel and Canaris pursued the special forces concept, but this time with professional German commando volunteers. A new unit was formed, the *Lehr und Bau Kompagnie z.b.V. 800* (800th Special Purpose Training and Construction Company), which became known as the Brandenburg-800. It was a volunteer organisation that allowed in only Reich-Germans or persons of German descent. At their training camp in the town of Quenzgut on Quenzsee near the city of Brandenburg, recruits were given intelligence tests and their ability to orientate in a hostile environment was analysed along with their psychological stability, self-control, self-discipline and physical fitness. Gradually, the company expanded into a battalion consisting of motorcycle and parachute platoons, as well as four companies:

1. Kompanie (Baltic/Russian)
2. Kompanie (English, Portuguese and French speaking from North Africa, UK and USA)
3. Kompanie (Sudeten and Yugoslav Germans)
4. Kompanie (Polish Volksdeutsche)

The men were given language training and were intensively trained in sabotage, all types of weapons, hand-to hand combat, handling explosives, basic medical skills and photography, as well as forging of documents. They were deployed in small units of five to twelve at a time. For a short spell in October 1940, Major Hubertus von Aulock took command, but it was passed on to Lieutenant Colonel Paul Haehling von Lanzenauer who led the unit until February 1943.

Recruiting and training focused on the Soviet Union despite the Molotov-Ribbentrop Pact but the new unit had first gone into action in the Netherlands, Belgium and France during *Fall Gelb* (plan for the Battle of France). Their operations relied on surprise and subterfuge to achieve their objectives. Wearing enemy uniforms over their Wehrmacht uniforms, they would penetrate enemy lines using their language skills and local knowledge to get close to their objectives, before taking them by surprise. They would then hold on until the advancing main thrush would catch up. They emerged with a high reputation for daring and success. With the west front relatively secure, von Hippel set up training camps *Krinitsa*, *Barvinek*, *Dukla* and *Kamenitsa*, where Ukrainian nationalists and volunteers from the North Caucasus formed special *Nachtigall* (nightingale), *Roland* and *Bergmann* battalions. In 1941 the Brandenburgers went into action in the Balkans where a detachment of 54 Brandenburgers of the II. Battalion took the *Iron Gates* at Orsova on the Danube during the invasion of Yugoslavia. When Barbarossa was launched, they would later move into the Baltics as part of German Army Group North. Once the invasion of the Soviet Union was launched the Brandenburgers carried out various acts of sabotage including capturing bridges and bridgeheads, obstructing evacuation and destruction of classified documents by Soviet military and civilian agencies. The 1st Battalion of the Abwehr's Brandenburg-800 Regiment, in cooperation with a reinforced company of the Ukrainian nationalists' *Nachtigall* Battalion, were involved in the taking of Lviv and the mass extermination of Lviv's Jews.

Abwehr III (Abt III) was commanded by the meticulously turned out 'stiff and typically Prussian' Colonel Franz-Eccard von Bentivegni. It was the counterintelligence division responsible for security and counterespionage within German industry, planting false information, penetration of foreign intelligence services and investigating acts of sabotage on German soil.[9] In many cases, von Bentivegni often found his department's operations overlapping uncomfortably with those of Himmler's Gestapo who wasted no opportunity to denigrate the whole Abwehr structure and mock his Junker-class demeanour. All Abwehr sections worked well alongside armed forces intelligence services, however, and continued to do so throughout most of the Second World War.

Chapter 4

SECRET GERMAN-SOVIET COOPERATION

'The great value of these institutions for our military
preparations is beyond a doubt [and even though] the Russian
interest in them is considerable, the advantages from these
installations predominantly favour the German side.'
Field Marshal Werner von Blomberg,
German Minister of Defence[1]

Along with the Russian Karl Radek, General Johannes Friedrich
Leopold 'Hans' von Seeckt had laid the foundation of Soviet-German
partnership in the realms of sharing intelligence, economic partnership
and military research almost before the ink was dry on the Versailles
armistice agreement of 1918 (the Treaty of Versailles) that ended the First
World War. Russia had signed a separate peace with the Axis Powers
in 1917, which had threatened to undermine the Western Alliance war
effort by releasing a million German troops for redeployment to the
Western Front. No longer an ally, Russia was vilified and shunned by
Britain and France not least because of its adoption of communism as
a political and economic challenge to Western capitalism. Isolated but
threatened by its erstwhile allies, the Bolsheviks saw reconciliation
with its former enemy, Germany, as a first step towards consolidation
of its fragile regime. The two countries had earned pariah status, which
encouraged them to identify in a common challenge. While the Treaty
of Versailles went on to strip the former German Empire of huge
tracts of territory and populations, Russia, alone amongst Germany's
neighbours, made no territorial claims on the defeated nation. Indeed,
like Germany, it had also lost land to newly formed countries, such as
Ukraine and Poland. This *Ostpolitik* strategy adopted by von Seeckt

was very much in the tradition of Iron Chancellor' Otto von Bismarck for whom German-Russian friendship was a cornerstone of German foreign policy but, of course, von Bismarck had dealt with Tsarist Russia, which was quite a different matter. It was a unique initiative by von Seeckt's in as much as he wanted to continue that tradition despite the deep ideological differences between Germany and Soviet Russia that had sprung up after the 1917 Bolshevik Revolution.

Both Russia and Germany had been, to some extent, reborn as a result of the war. Political ballast had been dispersed and the spiritual centres of both nations evaporated when the Tsar and the Kaiser, who had taken their countries to war in 1914, were both gone along with their autocratic regimes and both countries were embroiled to a greater or lesser extent in civil wars. What bonded them also was a visceral hatred of the new Polish state that had been created between them. The Bolsheviks would go on to consolidate their power in Russia but communism could not gain advantage in the street battles against the right-wing German *Freikorps* militias in the German cities despite getting moral and political support from Moscow.

Von Seeckt, a typical representative of the reactionary Junker-caste of Germany, was made *Chef der Heeresleitung* (head of the German armed forces) after the suppression of the Kapp-Luttwitz Putsch in 1920.[2] One of his main preoccupations was a fear that the Western Powers might force Germany into an alliance against the Bolsheviks, but he was convinced that 'the future understanding with Greater Russia was to be the permanent target of Germany's foreign policy [and] it was inappropriate to antagonize Russia's new masters.'[3] The lack of alternatives was a powerful factor that had led von Seeckt to look on Russia, which had not signed up to Treaty of Versailles, as probably the only country that would collaborate with him in developing a modern German army.

The Russians, meanwhile, had suffered a humiliating defeat at the hands of the newly emerged Polish nation under Józef Piłsudski, in the summer of 1920 and the ensuing Russo-Polish peace treaty, which tipped the scale once more in favour of the Allies. They were, therefore, receptive to the proposals brought to Moscow by von Seeckt's envoy, Enver Pasha, to engage with a highly secret *Sondergruppe R* (Task Group Russia) the purpose of which was to explore the prospects of military-industrial collaboration. The Soviet representative, Karl Radek, who had worked hard to arrive at this juncture saw it as a unique opportunity to utilise German economic power to help in the rebuilding of Russia's war industry. One of the aspects of the talks that appealed to him most was an arrangement between the Russian and

German general staffs for the training of the Russian officer corps by German instructors.

The first agreement was signed on 15 March 1922 between *Sondergruppe R* and the German Junkers manufacturer to set up a factory deep inside Russia, away from prying Western eyes, to build military aircraft, which the Germans had been strictly forbidden to do under the terms of the Treaty of Versailles. While there was significant political support for von Seeckt's strategy from German leaders, such as Baron Ago von Maltzan, head of the Eastern Department of the *Auswärtiges Amt*, and Ulrich von Brockdorff-Rantzau, the former Foreign Minister, the President, Friedrich Ebert, along with many in his cabinet, were opposed to cooperating with the Bolsheviks and so to prevent them blocking developments they were given no more than the barest outlines of what was going on behind the scenes. Under the utmost secrecy, most of the major German engineering firms had teams working there at the height of cooperation, seven of Germany's eight aircraft manufacturers were doing research at Soviet facilities.

Despite doctrinal opposition to Bolshevism within much of the German government, and much to the dismay of the Western Powers, the Treaty of Rapallo was ratified on 4 July 1922 under which Germany and Soviet Russia renounced the compensation claims for war expenditures and war damages. Diplomatic relations were to be resumed, and trade and economic relations were to be established within the framework of the *Gesellschaft zur Forderung gewerblicher Unternehmungen* (Trade Enterprises Development Company – GEFU) on the most-favoured-nation principle but concealed behind this cloak of economic agreements, the covert military cooperation began. The Reichswehr secretly bought fifty single-seat Fokker D.XIII fighters from the Netherlands and had them shipped directly to a flight school that had been set up at Lipetsk. Deep inside the Russian steppes and well away from prying Western eyes, this facility was referred to as the 'scientific aviation testing station' or simply 'the station'.

This early collaboration proved popular and successful as shown by the comments of Lieutenant Wilberg, Chief of the Reichswehr Aviation Department who announced plans to expand the fighter school to include the training of reconnaissance aircraft crews and to conduct experiments in aerial photography. Numerous technical innovations in military aviation were also tested and evaluated while battle strategies and new air combat tactics evolved. During summer 1931, experiments and training extended to the point where German and Soviet squadrons participated in mock attacks against daylight bombers to develop optimal attack and defence techniques. By 1933, when Lipetsk was closed down, over 1,200 Luftwaffe pilots had been trained at Lipetsk.

A German-Soviet chemical warfare project, *Gas-Testgelände Tomka* (code-named Tomka) based at Ivshchenkovo in the Samara Region of the Volga near Podosinky was, on the surface, operated by a fictitious joint German-Soviet company Bersol but was, in reality, a branch of the German chemical and pharmaceutical giant I.G. Farben. Its function was to manufacture poison gas, such as mustard gas and phosgene. Then, in 1926, Hermann von der Lieth-Thomsen, head of *Sondergruppe R*, signed a three-year agreement with the Chief of Soviet Army Intelligence, Jan K. Berzin, to establish a *Panzerschule* (tank school) named Kama in Kazan.

Apart from the immeasurably important objective of developing military capabilities through joint ventures with the Soviet Union, the German also had a clear objective of getting close to the inner circle of Soviet command to get some understanding of Soviet military capabilities and long-term strategy. By 1928, they were picking up indications that the Soviet military High Command under Mikhail Nikolayevich Tukhachevsky was trying to loosen the grip of communist control and extend collaboration with Germany. The Kremlin, however, was anxious to maintain some political distance from the Weimar Republic, which they were still actively trying to destroy through political violence and revolution.

In a relationship nourished more by self-interest than philanthropy, both sides were angling to get maximum benefit at the other's expense and, importantly, neither side lost sight of the fact that sooner or later ideological differences and geopolitical imperatives might see them on opposite sides of an East European conflict. The relationship was cordial enough to work but far from comfortable. It was clear also that as the economies of both countries improved and international scrutiny of German military developments became desultory the importance of cooperation was diminished. Soviet industry was being restructured in ways that made the country less reliant on German technological expertise and, at the same time, Germany was using the knowledge and experience it was getting from the collaboration to inform its own industrial development on home ground.

The arrangement essentially saw Germany providing the technical expertise while the Soviet Union provided the facilities and manpower for industrial production, which gave opportunity to both sides to exploit the trade agreements for economic and military espionage. There was a lot of common ground around military developments given the level of cooperation going on but still both sides knew quite well that each was pursuing its own agendas beyond what was happening at Lipetz, Kazan and Tomka. That said, it was a bone of contention within the Abwehr that companies like Krupp who had huge investments in the Soviet Union were making little effort to obtain and pass on intelligence about Soviet industry. Rheinmetall, some of whose executives working in the Soviet Union were also clandestine members of German Intelligence, were much more productive in that regard.

Von Brockdorff-Rantzau was clearly of the opinion that 'the Soviets needed the German more than the Germans needed them', which had been a guiding principle for the Germans throughout. With all collaborative operations taking place in the Soviet Union for security reasons, however, the Germans found themselves at a disadvantage once the arrangements came under stress and were first to react by slowing down supply of materials and denying the Soviets full access to the most advanced technical innovations under development in Germany. Already Junkers had pulled out of the deal having incurred crippling financial losses. Stalin began to think that he was being outmanoeuvred and felt that he had to make a statement to warn the Germans that they could not treat him with contempt. Not for him the role of the poor relation having to rely on Germany's munificence.

He decided to remind the Germans that they were guests on Soviet territory and needed to be a little more appreciative of Soviet hospitality. He authorised a show trial of five German technicians working for AEG and Knapp in the North Caucasus who were accused, along with around forty Soviet workers, of espionage and sabotage. It sent ripples of unease through the *Auswärtiges Amt* and was effectively the beginning of the end of the whole enterprise, but it would take some time to for it die completely. Germany was anxious to continue reaping the rewards of their considerable financial investment in the joint venture and played down the incident in the hope that there would be no repetition.

On 17 April 1928, Politburo member Nikolai Bukharin, in an undisguised threat, claimed that Soviet intelligence had uncovered a plot by foreign capitalists to sabotage Soviet industry. The arrested German engineers were complicit, he said, and were members of the German fascist organisation, the *Stahlhelm* (steel helmets). When the accused came to trial on 18 May 1928, von Brockdorff-Rantzau, observing, could see that the verdict was a foregone conclusion and threatened to take retaliatory action through diplomatic channels despite the risk of the Soviets letting the cat out of the bag by whistleblowing on Germany's illegal breaching of the Treaty of

Versailles. His strong representation seemed to have had some effect when the German accused were eventually acquitted while eleven Soviet defendants were sentenced to death.

Later that year, von Brockdorff-Rantzau, who had been one of the key advocates of German-Soviet collaboration died, but his policy of cooperation survived, especially at the flight training school at Lipetsk where new doctrines of aerial combat were steadily being developed and new types of aircraft tested. Tank warfare doctrine was of great importance to both sides also. The future Panzer leader Heinz Guderian was most enthusiastic and said that Kazan was 'the only place where really positive work on the area of tanks can be achieved'.[4] Almost every tank that the Germans used in the Second World War owes its development to work carried out at Kazan.

Things still seemed to be going well at Lipetsk, Kazan and Tomka with exchanges of personnel increasing against a background of generally smooth cooperation in the factory and in the field but all that was to change in 1933 when Hitler's Nazis took power in Germany.

The OGPU had never been comfortable with the influx of German military and civilian specialists inside the Soviet homeland. The KRO considered GEFU to be no more than a front for German intelligence engaged in espionage and reporting to Berlin on Soviet military and political conditions and industry, but clearly the concerns of the OGPU were overridden by foreign policy considerations in Moscow. The OGPU could be confident that their analysis of German intentions was accurate because it was exactly what they were doing from the other side.

In the Soviet Union it was now becoming a distinctly uncomfortable position to be seen as too close politically to the new Nazi power structure in Berlin. When, in 1933, German industry under the Nazis began a programme of heavy investment in military hardware with growing contempt for international condemnation, a death knell was sounding for the last remaining collaborative venture at Lipetsk.

Even as Hitler was made Chancellor of Germany, however, Stalin held fast to the belief that real power still lay with the German capitalists, aristocrats and military who would combine to thwart the extreme right-wing political ambitions of the NSDAP. Whatever stresses were developing in the collaborative venture, Soviet reticence was not necessarily a consequence of Hitler's elevation, but more to do with the military threat posed by a revanchist Germany and the enduring political instability in eastern Europe.

German-Soviet cooperation continued at Lipetsk, albeit with diminished enthusiasm on both sides, but by summer 1933 significant tensions were building. Official visits were cancelled by both sides and the Germans began repatriating men and equipment. The relationship stumbled on but there was a growing reluctance on the part of the Soviets now to cooperate in ways that might give Germany an advantage in the development of military hardware and doctrine. By the end of September 1933, all German military personnel had left Soviet soil and with that had ended any hope for renewed contact with both militaries now coming firmly under the control of governments that were moving further and further apart.

The Reichswehr intelligence officer Lieutenant Colonel Hartmann concluded that his experience in the Soviet Union had convinced him that the country was incapable of successfully fighting a defensive war.[5] The Abwehr, as a whole, however, during all the years of cooperation, had totally failed to establish agents inside either the higher levels of the *Stavka* (Soviet Armed Forces High Command) or the Soviet Communist Party. Unsurprisingly, that would not be Stalin's paranoid take on the situation. For him the close involvement of his top generals with the German military was deeply suspect and would see many of them cut down in his later purges as a result.

The level of growing unease in Moscow was illustrated by a speech to the Central Committee of the Soviet Communist Party on 29 December 1933, by the Soviet People's Commissar for Foreign Affairs, Maxim Litvinov, who said that the world was 'standing at the junction of two eras [one of] bourgeois pacifism [and] a new era of wars of imperialist redivision'. 'Peace', he continued, 'requires the collaboration and cooperation of other states.' He was scathing about the Nazi regime for 'preaching the most extreme anti-Soviet ideas' and whose leader openly aspired to 'enslave the Soviet peoples' but was careful not to go quite as far as to close the door completely on future cooperation.[6]

Any hope of that happening, however, was brutally swept aside when around eighty of Hitler's political opponents, including Reichswehr officers who had been amongst those most friendly to the Soviet Union, were cut down in Hitler's Night of the Long Knives (a violent purge) on 30 June 1934. It was a turning point for German-Soviet relations in as much as it was a clear indication to Stalin that Hitler was every bit as ruthless as he was. Although collaboration had been rapidly dismantled at the end of 1933, the Red Army, with Stalin's full approval, still made gestures indicating a willingness to retain some level of contact with the Reichswehr. The message was that 'no injurious intent' had been intended by Soviet withdrawal from collaborative ventures. In 1936, despite Hitler's hard-line policies against the Soviet Union, a two-year credit agreement was concluded, which allowed further improvement of trade relations. Having broken all Weimar sponsored ties to the Soviet Union, Hitler was now intent on developing a new relationship based on his own priorities. It was important to him that Stalin should feel no immediate threat from Germany and, hopefully, take a back seat politically while he manoeuvred and plotted against Austria and Czechoslovakia. Furthermore, Germany needed to draw on the Soviet Union's vast resources of raw materials such as oil, metal ores and timber to feed into its rearmament programme and to this end long-term trade agreements were signed.

One of the consequences of the whole German cooperative venture within the Soviet Union was that many Soviet air force leaders who had close contact with German businessmen and military leaders came under Stalin's baleful glare making them prime targets for his paranoia during the purges. Many would be executed for their 'friendship' with the Reichswehr.

While German-Soviet relations blew hot and cold during the late 1930s, it was on 23 August 1939 that the world was shocked to find that the two nations had made a deal that left the fate of Poland hanging in the balance. That country had hoped against hope that fear of Soviet countermeasures would make Hitler stay his hand against them but on that fateful day, two Luftwaffe Fw 200 Condor aircraft landed at Moscow's Khodynka airfield to a spectacular welcome. On board were the German Foreign Minister, Joachim von Ribbentrop, accompanied by about forty officials, advisors, photographers and translators. They were met by a high-powered delegation of Soviet officials before being driven to the former Austrian legation building, which had been allocated to them during their stay. Very soon, von Ribbentrop and the German ambassador to Moscow, Friedrich-Werner Graf von der Schulenburg, were taken to the Kremlin where they sat down with Stalin and Vyacheslav Molotov, the Commissar for Foreign Affairs. The importance of the meeting was clear to von der Schulenburg who, during the whole of his five years at the Moscow embassy, had never before laid eyes on the Soviet leader. Talks between the four men began immediately.

Talks ended with an alcohol-fuelled reception at which Stalin toasted Hitler's health and said that 'the Soviet Union would not betray its partner'.[7] With that the Molotov-Ribbentrop Pact was signed. Its clauses included a guarantee of peace between both countries and a commitment that neither government would ally itself to or aid an enemy of the other. In addition to the publicly announced terms, the treaty also included the Secret Protocol, which defined the borders of Soviet and German spheres of influence after the German attack against Poland.

Chapter 5

SOVIET INTELLIGENCE BEFORE BARBAROSSA

'An intelligence officer must be steeped in venom,
in bile; he should trust no one.'

Joseph Stalin[1]

It is a recurring problem when looking at Soviet intelligence organisations that departments were constantly in flux with frequent structural changes and overlapping of responsibilities. Individual agents were liable to appear in the reports of different organisations and often seemed to have no permanent connection with any one of them in particular. Another aspect of Soviet intelligence was that it did not have any top-level agency equivalent to the German *Abwehr II* special duties section to carry out activities, such as sabotage and sedition.

Soviet intelligence officers working abroad were based in *rezidentura* (residencies) from where they were expected to familiarise themselves with the military, political and economic situation in the countries concerned, know about effectiveness of indigenous counterintelligence, and research the backgrounds and potential of agent sources. Vasily M. Zarubin had been an 'illegal' *rezident* working in Berlin, who paid a brief visit to Moscow before transferring to the United States in March 1937. While in Moscow he was unexpectedly summoned directly to the Kremlin, an instruction that cannot have been a wholly welcome. Once there he was closely questioned about a report he had recently sent concerning an extremely rare written memorandum carrying Hitler's own name as opposed to one 'in his name'. He was asked exactly how much confidence he had that it was genuine. He had every faith in the source, Zarubin told his chief Nikolai Ezhov. Many times he had checked and cross checked intelligence from this particular source and had always found it to be reliable. Zarubin was an officer with years of experience, who had been at the Berlin *rezidentura* since 1934 and his sound reputation was well founded. When asked how sure he was that the words attributed to Hitler were not malicious misdirection and a provocation to disorientate Moscow, he replied that he was as sure as he could possibly be. What was it about the memorandum that had so disturbed Moscow? It was the fact that Hitler, once in power, so rarely stated his views in writing, which made his memorandum of great significance. 'The world was moving towards a new conflict, centred upon Bolshevism', Hitler had dictated in August 1936, 'this crisis cannot and will not fail'. He continued and concluded by saying that 'all other considerations must recede into the background as being completely irrelevant'.[2]

Not willing to take personal responsibility for handling this incendiary piece of intelligence, Ezhov quickly passed it further up the line of command and when it landed on Stalin's desk, the *Vozhd* personally interviewed Zarubin. He asked the same question. First of all, he asked how Zarubin could know that the memorandum really existed if he hadn't actually seen it. All Zarubin could do was repeat that his source was reliable. If it was genuine then Stalin wanted reassurances that it was not one of Hitler's tricks to mislead and confuse. To this Zarubin had no answer. He knew Hitler's mind no better than Stalin did.

Stalin did not reject Zarubin's intelligence out of hand but he needed further corroborating evidence from other sources. His hope of getting any, however, was summed up when he told Ezhov that, despite Zarubin, Soviet intelligence was 'poor, weak [and] infested with spies'. At a time when Stalin's paranoia was reaching staggeringly murderous heights, it should have been a warning sign that caution, rather than wholesale purging of military and intelligence officers was required, but that was not Stalin's way of doing things.

One of his most important 'illegal' *rezidents* was the Hungarian-born Sándor Radó (codename Dora) who ran *Die Rote Drei* (The Red Three) spy ring in Switzerland. He had apparently been idling his time away until April 1939 when the newly appointed chief of *Glavnoe Razvedyvatel'noe Upravlenie* (Soviet General Staff Intelligence Department – GRU) Ivan I. Proskurov took him to task for his failure to produce anything of value and, with tensions rising in Europe, called on him to gather intelligence on 'military activities in Italy and Germany [for action] against France' and to 'determine where, how and for what purposes' said forces would be employed against the

French.[3] Another 'illegal' called on to get intelligence on the French was Henry Robinson (codename Harry) at the Paris embassy. Colonel Maksim Purkaev (codename Marble) and Captain Nikolai Zaitsev (codename Bina), who ran the Alta spy ring, were 'legals' in the Berlin embassy run by GRU *resident* Filipp Ivanovich Golikov. With a major European war looming, these men were also urgently called on to get intelligence on Germany's military capabilities and, crucially, what German and Japanese intentions were against the Soviet Union. Along with the Ramsay spy ring in Tokyo, Alta was particularly productive, but offered few prognoses.

Stalin 'immersed himself directly into the intelligence process' by demanding access to raw intelligence before it had been collated, analysed and assessed.[4] He personally received nearly every report from Soviet intelligence officers and their sources stationed abroad, which meant that he relied only on his own judgement about how reliable any particular piece of intelligence was and how well it was supported by numerous other sources. His aversion towards accepting information that differed from his own conclusions and his penchant for taking a dim view of anyone who presented him with it inevitably led to a filtering of intelligence reaching his desk.

Soviet and German officers had worked side by side during the years of clandestine military cooperation and, later, the Spanish Civil War had seen many Soviet military and intelligence officers deployed in that country facing German and Italian foes. All this German-Soviet contact was a growing concern for Stalin whose position in the Politburo was still anything but secure. He suspected that German intelligence had penetrated Soviet intelligence to a significant degree, and was manipulating him and doing it successfully while his own agencies were providing him with little of value. The Hitler memorandum was just another manifestation of German attempts to destabilise the Soviet Union and destroy it from within. Stalin's view was that the GRU needed purging of traitors. All he could really count on was his own judgement and that would become his default position.

Throughout the years leading up to the German invasion of the Soviet Union there was a clear distinction between what the Soviet intelligence sources were reporting and what Stalin, judging by his actions, seemed to believe. Being head of the GRU was a thankless task and one that required tact and forbearance. Ivan Proskurov an independently mind, talented but modest and unassuming military pilot and air force commander who had fought in the Spanish Civil War was amongst those least likely to conform to that description, but it was he who found himself in the hot seat. Born in Ukraine in 1907, he escaped the murderous famines of the 1930s resulting from the collectivisation of farming there through his attendance at the prestigious Zhukosvky Air Academy in Moscow. Graduating from there, he had volunteered to serve in Spain on 'special assignment' under the control of the GRU. During his time in Spain, he proved to be an extraordinarily efficient air force commander and came to Stalin's personal attention after conducting a bombing operation against the German battleship *Deutschland* near Ibiza on 29 May 1937. When he returned from the war, he was promoted to major and made a hero of the Soviet Union and later on 14 April 1939, despite a total lack of intelligence experience, he was made chief of the GRU. Stalin's was short of options after his vicious purges had decapitated the GRU Directorate whom he accused of having 'fallen into the hands of the Germans.'[5] During the three or four years prior to Operation Barbarossa, as many as 20,000 Soviet intelligence and counterintelligence officers had disappeared. Semyon P. Uritsky, also a person with little intelligence experience, had been chief up until June 1937 when he was fired, arrested and subsequently executed in January 1938. Berzin, who had been with Proskurov in Spain, briefly occupied the top spot from June until August of that year before he, too, was arrested in November 1937 and executed in July 1938. It was clearly a demanding role requiring its holder to tread a fine line between keeping abreast of foreign affairs, often through travel, and falling foul of Stalin's acutely suspicious nature.

Initially, Stalin seemed impressed by Proskurov's reporting on the German invasion of Poland and the way he had contributed to the negotiations preceding signing of the Molotov-Ribbentrop (German-Soviet Non-Aggression) Pact on 23 August 1939. Leading up to this, Proskurov's sources in Warsaw had provided the GRU with some of its best intelligence on German plans and activities. Only days into his new role, Proskurov's report of 17 May 1939 had included an appendix entitled 'The Future Plans of Aggression by Fascist Germany in the Estimation of an Official of the German Foreign Ministry, Kleist.' The top secret report gave details of a briefing given by Dr Peter Kleist, head of the Eastern Department of von Ribbentrop's *Auswärtiges Amt*, to senior officers of the German Embassy in Warsaw on 2 May 1939. Kleist had told them that

> Germany at the present moment [was] in the first phase of its military consolidation in the east, which, without regard to ideological considerations, must be achieved by whatever means. [There will be] merciless cleansing of the east [then] the western phase that must end

in the defeat of France and England [after which] one can count on the feasibility of the destruction of the Soviet Union.[6]

Kleist went on to explain how the Germans had made common cause with Ukrainian nationalists in connection with a German attack on Poland, which was set for July or August 1941. Kleist assumed that Britain would be crushed by the Luftwaffe, America would not intervene, and the Soviet Union would remain neutral.

Proskurov had three Soviet agents in the German Embassy in Warsaw operating as part of his *Arbina* network. Rudolf von Scheliha, Gerhard Kegel and Kurt Völkisch, and it was probably von Scheliha (codename Arietz) who had provided the Kleist intelligence. Von Scheliha was later made Deputy Head of the Economics Department of the German Embassy in Moscow. Having read the report, Stalin seemed to place a modicum of credence on it and accepted that Hitler was serious about attacking Poland. He agreed that Britain and France could do little to prevent Poland's defeat and saw that his best chance of delaying any German move against the Soviet Union was to pursue a non-aggression pact with them to stabilise relations while Hitler secured his western flank. Diplomatic exchanges then took place to establish trade agreements and an understanding about the future fate of Poland and Lithuania that was incorporated into the secret protocol accompanying the Molotov-Ribbentrop Pact. This had put Latvia, Estonia and Finland in the Soviet sphere of interest and left Lithuania to the Germans while the border between their spheres of interest in Poland was also agreed. Stalin's thoughts were aired on 7 September 1939 when he said, 'A war is on between two groups of capitalist countries … for the redivision of the world, for the domination of the world. We see nothing wrong in [Britain and Germany] having a good fight and weakening each other.' When the German attack went in against Poland, Stalin bullied the Baltic states into signing mutual assistance treaties allowing for Soviet troops to be stationed there. He had no way of knowing that France would fall so quickly and held fast to his belief that Hitler would not attack the Soviet Union before 1942 at the earliest.

GRU officers were trained to be totally objective in their analysis of intelligence. The inevitable result was that their reports often failed to find favour in the Kremlin. It was against this background that the integrity and competence of the GRU chief was constantly challenged by the Soviet leadership and would prove to be a crucial factor in the way that the service responded to German-Soviet relations between 1939 and 1941.

Proskurov's position was soon undermined. Stalin told him that he was too honest and naïve to be an intelligence officer. In reply, Proskurov complained of inadequate resources and that some commanders simply locked his reports up, unread, in their safes for months on end. Out of fifty reports sent to the Artillery Directorate, he said, only seven were read and then only by a couple of people apparently on the assumption that the Intelligence Directorate would distribute them to units directly. He also began to suspect that Stalin did not understand the first thing about what intelligence was and how it should be used. Neither, for that matter, did he think that Stalin had much grasp of military matters.

When Proskurov complained at one conference in April 1940 that ORBs (Separate Reconnaissance Battalions) were not being properly trained to collect intelligence, it was immediately clear to the room that Stalin had no idea what Proskurov was talking about. The *Vozhd* also kept very quiet when discussion turned to who was responsible for the horrendous death toll of the Soviet-Finnish Winter War. Proskurov blamed the 'idiotic' situation whereby the commanders of the adjacent Eighth and Ninth armies had refused to share intelligence with each other. He went on to infuriate Stalin by complaining that agents who had been despatched behind enemy lines and returned with intelligence had been received, not with accolades, but suspicion. He was clearly a man who was not intimidated by Stalin and continued to challenge him in front of others, which was leading him into what would soon become a very uncomfortable place when Stalin chose to place all the blame for recent failures on him and his Intelligence Directorate. Undaunted, or perhaps just naïve as Stalin had said, Proskurov, continued to criticise senior officers by name in defence of his and his department's reputation.

This was never going to be allowed to pass without reprisals. In May 1940, a reports of the Soviet Chiefs of Central Directorates on The Condition of Intelligence Work described intelligence as one of the weakest sectors in the Defence Commissariat. There is no organ providing the Red Army with information on the resources and state of readiness of foreign armies, they said. On 27 July 1940, Proskurov was dismissed for, among other things, embarrassing Stalin at the April 1940 conference. The failure of the Finnish campaign, the details of which were widely known within the Soviet Union could not be allowed to reflect on the political or military leadership, so the finger was pointed at Proskurov's Intelligence Department but, predictably, Proskurov refused to shoulder the blame. Seemingly not content with one implacable foe, he publicly defended himself by ridiculing the military performance in Finland, which riled the new Defence Commissar, Marshal Semyon Timoshenko.

Proskurov's days as Red Army intelligence chief were coming to an end, but it was at this time that Germany chose to launch *Fall Gelb*, its attack against France and the Low Countries. When French resistance collapsed at Sedan, Stalin's hopes for a long, drawn-out debilitating war between Germany and the Western Allies began to crumble. Intelligence about Hitler's next move had suddenly become critically important but Stalin's reticence to accept anything that contradicted his own analysis became the deciding factor in how the Soviets would use that intelligence.

Little seems to have changed by 7 December of that year when the leadership of the People's Commissariat of Defence was being transferred from Marshal Kliment Voroshilov to Marshal Semyon Timoshenko. Documentation of the transfer included an assessment the state of Soviet military intelligence. It said,

> The organization of intelligence is one of the weakest spots in the work of the People's Commissariat of Defence. There is neither organized collection of intelligence nor systematic transmission of information on foreign armed forces. The work of the Intelligence Directorate is not connected with the work of the General Staff. The Intelligence Directorate falls short of the People's Commissariat of Defence's need for an agency that would provide the Red Army with information on foreign armed forces' organization, condition, armaments and preparations for deployment. The People's Commissariat of Defence does not have such information at the time of this transfer. Theatres of operations and preparation of these theatres have not been studied.[7]

Intelligence provided by Soviet Military residencies in Eastern Europe was a mixed bag of solid intelligence, rumours and gossip. The best came from Bucharest where third secretary, Colonel Grigory M. Yeremin, had the German Embassy Press Officer Kurt Völkisch (codename AVS) and his wife (code name LTsL) on his books. Bucharest and Sofia had risen to prominence as the Soviet Union became increasingly concerned about the nature of their relations with Germany. Romania and Bulgaria were the last Eastern European states through which the Soviet Union could run effective intelligence operations. It was from Colonel Dergachev, the Soviet military attaché to Bulgaria and legal *rezident* on 6 June 1940 that the Kremlin received its first report, which broke through the fog of rumour and vagueness to specifically predict a German attack against the Soviet Union 'within one or two months'.[8] Three weeks later, Proskurov submitted a report to Stalin, which supported Dergachev's prediction but questioned the timing. Other intelligence from the legal *rezidents* in Berlin indicating that the German Ministry of Railways had received orders to 'develop a plan ... of military transport from the West to the East' by no later than the end of 1940. While Stalin had read this report, nothing indicates that either he or the GRU took it seriously.

The NKVD had been disbanded in 1930 but reformed again in 1934 and was responsible for executing hundreds of thousands of peasants, government officials and Red Army officers during then great purges of 1936–1938 before it was purged itself by Lavrentiy Beria in 1938. The First (Railroad) Department of the NKVD's Chief Transport Directorate (GTU) was charged with the collection of intelligence on the buildup of German forces in occupied Poland. A report from the GTU on 12 July 1940 contained information from agents in Hamburg, Lübeck, Stettin, Memel, Tilsit, Königsberg and Danzig concerning an increase in the number of locomotives being used to haul construction materials to build fortifications along the Soviet frontier. Eighteen German divisions were reported to be concentrated in the area around Terespol. Other reports warned of extensive movement of artillery towards the Soviet along the Bug river. Troops brought from France ostensibly for leave were instead being sent directly to Poland. Five new airfields with concrete hangars had been constructed close to Warsaw.

The precipitous capitulation of France and the routing of the British Expeditionary Force at Dunkirk had surprised and shaken the Soviets. Proskurov sent a comprehensive memo to staff of the Intelligence Directorate of the Soviet General Staff in June 1940 reporting on the 'power and speed' of the German blitzkrieg and the contribution of German special forces. The report clearly challenged the Red Army leaders to question whether they would be able to withstand such an assault without developing a system of mobile and fluid defence. In June also came the first reports of German troop movements into East Prussia. While Proskurov raised no alarm over this, others on the frontline had warned that Baltic troops could not be relied upon to stand firm against a German attack.

When Hitler came to power in Germany, the GUGB had expanded its residencies abroad to meet the new threat, but it was eviscerated in Stalin's purges when hundreds of its members were arrested, tortured and then either shot or sent to the Gulag. Replacements were drafted in from both civilian life and the military and sent to special training establishments. By May 1939, the NKVD's Foreign Intelligence Service chief was a man of peasant stock, Pavel M. Fitin, who had served as a private in the Red Army. The paucity of experienced and qualified staff after the purges saw him elevated rapidly to become chief of the *Naródny Komissariát Gosudarstvennoi Bezopasnosti* (Ministry of State Security – NKGB) Foreign Intelligence Directorate. The GUGB was the main directorate of the NKVD until February 1941 when it became the independent NKGB and the Fifth (Foreign Intelligence) Department became the First Directorate. It was reabsorbed by the NKVD on 20 July the same year.

It had eight directorates including *Innostrannoe Upravleni* (*Razvedyvatel'noe*) (First Directorate – INU), the Foreign Intelligence Directorate responsible for conducting clandestine operations abroad using embassies and trade missions, and targeting foreigners inside the Soviet Union for recruitment as agents. Also responsible for all espionage and counterintelligence operations against non-military targets and collection of foreign intelligence. It was the primary agency for running informant networks inside the Soviet Union, for prosecuting crimes against the state and apprehending German agents in Soviet-held territory.

Kontrazvedyvatel'noe Upravleni (Second Directorate – KRU) was responsible for counterintelligence (excluding military counterintelligence) within the Soviet Union. It ran thousands of informants and was the backbone of the Soviet police system among the civilian population. Duties included the apprehension of foreign spies infiltrating foreign intelligence services inside and outside the country and surveillance of agents of other Soviet agencies. Agents returning from assignments in enemy-held territory were screened by KRU before being allowed to return to duty.

Sekretnoe Politichesko Upravlen (Third Directorate – SPU) undertook no operational missions behind German lines but employed its extensive internal informant network to monitor all anti-Soviet activities in political, religious and cultural organisations where German infiltration was likely.

The UOO/NKGB had responsibility for counterintelligence within the Partisan movement to maintain political reliability and security while the Fourth Directorate was the Directorate for occupied areas, guerilla operations and maskirovka.

Fitin proved to be a careful, meticulous leader, well-liked by his subordinates. His deputy was Pavel Anatolyevich Sudoplatov, a special operations operative well versed in the dark arts of sabotage, kidnapping and assassination of Stalin's enemies including Leon Trotsky. Sudoplatov was a close ally of Beria and both men were careful to reinforce Stalin's view that Hitler would not invade the Soviet Union.

Fitin reported that the Germans were laying down 'strategic highways … from Kraków to Tarnuv, Tarnuv to Iaroslav, and Iaroslav to Zasane.'[9] In Poland, new cement and armament factories were being built. He also warned that the Germans were recruiting officers and other ranks with knowledge of Russian, Serbian, Croatian, Bulgarian and Romanian, and were training up Ukrainian and White Russian mercenaries in covert intelligence gathering. During the four weeks up to 14 July 1940 agents had recorded a total of 860 special troop trains heading from the West in easterly and southeasterly directions. All this was reported to the People's Commissar for Internal Affairs, Lavrentiy Beria who passed it along to Stalin.

While this was of some concern, intelligence from Romania and Bulgaria included statements such as, 'Concentration [of German troops in the east] is not of a serious scale'[10] and 'redeployment of forces eastward was not directed against the USSR.'[11] On 20 July 1940, Golikov explained that the growing number of German divisions in Eastern Europe, particularly in Poland, was no more than a redistribution of forces following the fall of France. Richard Sorge (codename Ramsay), however, pointed to the recent Tripartite Pact between Germany, Japan and Italy, which was aimed primarily at the United States, but which could be redirected against the Soviet Union should it 'pursue policies undesirable from the standpoint of Germany', and, at this point, GRU began to show nervousness about the large number of German divisions in Eastern Europe.[12] Subsequent intelligence summaries no longer ended with bland assurances that German forces in the east were 'not of a serious scale' and that movement of troops eastward into East Prussia, Belorussia and Ukraine now 'required scrutiny'.

A Soviet Critical Intelligence Assessment report of 19 August 1940 warned that 'The unfolding political situation in Europe is creating the probability of an armed confrontation on our western borders.'[13] Unlike Stalin, the Red Army General Staff accepted that the ongoing German threat of a seaborne invasion of the British Isles was no more than a diversion from Hitler's primary goal and if he chose to deploy all available Axis German forces in the east, the overall prospects for the Soviet Union were daunting. Actual numbers were hard to come by, however, but estimates put infantry divisions at more than 250, aircraft at 12,000 and tanks at more than 10,000. In the event of an attack, it was expected that the bulk of German forces would strike north of Sandomierz where the San joins the Vistula.

The one agency that was best placed to see what was going on along the border was the Directorate of Border Troops (GUPV) that, amongst other things, was responsible for apprehending Abwehr agents who tried to cross the border or who were recruited from anti-Soviet elements of the local population. When interrogated, these agents often inadvertently provided important intelligence. For instance, when some were asked to return to German territory with samples of oil and fuel used by the Soviet military, they had no idea why, but it was a clear signal that analysis of the samples would indicate whether Soviet fuel dumps could be used by German Panzer tanks, military vehicles and aircraft or whether they would require modification before use.

By October 1940, there were clear signs that the Red Army High Command, at least, was taking a dim view of developments. They were obviously unnerved by Golikov who, stressing the reliability of his source, reported on serious shifts toward 'deterioration in relations between Germany and the Soviet Union' and the possibility that Germany might default on its obligations to meet its contractual obligations under the Molotov-Ribbentrop Pact by diverting materials to its own armed forces.[14] Since there was no diminution in the number of reports of German military build-up in Poland and Romania they called for the main transport agency of the Soviet Union to prepare a detailed rail schedule for rapid deployment of forces to the border. Measures were taken to increase the detection and interrogation of German agents operating in the Soviet Union. Most were Ukrainian or Belorussian nationalists who had 'great experience in operating against [the Soviet Union] with an excellent knowledge of territory and with a large number of contacts', but Poles also featured in significant numbers.[15]

When a Soviet agent, who had been working as a conscripted labourer in Warsaw, returned he reported that airfields were being built without hangars, close to forests and with very large landing strips. Roads were built for the transport of aviation fuel, which was stored underground in concrete bunkers. He also reported on the mass round up of Jews and their incarceration in ghettos. By December 1940, Golikov saw war between Germany and the Soviet Union as inevitable in the not too distant future, but he was reluctant to share his thoughts with Stalin.

On 29 December 1940, only eleven days after Hitler had signed off *Wehrmachtsbefehl Nr 21* calling for OKW to 'prepare all parts of the Wehrmacht for the overthrow of Soviet Russia in one rapid campaign', Alta reported its contents to the GRU through Colonel Nikolai Skorniukov (codename Meteor), assistant air attaché and 'legal' *rezident* at the Berlin embassy. Hitler will invade the Soviet Union in March 1941, the message said. There was a flurry of reaction as Golikov, not willing to take a single source as definitive and looking for scraps to mollify Stalin, urgently requested more information, hoping that the Alta report was an exaggeration. Although Alta got the date wrong, it is indicative of the high level of Soviet penetration of OKH that essentially all other details of Hitler's *Weisung für die Kriegführung*'s were entirely accurate. Meteor vouched for the intelligence that was not 'based on hearsay' and had come from 'a military official'.

Supporting intelligence was not long in coming. The military attaché and GRU legal *rezident* in Belgrade, Major General Aleksandr G. Samokhin (codename Sophocles), also produced valuable intelligence on the German presence in the Balkans and German intentions to invade the Soviet Union. On 27 January 1941, he reported that there were fourteen German divisions in Romania presumably to protect the Ploesti oilfields. The German ambassador in Belgrade was reported as saying in a private meeting that the Soviet Union would never agree to inclusion in the 'New Order in Europe' and, therefore, 'war [against them was] inevitable'. In early February, Sophocles reported that Germany now saw the Balkans as their new 'decisive centre of political events' after which Hitler would turn toward the Soviet Union.[16] Dora reported from Geneva on 21 February that, according to Swiss intelligence, Germany already had 150 divisions in Eastern Europe and would attack the Soviet Union in late May. Golikov dismissed it as misinformation. When, a week later, another 'legal' in Berlin concluded that 'There are no specific signs of impending aggression against us.' Golikov was pleased and wrote, 'This is a helpful report.'[17]

More reports came in about the transfer of large German units, the movement of munitions, and the completion of airfield construction on the Soviet frontier in early 1941. The movement of tanks and mobile river crossing pontoon bridges increased all through the early spring indicating what one report to Nikita Krushchev called intensive preparations for war. But there was still no sign that Stalin was taking things seriously. Soviet historian Alexandr Nekrich saw Stalin's 'blind faith in his own power' and 'ignorance of the outside world' as the significant factors alongside his 'utter dependence' on only such intelligence as 'he wished to receive'.[18] Beria tried to rouse him with a report circulated to the Central Committee VKP(b), the Council of People's Commissars (SNK) and the Defence Commissariat (NKO), itemising German troop movements in East Prussia, and the Government General. Report after report gave the same message of new German troops, munitions and other supplies mostly conducted at night. All schools along the border were closed and used military barracks.

Article I of the Molotov-Ribbentrop Pact had stipulated that both Germany and the Soviet Union would refrain from 'from any aggressive operation'.[19] It is hard to see German provocations as anything other than an obvious disdain for such an understanding, but there was absolutely no indication through diplomatic circles that Berlin was contemplating a unilateral withdrawal from the pact.

When intelligence continued to be contradictory, it was a simple matter for Golikov to ascribe to each report a comment in line with Stalin's prejudices. In early March, Alta put the invasion date sometime between 15 May and 15 June. Colonel Nikolai Liakhterov (codename Mars), the Soviet military attaché in Budapest, wrote that, according to his German sources, an attack against the Soviet Union was 'unthinkable' while Britain remained belligerent and that Wehrmacht deployments to Romania were aimed only at the Balkans.

Mars went on to say, on 14 March, that Hungarian intelligence told him that talk of Germany attacking the Soviet Union were mere propaganda. On 10 March 1941, Sophocles had reported that the German General Staff had 'refused' to attack Britain and were deep in discussion instead with Hungary, Romania and Bulgaria over plans to invade the Soviet Union. Golikov sent back a sharp reply telling Sophocles to be more discerning about where he got his information. It was Golikov's default response to unwelcome intelligence. March also saw a flurry of reports from Colonel Grigorii Eremin (codename Eshchesnko), the 'legal' military attaché at the Soviet Embassy in Romania all of which pointed to the Soviet Union as Germany's real target. It is remarkable that on 11 March, Golikov authored an intelligence summary of German forces in Eastern Europe that made no mention of intelligence warning of an attack against the Soviet Union. When, a week later, he was forced to acknowledge doubts, he wrote, 'I consider that the most probable time operations will begin against the Soviet Union is after the victory over England or the conclusion of an honourable peace treaty'. Rumours to the contrary should be regarded as misinformation emanating from Britain and Germany.[20]

It was a central feature of German planning for Barbarossa that the Abwehr should attempt to confound Soviet intelligence and keep them in the dark about Hitler's true intentions. Deception was at the core of the planning process with all parts of the German government playing a part and even the Führer, himself, making significant contributions to the process. The most important element of the subterfuge was a concerted effort to persuade the Soviets that Hitler's primary objective at the start of 1941 was the complete subjugation of Britain, which would be accomplished by an invasion of the British Isles.

Stalin, like many others, was shaken by the swift capitulation of France and the rout of the British Expeditionary Force in May and June 1940. He had hoped for a more spirited defence and a much longer and costly war in the West, but even after the French surrender at Compiegne, he was inclined to believe that Hitler would not open a second front in the east while the British, albeit subdued, remained as a belligerent foe in the West. Hitler was smart enough to realise that Stalin was playing for time and authorised a programme of deception that would play to Stalin's paranoia and give the Soviet leader hope that his armed forces would be given a breathing space to prepare a defence. Even as, or especially because of, the increased Wehrmacht build up on the Soviet border in May 1941, extra effort was expended to give the impression that it was itself a double-bluff and deception designed to disguise preparations for an invasion of the British Isles. Golikov was only too willing to take this at face value even though the London GRU residency was reporting that the Luftwaffe had closed down many of its facilities in France and the Low Countries.

That Hitler would invade the Soviet Union at some point was never questioned in Moscow and never seriously denied in Berlin, however, and the Germans made no effort to disabuse the Soviets of that which brings us to the second phase of the deception, where the eventual blow would fall. Stalin believed that the Germans were planning for a long war and would prioritise occupation of the Ukraine and the Donbas to control their food, mineral and industrial resources but that was far from the truth of the matter. Hitler planned a Blitzkrieg operation similar to the one that had destroyed the French army in a matter of a few weeks. He anticipated a lightning advance against a weak and disorganised enemy and a triumphal occupation of Moscow before Christmas 1941 and to this end it was not the Ukraine that would feel the main force of the attack but the Brest-Misk region north of the Pripet Marshes.

The Red Army, however, was concentrated in the Ukrainian Special Military District, despite the objections of Timoshenko and Chief of Staff Kirill Meretskov. They had anticipated exactly what Hitler would do but Stalin had overruled them. German intelligence had a pretty good idea about Red Army deployment in those areas close to the border. It was now imperative that nothing was done to alert Stalin to the error of his ways and the Germans just hoped that he would not suddenly start listening to his General Staff rather than getting rid of any within who challenged his decision. To this end, everything was done to suggest that when the attack went in it would be across the Ukraine. As the invasion date approached, ever more German disinformation seemed to confirm that German troop movements in the east were no more than enhanced diplomacy designed to confuse the British and put pressure on Stalin to avoid any possibility of rapprochement with British Prime Minister Winston Churchill.

The Bucharest Tass correspondent Mikhail Sharov learned that AVS had been directed by German intelligence to maintain contact with Ukrainian anti-Soviet organisations in Romania and report on German plans directed against the Soviet Union. Sharov saw to it that these reports went directly to Stalin, Molotov and others in the top leadership. AVS had already reported that there was much talk in Berlin of an impending German attack on the Soviet Union, but warned that this may be no more than rumour deliberately planted to create uncertainty in Moscow. He also discounted the likelihood of an all-out attack against Britain because of a predicted high casualty rate, but it was certain that Hitler would not sit on his hands for long. Reports emanating from other sources in Bucharest supported the idea that Hitler had abandoned all thought of an invasion of Britain and that an attack against the Soviet Union was imminent. AVS also reported that during meetings in Vienna, intoxicated by the success of *Fall Gelb*, Göring and the Romanian leader Ion Antonescu had discussed Romania's role in a forthcoming war against the Soviet Union that could start as early as May 1941. Stalin had never doubted that the Molotov-Ribbentrop Pact was a temporary measure and that it was a case of when and not if the Germans would attack the Soviet Union, but balancing the evidence, he stood by his conviction that it would not happen before Hitler had resolving the issue of Britain. What Stalin needed was time. Time to prepare and he seemed determined to do everything to refrain from provoking Hitler while he got it.

On 26 March 1941, yet another source had stated that the Romanian general staff had been given precise information about a simultaneous attack planned to take place against the Ukraine and the Baltic States, some few months hence, that, it was hoped, would stimulate an uprising there against their Soviet overlords. While German troops would redeploy from Yugoslavia, Ukrainian groups would prepare for espionage and sabotage missions to foment unrest. The Romanians would take part by providing twenty divisions armed by Germany and, in return would be given control over Bessarabia. In every sector there was a growing threat of German aggression towards the Soviet Union. Preparation for military action were reportedly going forward 'like clockwork' and there was much reporting of German boasts that any war with the Soviets would start in June 1941 and be over within a few months.

Meanwhile, Stalin perpetrated another act in the theatre of deception. On the eve of Barbarossa it was perhaps one of his cutest devices. On 13 April 1941, the Japanese Foreign Minister Yosuke Matsuoka and Ambassador Yoshitsugu Tatekawa together with Molotov signed the Soviet-Japanese Neutrality Pact. It was designed to appear as a friendly gesture towards Germany and a blow to any possibility of deal with the British. Stalin even put in a personal appearance alongside Molotov to see Matsuoka off at the railway station afterwards.

On 14 April, Sophocles had reported to Moscow on the build-up of German forces in three main concentrations at Königsberg under Gerd von Rundstedt, at Kraków under Johannes Blaskowitz or Wilhelm List, and at Warsaw, under Fedor von Bock. They were also sending troops into Finland and at least ten infantry and three tank divisions into Hungary. Furthermore, Germany seemed to be putting pressure on the Balkan countries to support an attack on the Soviet Union. With them as allies, the Germans would have succeeded in establishing themselves on the shores of the Adriatic and Aegean.

The GRU resident in Prague, Leonid A. Mikhailov ran various agent who had contacts with the Czech resistance. On 15 April 1941, he reported that sources confirmed a provisional date of 15 May for the start of an invasion of the Soviet Union, which would be masked by large-scale preparations for a massive attack against Britain. When he was given a copy of the report, Stalin refused to believe it and scribbled across it 'English provocation! Investigate'.[21] Two days later Mikhailov reported that a Czech agent of the Soviet military intelligence called Shkvor told him that the Skoda firm had been ordered to immediate halt the manufacture of heavy armaments that were being produced for the Soviet Union at their plants.

By mid-May, the weight of evidence was piling up to suggest that an attack was imminent, but it is doubtful if he had the nerve to say as much to Stalin and incur the sort of retribution that would follow any undermining of the Vozhd's increasingly fragile hold on a version of events that looked ever more spurious in the face of reality. There was still enough ambiguity to stay Golikov's hand, however, especially in the timing of an attack that varied between a few days and a whole year, and doubt raised by so many predicted invasion dates having come and gone.

Marshal Georgy K. Zhukov and Timoshenko were sufficiently disturbed by the intelligence to put forward the idea of a pre-emptive attack against the German forces massing on their border. In

May, Zhukov warned that Germany had the potential to anticipate Soviet deployment and deliver a surprise blow. To prevent this, he recommended a pre-emptive strike to prevent enemy deployment and to attack the German army at the point at which it is deploying. The whole idea was quite impractical and Zhukov, above all others, must have known it. Had preparations been made, German reconnaissance would have picked it up almost immediately and launched their own pre-emptive strike to prevent the Soviet pre-emptive strike.

By the end of May, there was less and less divergence in the various intelligence reports Golikov was getting. Intelligence from all sources predicting an imminent attack was approaching unanimity. Enshchenko reported from Budapest that German troops, artillery and ammunition trains were heading north towards the Romanian-Soviet border. The idea of a German attack against Britain, one of the pillars of Stalin's hypothesis, had dropped right off the agenda and the reported movement of German forces left little doubt as to their purpose. Speculation was giving ground to expectation.

On 7 June 1941, in a report circulated to all top Soviet officials, AVS said that, on the basis of current rumours, Romania would be at war with the Soviet Union 'very soon'. All railways in that country were mobilised towards transporting troops to the Soviet border. Golikov's nerves must had been stretched to the limit when he wrote to Stalin saying, 'Considering that Romanian mobilization is meant to strengthen the German right flank in Europe, SPECIAL ATTENTION must be paid to the ongoing strengthening of German forces in Poland.' The capitalisation was tantamount to shouting at the *Vozkd*. Golikov survived, but his warning had no discernible effect on Soviet strategy. After 7 June, if Golikov wrote any further summaries for Stalin's attention, none have subsequently come to light, and the implication is that he simply passed on the raw intelligence as it came in.

When the German attack went in two weeks later, members of the Soviet Embassy in Bucharest had been sent back home and contact with AVS was ruptured until the arrival in Romania of the Red Army in 1944, when he resumed working for the Soviets and continued to do so until the end of the war. In 1952, he and his family were rewarded with a trip to the Gulag and only released after Stalin's death.

The pressure was building on Stalin to take the idea of an imminent German attack seriously but changing his mind after such a long period of stubborn resistance would not come easily. Apart from anything else it would expose him to political attack from those in the Politburo who were looking for an opening to unseat him. A report of 6 June 1941 from Sofia, which supported the idea of a German attack on the Soviet Union, further chipped away at Stalin's confidence when he was already agitated by Proskurov's dismissal of any possibility of a German attack against Britain. More than anything else, it was Proskurov's intelligence that was undermining Stalin's conviction. He simply could not control this man who persisted in giving him unwelcome news so he had ordered Timoshenko to fire him and replace him with Golikov, someone who Stalin saw as one on whom he could rely completely to reassure him and furnish him with intelligence entirely consistent with his own views.

Soviet counterintelligence agencies were also very active against foreign missions in Moscow with agent penetrations, telephone taps, the installation of listening devices. Of particular importance was the home of German military attaché General Ernst Köstring. In late April 1941, they started work on a neighbouring house ostensibly to fix burst pipes and from there they tunnelled into the basement of Köstring's home accessing his office and planting microphones. Conversations they monitored included discussions between the Germans and with their Italian, Hungarian and Finnish allies pointing to the likelihood of a German attack on the Soviet Union.

By early June 1941, the evidence of an impending German invasion of the Soviet Union was becoming overwhelming. The fuel and oil samples, the machinery being brought up to adapt German railcars to the Soviet gauge, the camouflaged river crossing equipment and massive movement of troops, were all pointing to the same conclusion. Beria, at least, was taking the warnings at face value. He reported to Stalin on German troop movements in eastern Poland and the presence of pontoons, wooden bridge components and dirigibles, all essential for river crossings, facing Brest and Lvov. May had seen increased Luftwaffe activity at new airfields constructed near the border and then German authorities started delaying or blocking the movement of Soviet trains bound for Germany carrying trade goods provided for under Soviet-German agreements.

However, when Red Army leaders ordered troops to occupy forward defensive positions on 9 June it was immediately revoked by Stalin for fear of antagonising the Germans and provoking a border incident. The British Foreign Secretary, Anthony Eden informed the Soviet ambassador in London, Ivan Maisky, on 10 June of other intelligence, derived from Enigma intercepts, that had identified all German units concentrated on the German-Soviet border.

An agreement reached on 10 June 1941 had given almost free rein to Luftwaffe reconnaissance flights. The Soviets were now aware that large-scale German efforts were under way to photograph the entire border area of the western Soviet Union for the purposes of producing accurate maps. Intelligence had come from an intelligence source in the Luftwaffe, Harro Schulze-Boysen (code name Starshina) who had been passing intelligence to the Soviets since the time of the Spanish Civil War. Shulze-Boysen, along with Arvid Harnack (codename Korsikanets), an official in the German Economics Ministry controlled a disparate group of communist sympathisers who worked in a variety of departments. Horst Heilmann was a signals decoding analyst, Johann Gradenz was intimately involved in aircraft production while Herbert Gollnow was in counterespionage. Other worked in the *Auswärtiges Amt*, The Ministry of Labour and the Berlin Council. At the time of the Barbarossa invasion, Shulze-Boysen was a lieutenant in the Reich Aviation Ministry at Potsdam processing reports from the Luftwaffe attachés attached to foreign embassies. In March 1941, he had been contacted by the Soviet intelligence agent Alexander Korotkov to whom he passed on information about intended Luftwaffe bombing targets in the Soviet Union. Berlin was highly impressed by the quality of Shulze-Boysen's intelligence that continued to flow after the invasion had started.

Shulze-Boysen reported that Luftwaffe reconnaissance missions were being flown from bases at Bucharest, Königsberg and Kirkenes in northern Norway but the main base was at Oranienburg. These reconnaissance operations, run by Lieutenant Colonel Theodor Rowehl used Heinkel He111s flying over Belorussia from bases in East Prussia, Dornier Do 215 B-2 covering the Baltics and both types flying out of Bucharest over the Black Sea. Specially modified Junkers Ju 88B and Ju 86P aircraft based in Cracow and Bucharest, covered the area between Minsk and Kiev. Aircraft fitted with long-range fuel tanks ranged far and wide from Leningrad and the nearby naval port of Kronstadt in the north to the industrial areas on Pskov and Minsk and the naval base of Nikolyev on the Black Sea.

In the two months up to the invasion, the Soviets had logged almost 200 Luftwaffe violations of Soviet airspace. On 12 June 1941, Beria told Stalin and Molotov that these were clearly not accidental and probably part of a broader agenda. Some flights went as far as 100 kilometres into Soviet airspace seeking areas where defence construction was under way or over the locations of large Red Army garrisons. Soviet leaders felt it necessary to at least make diplomatic protests if only to save face but were extremely reluctant to order countermeasures. The lack of retaliation and the absence of public protest was also meant to impress the Germans with the Soviet Union's non-belligerent approach. By 20 June 1941, there were exchanges of fire between German and

Soviet aircraft prompting the commander of the Twelfth Army in the Kiev Special Military District to ask for clarification on when it was permitted to open fire with antiaircraft weapons on German aircraft. It was reiterated to him in no uncertain terms that firing on German aircraft in peacetime was strictly forbidden. This was the day on which Soviet intelligence sent a report to Stalin, Molotov, Timoshenko and Zhukov entitled 'On Signs of Inevitability of the German Attack on the Soviet Union in the Next Several Days'.[22]

On 13 June, the Soviet Ambassador to Berlin Vladimir Georgievich Dekanozov had sent a telegram to Molotov describing the growth of German military strength along the Soviet border. This amounted to at least 140 divisions with another 30 to 40 divisions in reserve. Trains loaded with troops continued to move east, he wrote, but Molotov locked the telegram away and showed it to nobody. Two days later, Dekanozov followed up with a confirmation of his earlier intelligence supported by Danish and Swedish attachés who had no doubt that it indicated serious preparations for war. This time Beria saw it and showed it to Stalin urging him to recall Dekanozov. What Stalin actually did was to draft a TASS report for transmission over Moscow Radio, which said, 'the rumours of Germany's intention to tear up the Pact and to undertake an attack on [the Soviet Union] are without any foundation'.[23] Zhukov would later say that this transmission created a 'dangerous sense of complacency' among the border troops.[24]

At the start of 1941, Britain was suffering under the 'Blitz' as major cities were nightly targeted by Luftwaffe bombers in what was seen as a precursor to an amphibious invasion in the spring. It was entirely in Britain's interests to remind Hitler that any prolonged engagement with British forces would expose his eastern border to Soviet adventurism. The British would do everything they could to divert German attention to the east where a Nazi-Bolshevik war as Britain's best possible route to survival of its empire but feared that it might be a brief encounter resulting in rapid Soviet capitulation. If Germany did attack the Soviet Union, anything the British could do to stiffen Soviet resistance would undoubtedly prolong the war and act very much in Britain's interests. To that end the British government did all they could to urge the Soviets to galvanise their armed forces.

British intelligence had, by this time, developed a sophisticated system of breaking German Enigma military codes at Bletchley Park. Through Enigma intercepts in March 1941 they discovered indications that three German armoured divisions were on the move up to the Soviet border. And chose to share this intelligence with the Soviets. Initially, the British had taken seriously the idea that German activity in the east was a deception to cover preparations for an invasion of the British Isles in spring 1941, but their information was now leading them to believe, with some relief, that the Soviet Union was German's immediate target. If and when the Germans' turned on their allies, it was inevitable that the Soviet Union would look to the West for immediate military assistance. In that light it seemed prudent to indicate to the Soviets that such help would be forthcoming, and they were quick to send warnings of what they had learned. A few weeks later, Sir Stafford Cripps, the British Ambassador to Moscow, warned the Soviet Deputy Foreign Minister, Andrey Vyshinsky, that more intelligence showed a significant increase in German signals traffic on the border although neither he nor Vyshinsky mere made aware of the source. Churchill sent a personal, emphatic and urgent message to Stalin on 3 April concerning intelligence that, he said, had been received from 'a trusted agent' – by which he meant Enigma intercepts, but he was certainly not going to tell Stalin that Britain had cracked German codes. He warned that Hitler planned to move three Panzer divisions from Romania to southern Poland. Stalin still held firm to his conviction that this was British 'provocation' as was a similar warning from the United States' Deputy Secretary of State Sumner Welles. Politically Stalin was still playing both sides against the middle in terms of resisting overtures from the British to enter into an alliance against Germany.

Britain had sent repeated warnings to Stalin about German troop movements that suggested an intensifying concentration along the German-Soviet border but Stalin was sceptical, believing that Hitler's primary target was Britain and that any suggestion pointing elsewhere was German (and possibly British) misdirection. Stalin had developed a deep-rooted mistrust of British diplomacy after the collapse of the Munich Agreement and British aid to Finland during the Winter War.[25] The British and Polish cryptographers had broken German Enigma secret codes and, in spring 1941, were getting increasing levels of intelligence about their strategic objectives. This intelligence was derived from Enigma decrypts and codenamed ULTRA. It was distributed to relevant agencies, but its source was to remain a closely guarded secret throughout the war and for many years after. When Churchill chose to pass on some ULTRA intelligence to Stalin, he had to tread a fine line. Whilst his purpose was to persuade Stalin to abandon the Molotov-Ribbentrop Pact and join the Western Alliance, he could not reveal that his level of confidence in ULTRA was derived from the reliability of its source; neither could he pass on information that, if acted upon, might reveal to the Germans that their codes had been broken.

On 3 April 1941, Churchill sent a message to Stalin,

> I have sure information from a trusted agent, that when the Germans thought they had got Yugoslavia in the net, that is to say, after March 20, they began to move three out of the five Panzer divisions from Romania [sic] to Southern Poland. The moment they heard of the Serbian revolution this movement was countermanded ... Your Excellency will readily appreciate the significance of these facts.[26]

Churchill's 'trusted agent' was ULTRA decrypt JQ/803/T2 and his reading of the situation, which he also intended to persuade Stalin of, was that although Hitler had been forced to concentrate his five Panzer divisions against Yugoslavia, his ultimate objective was to move three of them north in preparation for an attack against the Soviet Union.

Over the next days, Churchill also instructed British Foreign Secretary Anthony Eden to pass on to the Soviet Ambassador in London, Ivan Maisky, details of German military and air moves and preparations towards the Soviet frontier. The most detailed of these was on 10 June giving the Soviet General Staff a list of German troops concentrated on the German-Soviet border, identifying all German units.

British and Polish cryptographers at Bletchley Park had broken the German 'Vulture' codes used to send daily orders to the Eastern Front from Berlin. At the start of July 1941, they also told the Soviets that German intelligence had broken some Soviet air force and naval codes, and were reading daily Soviet despatches in the Baltic region. By 16 July, Britain was giving the Soviets details of German plans for the encirclement of Soviet forces at Smolensk and Gomel.[27] This had important implications, however, in as that high-level real-time intelligence of this importance could only have come from an extremely well-placed informant. Avoiding all mention of the Bletchley Park operation, SIS chief Menzies told the Soviets that they had such an agent in Berlin. Details of the German armoured and motorised divisions about to be committed to the battle for Moscow were on Stalin's desk on 9 September, a full three weeks before the actual attack took place. Updates on the proposed attack were sent on an almost daily basis over the following days and weeks.

Then on 2 January 1942, Bletchley Park broke the German 'Kite' cipher and a month later the 'Orange Two' cipher both of which were used alongside and in a similar capacity to 'Vulture'. Surveillance of these communications revealed, a few days later, the scale, direction and date of the second German summer offensive against the Soviet Union, including Luftwaffe operational orders. Intelligence indicated German anti-aircraft units in Romania being transferred to the Ukraine and heavy German military rail movements from Romania to the Eastern Front. On 10 May, the Soviets were told of the transfer of German bomber and dive bomber units to the Eastern Front together with details of German assessments of Soviet troop concentrations.

The next significant ULTRA contribution to the Soviet war effort was on 23 May 1942 when the Soviets were given details of where the German Summer offensive would be and where the main concentrations of German forces were. Further intelligence during July indicated that, as a result of a change in German strategy, armoured units were scheduled to move in the direction of Stalingrad. It is likely that the German Panzer commanders received these orders at the same time as Timoshenko on the Stalingrad Front.

In September 1942, Bletchley Park broke the 'Tunny' cipher, which carried a large amount of strategic, as opposed to tactical, traffic. Over the course of the Stalingrad battles, intelligence was passed on without delay and the Western Allies timed a series of initiatives, such as General Montgomery's El Alamein offensive and the Allied amphibious landings in North Africa, that forced vital German resources to be diverted elsewhere. When 400 warplanes – that Göring called 'the core of the German bomber fleet' – and several hundred transports were transferred from the Eastern Front to Tunisia, the Soviets were able to factor that into their strategy.

When, on 7 November 1942, Bletchley Park picked up intelligence that the Luftwaffe was planning to bomb the Baku oil facility they passed the intelligence to Stalin. The Soviet leader, in contrast to his normal perverse refusal to offer acknowledgement, cabled back 'Many thanks for your warning, We are taking the necessary measures to combat the danger'.[28] What he was referring to was the increase in Red Army personnel from 1.5 million in 1938 to more than 5 million three years later and the creation of 31 motorised divisions, 61 tank divisions, 16 airborne brigades and almost 100 rifle divisions.

Further work at Bletchley Park saw the Luftwaffe 'Ermine' code broken on 25 February 1943, which coincided with the start of the first large-scale British and American bombing raids over Germany. In the spring, the Wehrmacht started planning what would prove to be its last attempt to break through Soviet lines and advance eastward. On 25 April a 'Tunny' decrypt detailed a German analysis of the Soviet forces facing them at Kursk. The Soviets could see from this where the Germans perceived the Soviet weaknesses to be and by anticipating an attack towards those areas, the Soviets were given two months to develop a strategic defence accordingly. At the same time real-time intelligence was passed to the Soviets concerning the orders going out to German forces as the attack date approached.

In June 1943, it would be the Soviets themselves who captured a German naval Enigma coding machine and broke the German ground to air signalling codes. To help Soviet intelligence make best use of this breakthrough, Churchill sent a number of British naval intelligence experts to Murmansk. Later that year, the British gave the Soviets one of the Enigma machines that they had reproduced.

The Luftwaffe had begun flying over Soviet territory along the new border in Poland as early as September 1939 and, initially, had not been a subject of concern for the Soviets but within a few months these flights started to look ominously like systematic reconnaissance. By February 1940, the Soviets had started firing on them if they ventured more than a few kilometres into Soviet airspace, but incursions continued and retaliation escalated with the inevitable result of the downing of a Luftwaffe aircraft on 17 March all of whose crew were killed in the crash. When cameras and maps were recovered from the aircraft, the matter was brought Stalin's attention but rather than a spirited reaction authorising effective preventative measures, two weeks later Beria simply directed that firing on German aircraft over Soviet territory must stop and oral and written protests were to be the only response. Unsurprisingly these were ignored by the Luftwaffe. During the months April to June, the Soviets logged an average of three flights violating Soviet air space every day.

Border guards were reduced to passive observers while the aircraft continued to fly overhead and Stalin continued to employ a rigid policy of extreme caution to avoid any risk of an 'accidental' provocation, which might present the Germans with a *cassus belli*. This was in addition to their emasculation ordered by Stalin after the Molotov-Ribbentrop Pact. Before that they had been in a state of immediate readiness with enough food and ammunition for three weeks but after the German invasion of Poland, these had been reduced to no more than three day's supply and had not subsequently been increased.[29]

Regarding ground incursions of saboteurs and agents, Beria also demanded that no bullets were to be fired that might fall onto German territory. Naturally, this severely restricted what border guards could do to deter heavily armed insurgents. The result of Beria's directive was that thousands of heavily armed saboteurs would later cross the border in the period leading up to the invasion and on the night before the German attack, they managed to cut hundreds of Soviet telephone lines.

The German diplomat Gerhard Kegel, who had been recruited to the GRU in 1933 was a member of the *Arbina* network now working at the German Embassy in Moscow. He sent a blizzard of warnings on 19 June saying that wives and children of the embassy staff were ordered to return to Germany, and representatives of German industrial firms within the Soviet Union were given urgent instructions to leave immediately for Berlin. Hours later, he notified the GRU that the embassy staff had been ordered to destroy all classified documents and pack their personal belongings.

There were plenty of signs of developments in German strategy. On 14 June 1941, the Soviets intercepted a radio transmission ordering all German merchant ships to steer clear of Soviet ports and any there were to leave immediately. Zhukov and Timonshenko were taking the intelligence very seriously now. 'German divisions were manned and armed on a wartime footing' they said on 14 June, and urged Stalin to alert troops stationed on the border and deploy them to their defensive positions. Stubborn as ever, Stalin dismissed their fears by saying, 'You can't believe everything you read in intelligence reports'.[30]

War would begin between 15 and 20 June, Arietz reported, but Arnold's information put it a week later between 22 and 25 June. Ramsay further clouded the picture by saying that the invasion date had been put back to the end of June. From Budapest, Mars chipped in with a report saying that the Wehrmacht's strategic deployment was complete. On 16 June, Shulze-Boysen confidently reported that all necessary reparations for an armed attack on the Soviet Union had been completed but Stalin still seemed to pin his hopes on negotiations believing that a German attack would be preceded by an ultimatum allowing time for talks. It should have been plain to Stalin that this was a vain hope given that all official approaches to Berlin to open negotiations were hitting a brick wall despite persistent rumours circulating about Hitler's willingness to open talks with him. Shulze-Boysen warned that rumours that Hitler was preparing to open negotiations with the Soviets had been cooked up by Goebbels's Ministry of Propaganda and should be treated with scepticism.

Golikov was responsible for the dissemination of reports from GRU field residencies and the preparation of periodic intelligence summaries. Significantly, his handling of this information reinforced Stalin's view that Hitler would not attack the Soviet Union until he had defeated Britain. This was reflected in the way he distributed his reports. Some he passed along to the Soviet leadership 'as seen', such as a report from

Bucharest reinforcing the belief that German army concentrations in the east were simply a devise to destabilise the Soviet decision-making process. Others such as one from the spy Richard Sorge in Japan had the following section removed before circulation: 'German generals evaluate the combat readiness of the Red Army so low that they estimate the Red Army will be destroyed in the course of a few weeks. They believe the defence system on the Soviet-German border is extraordinarily weak'.[31] Overall, Golikov only allowed through reports repeating the German deception theme that an invasion of the 'English Isles' was Hitler's primary objective. Khrushchev later referred to a leadership that was 'conditioned' to disregard intelligence that supported the idea of a German offensive against the Soviet Union and that the intelligence community at all levels handled any such data with 'fear and assessed [it] with reservations'.[32]

Much to the annoyance and puzzlement of the German Section of Foreign Intelligence in Moscow, Amaiak Zakharovich Kobulov had been appointed NKVD/GUGB resident in Berlin on 26 August 1939 despite never having previously served abroad, spoke no German and had no background in intelligence. His credentials, however, were of little concern to Stalin and Beria, who had chosen him for his complete trustworthiness. It was the timing of the appointment that was significant. He arrived in post just three days after the signing of the Molotov-Ribbentrop Pact and four days before the German invasion of Poland.

The NKVD was to regret urging Kobulov to develop new agent sources when he came up with a young Latvian journalist, Oreste Berlinks, who offered to share information he had gathered from the German Foreign Ministry. Berlinks (codename Litseist) had come recommended by a TASS correspondent I.F. Filippov (code name Filosof), a member of the NKVD Foreign Intelligence Residency in Berlin. It was soon clear that all intelligence furnished by Litseist was bypassing them altogether, and going straight to Stalin and Beria. Not only that but checks they had made indicated that Litseit had been involved with anti-Soviet activities in Latvia and had spread pro-Nazi propaganda there. They warned Kobulov to be wary but he ignored them.

Soon there was a steady flow of reports from Litseist about German plans to invade England, Hitler's nervousness about getting involved in a two-front war, his reluctance to consider an attack on the Soviet Union despite pressure from his High Command to strike and plans for Ukrainian independence all of which was music to Stalin's ears, but his monopolising of information had its drawbacks. It was unfortunate for him that when he used to say, 'an intelligence hypothesis may become your hobbyhorse on which you will ride straight into a self-made trap', he failed to include himself in its audience.[33] Litseist was a plant. The Gestapo had discovered very early on that Kobulov was an NKVD agent and had engineered the link-up with Litseist to channel disinformation from von Ribbentrop's Special Bureau to Moscow, but it came as a very welcome surprise for them when Litseist reported back that Kobulov boasted to him that his reports were going directly to Stalin.

The Kobulov posting had given Stalin a direct line to Berlin intelligence but its importance pales by comparison to one other avenue of communication. At the beginning of 1941, the constant reports of a German military build-up in the east had reached a level where Stalin felt that, although he did not believe they presaged invasion, the issue of these troop movements needed to be addressed if only to convince his own people that preparations for an attack were in place. It came as a surprise to Zhukov when Stalin told him that he had written to Hitler personally. He told Hitler that German troop movements were causing some concern and asked for reassurances that there was no hostile intent towards the Soviet Union. Hitler duly replied swearing on his honour that this was the case and that the troops were being manoeuvred for other, unspecified, purposes. Just how much faith Stalin was willing to place in Hitler's 'honour' is questionable, but Hitler's assurances were yet another small reinforcement of Stalin's views.

When Zhukov tried to convince Stalin of the danger with maps showing where the German forces were being concentrated Stalin took out the letter he had received from Hitler showed it to Zhukov and sent him away. It should be said that no archival records of this Stalin-Hitler correspondence exist, only anecdotal references to it. The writer Igor Bunich claims that there were at least six letters sent by Hitler to Stalin during a six-month period from October 1940 to May 1941. In one dated 3 December 1940, Hitler assured Stalin that his priority was resolution of 'the English question', but admitted that Goebbels was deliberately circulated propaganda about an invasion of the Soviet Union to keep the British off balance. The letter ends with a hope that the Hitler and Stalin might have a personal meeting sometime in July 1941.

The final masterpiece in the catalogue of disinformation, however, was Hitler's letter to Stalin of 14 May 1941, which was a masterful exploitation of Stalin's hopes and fears. Again, Hitler swore on his honour that Germany had no hostile agenda towards the Soviets but he warned that some Wehrmacht generals who were less than enthusiastic about fighting the British might use the build-up of forces in the east to deliberately provoke an incident. Stalin, he said, should show restraint in such an event and refrain from responding militarily. To deescalate and reduce tension, Hitler went on, some of the German forces in the east would start relocating back to Germany and France sometime after June 1941.

After his removal from the GRU, Proskurov had avoided the fate of his predecessors and instead had become chief of the Aviation Department of the Seventh Army and planned to take up his new role on 23 June. With two days still to go, however, with rumours of an imminent German attack growing ever louder he went to military intelligence headquarters and spoke to Colonel Ivan A. Bolshakov, head of the German desk, to find out what was really going on. Bolshakov showed him a report from Admiral Arseny G. Golovko, commander of the Northern Fleet, who complained about German aircraft flying at low level over the fleet base at Polyarnyi. Antiaircraft batteries had remained silent due to the instruction to avoid provocative actions. Another report from Shulze-Boysen on 16 June told that all the preparations by Germany for an armed attack on the Soviet Union were complete, and the blow was to be expected at any time. This was shown to Stalin and Molotov a day later along with two reports from Sorge in Japan warning of an imminent attack also. Proskurov heard and saw enough during his visit to cause him great alarm. He called the chief of staff of the Seventh Army's air force component and warned him to move all aircraft away from the main airfield since an invasion was imminent.

In Moscow on 22 June, the weather was perfect and many citizens had gone away for the weekend. The city was quiet. Proskurov was planning a picnic with his family but when he heard Molotov speak on the radio describing fighting that had been under way since dawn, he hurriedly packed and left for the Defence Commissariat. He said his goodbyes to his wife and two daughters who never saw him again.

Shulze-Boysen's report from Berlin, on 16 June, was accompanied by one from Harnack, which quoted Rosenberg as saying that the Soviet Union would be 'wiped from the map'. When Stalin read these reports he called for Fitin, frostily told him that they were German disinformation and sent him away. Fitin scurried off and ordered a review of all intelligence since September 1940. The sum total of findings indicated that the Germans were serious about invading the Soviet Union sometime in the summer of 1941, but Fitin suspected that passing this analysis to Stalin would cost him his job at the very least.

In the meantime, the Belorussian NKGB station reported details on final preparations for a German assault. Fitin sat on this also, but when he got reports from another of his agents, a Berlin police officer called Wilhelm Lehmann (codename Breitenbach), whose position in counterintelligence element of the RSHA allowed him to send to Moscow copies of all documents produced by his department, the tension was ramped up. Breitenbach had been considered a first-class source ever since sending intelligence about Werner von Braun's early 1936 experiments with rocketry, and he received special handling under the guidance of Beria himself. His report, on 19 June, showed that his Gestapo unit had been warned of a German attack against the Soviet Union starting at 03.00 hours on 22 June. Despite Breitenbach's reputation and track record, this too was filed as 'false and provocative', despite having reached Beria's desk. Breitenbach was exposed by a double agent soon after the invasion started and was executed by the Nazis. A final warning came in from Soviet military intelligence in Berlin that the invasion would begin within hours.

Belatedly, at midnight on 21 June, Timoshenko sent telegrams to staffs at all military districts ordering a state of readiness for an imminent German attack. Two hours later fleets of Luftwaffe bombers took off to bomb Soviet airfields and at dawn the mighty German army burst across the Soviet border. Stalin had only gone to bed two hours earlier. His first reaction was to stifle criticism by ensuring that all those who were already in his prisons who had foretold the tragedy would be permanently prevented from giving evidence. He then called a Politburo meeting for 05.45 hours. At the very least, Stalin had expected an ultimatum before any attack but all Molotov had got from von Schulenburg was a written protest about an 'intolerable threat to Germany's eastern borders brought about by the massed concentration of Red Army forces, which had demanded military countermeasures. After the meeting, it was still not fully accepted that an all-out attack was under way. The directive sent out to the border forces authorised defensive action but made no mention of 'a state of war'. Stalin refused to go on the radio to address the people and left it to Molotov to break the news. History would show that the barely half-measures ordered were completely inadequate to meet the situation. By 25 June, the Wehrmacht had advanced 200 kilometres into Soviet territory sweeping all before it.

Chapter 6

GERMAN INTELLIGENCE BEFORE BARBAROSSA

'No intelligence agency rests or ever lacks an enemy.'[1]

German intelligence had a long history of trying to peer deep into the Russian steppes to spy on the Red Army but with very little success. The only occasions during the First World War when they had come close to achieving any worthwhile intelligence was through the efforts of agents with total command of the Russian language and dialects who had intimate knowledge of the country's traditions. The intelligence chief at that time, Colonel Walter Nicolai even went so far as to say that the difficulties he encountered when up against the Russians were 'practically insurmountable' due to the vastness of the lands, the lack of good roads and the general hostility of the population.[2] The Abwehr in 1941 were about to find that little had changed in that regard.

In 1938, spying on the Soviet Union had low priority for Germany given that it was, in theory at least, a friendly state. Without specific orders to penetrate the Soviet Union, the German intelligence agencies were, in any case, unenthusiastic about operating in what was an exceedingly hostile environment. The border zone on the Soviet side was extensively patrolled by security guards and the local population was heavily encouraged to report any unusual activity or unfamiliar faces. Movement over long distances was difficult given that locals rarely travelled far from home, which caused itinerants to arouse immediate suspicion. Civilian radios were few and far between so again unusual radio traffic was quickly spotted by Soviet intelligence. Agents were severely restricted by the 'unrelenting suspicion' that was cast over everyone in Stalin's domain.[3] Also, the strictly monitored requirement for valid documentation throughout Soviet society meant that agents who were sent in needed to be extremely well supplied with relevant up-to-date papers to avoid immediate exposure.

The Germans had rather more success at the extremities of the Soviet border such as the Baltics and the Black Sea coast where communities were much more mixed with German heritage in evidence there.

The requirement for agents to appear normal and unobtrusive was obviously urgent but extremely difficult. A misunderstanding of local dialect or the wearing of clothing that looked rather newer or of different material or style would be a, literally 'dead', giveaway. Something as innocuous as the wrong buttons on clothing might not be overlooked. Anyone suspected of being a foreign agent would be subjected to extensive examination according to detailed directives circulated by the NKVD and NKGB. The climate was often dangerously cold for anyone who could not find suitable accommodation during storms or during freezing nights. Many agents were given identities that helped them overcome such difficulties. They might would pose as engineers, technicians or inspectors, the sort of people who would have good reason to move around from place to place and whose strangeness to the locals might arouse less attention. Even so, only the best agents survived.

After the military defeat and division of Poland, German agents took advantage of the chaos to infiltrate into the Soviet Union through the new and still permeable border. They had tried to infiltrate agents into Soviet territory across the Lithuanian border, but the Soviets had anticipated such a move and had already created very inhospitable environment for any German representatives living in that region who might be in positions to support clandestine operations. It was different in Poland, however, where agents had benefitted from the new German-Soviet border that ran through central Poland because, at first, the Soviets did not have extensive border controls established along the new line. Some of those chosen to cross the border were locals who knew the terrain and spoke local dialects. They mixed with Polish, Hungarian and Romanian refugees disguised as Polish soldiers, German defectors, Jews, and Communist sympathizers hoping to take advantage of the hostility of the Polish populations towards their new Soviet masters in those areas only recently occupied. Supplied with contraband goods, if caught they could claim to be smugglers.

Those who crossed posing as refugees could claim to be fleeing the German occupation of western Poland either to avoid persecution or dodge conscription into the army. The advantage of the refugee cover was that agents did not require local knowledge, but the Germans were clearly not aware that any refugees rounded up by the NKVD were likely to be immediately despatched to Siberian concentration camps. Where émigrés were recruited the success rate was probably the lowest of all agents. Few had the aptitude or skills to blend in with a political system that they had rejected. The fact that so many who were sent across into Soviet territory during the first few months of 1941 were intercepted and executed is indicative of both the dangers and the lack of adequate support.

The overall estimate of the numbers of agents employed by both sides is quite staggering given, on the German side at least, the dearth of useful intelligence accrued. Lieutenant Colonel Heinrich 'Heinz' Schmalschäger, the head of the German *Walli III* counterintelligence, claimed that up to 130,000 trained Soviet agents were deployed against the Germans during the course of the Second World War with many more less well-trained ones besides. On the German side, numbers are generally unavailable, but one source mentions up to 800 agents deployed behind Soviet lines at any one time and this together with other data suggests that there may have been between 36,000 and 45,000 German agents during the same period.[4]

On 10 November 1938, the OKH's *Abteilung Fremde Heere* had been split up into east and west sections with the east section, *Fremde Heere Ost* (FHO), created out of *12 Abteilung des Generalstabes des Heeres*, under *Oberquartiermeister IV* (*O. Qu. IV*). The Chief of O.Qu IV was designated as Assistant Chief of Staff for the Evaluation of Intelligence for the Army Staff. His function was to bring together intelligence from all available sources and provide OKH with analysis of operations, plans and intentions of the Red Army. This was to some extent hypothetical given that Piekenbrock later declared that OKH showed little or no interest in in reports from agents because they said they already had a complete picture of enemy forces obtained from PoW interrogations and captured documents.[5] On the counterintelligence side, FHO was charged with examination and analysis of the Soviet intelligence and security services.[6] Both east and west sections of *Abteilung Fremde Heere* got their information from three main sources:

- Attachés
- Army field intelligence (reconnaissance, air observation, PoWs, signals intelligence and captured documents)
- Abwehr

Army General Staff officers (Ic) were attached to each army group, army, army corps and division to direct the activities of the *Geheime Feldpolizei* (Secret Field Police – GFP) and propaganda officers. The GFP performed the functions of the Gestapo in the combat areas. Their task was to carry out arrests at the direction of military counterintelligence, conduct investigations into cases of treason, espionage, sabotage, anti-German propaganda and carry out reprisals against partisans. Almost all its members had been criminal police officers in civilian life and it employed large numbers of agents within the civilian population.

Despite its modest staff of fifteen officers under the command of the popular 'carefree bon vivant' Major Eberhard Kinzel, the FHO had responsibility for the Soviet Union, Scandinavia and the Far East.[7] The FHO found itself stuck between the OKH and the Abwehr right up until 1944 trapped between the 'millstones of competing organizations'.[8] All this meant that the FHO was forced to restricted much of its activities in the Soviet Union to the collection of statistical and technical intelligence about the Red Army, which it received through 'legal' sources. At this stage, it made no attempts to evaluate this intelligence leaving it instead to the *Operationsabteilung* of the General Staff. The general assumption that the war would be short and decisive as a result of German military superiority was clear example of egregious arrogance and, crucially, it meant that little was done to prepare for a prolonged campaign. When the Operations Chief of OKW General Alfred Jodl told Pieckenbrock and Canaris in January 1941 that intelligence about the Red Army was superfluous to requirements and they should restrict their activities to observing the border areas, he was merely expressing the conventional wisdom prevalent at headquarters. As a result, there had been few studies made of the sort of climatic conditions the German aircraft, tanks and motorised vehicles would have to contend with as they moved deeper into the Soviet Union and aerial reconnaissance was a poor substitute for detailed maps, of which there was a dire shortage, showing roads and potential supply routes.

One of Kinzel's first military assessments covered the behaviour of Soviet forces in occupied Poland and confirmed the common German prejudice that Soviet officers were poorly educated and unprofessional. Following on from this, the Chief of OKH, Franz Halder, called for a study of the way the relationship between Germany and the Soviet Union was developing together with an analysis of any Soviet military threat. Kinzel gave estimates of Soviet strength as 150 full Rifle (Infantry) divisions, but at least 30 were deployed in areas that made them unavailable to defend their western borders. It was unlikely, he told Halder, that the Soviets would be in any shape to launch an attack westward until they had significantly expanded their road and rail communications to facilitate troop movements. This report continued to form the basis of German assessments of Soviet capabilities throughout the coming months, but it was deeply flawed. Nowhere in the report was there any mention of extensive tests being carried out with the new T-34 battle tank, which had been in development since 1937 and which would play a decisive part in Soviet resistance after the German attack in 1941. Neither was there any significant analysis of Soviets industrial capacity for armament production.

Before German mobilisation in 1939, the Wehrmacht infantry divisions did not have *Aufklarungsabtellung* (reconnaissance battalions) but that changed when thirteen cavalry regiments were divided into battalions and attached to divisions for reconnaissance with each unit retaining its cavalry name. These became the 'eyes' of the division whose role was to protect the main forces from unnecessary 'surprises'. By 1942, these reconnaissance battalions were being used more and more to reinforce the infantry and after the Wehrmacht went on the defensive along the entire front in 1943, they practically ceased to carry out any of their intended functions.

In November 1940, operational groups were created within the Abwehr to carry out intelligence, counterintelligence and sabotage against the Soviet Union, but there is much speculation that Hitler banned his intelligence agencies from spying on the Soviet Union at this time to avoid any political fallout. No written evidence of such an order exists, which opens up the possibility that it was a fantasy created by the Abwehr to later excuse its lamentable performance in the months before Operation Barbarossa. Even if the order had existed, it is a poor reflection on Canaris and Kinzel if they had not made at least some effort to carry out their basic professional responsibilities by circumventing it. Canaris, however, may well have been more than happy to stick by the letter of Hitler's directive opposed, as he certainly was, to an invasion of the Soviet Union.

On 18 December 1940, Hitler signed the *Wehrmachtsbefehl Nr 21* order authorising the attack on the Soviet Union. It provided for an offensive by a strength of about 100 infantry divisions, 35 armoured and 30 fully motorised divisions. Heydrich's man Walter Schellenberg described the 'hectic atmosphere' in Berlin as a result of the order. SD intelligence resources were stripped from the Western Front up to the borders of Romania, Hungary and Finland and in Germany itself surveillance was stepped up against the many thousands of Russian émigrés, many of whom were suspected of being informants for Moscow.

The occupation of Poland had allowed the Germans to set up listening posts along the border with the Soviet forces, but this was hampered by the Soviet practice of using telephone communications in the border areas. Together with Luftwaffe reconnaissance, the rather tall order was to discover the distribution of Soviet forces all along the 1,000-kilometre border. During the weeks prior to 22 June 1941, the Wehrmacht paid great attention to aerial reconnaissance. They had developed high-quality cameras and film and devoted resources to training photographic analysts to very high proficiency. Rowehl's long- and short-range reconnaissance squadrons had been set up in late 1940, and suborned to individual armies and tank groups in anticipation of their invasion becoming a war of manoeuvre. Specially designed high-performance Focke-Wulf Fw-189 reconnaissance aircraft were brought in to operate alongside the Dornier Do 17, Henschel Hs 45, Hs 46 and Hs 128.

During the build-up to the invasion of Poland, the OKW had been anxious to survey the border areas, but scheduled civilian flights were banned from overflying the Polish controlled area. A former navy flyer, the 'lanky, easy-going' Rowehl, although no longer a serving officer, was a flyer of some experience, having made several reconnaissance flights over England in a Rhomberg C7 during the First World War. He had hoped to ingratiate himself with the military by privately hiring a commercial aircraft to secretly overfly the corridor, in blatant contravention of a 1929 German-Polish Treaty, at high altitude and photograph what were believed to be Polish fortifications under construction.[9] The mission was so successful that Rowehl, while remaining a civilian, was seconded to the Abwehr to form his own aerial photography company, the *Hansa Luftbild GmbH*.[10] The High-Altitude Flying Test Agency, as it was called in the early 1930s, was secretly set up as a civilian agency with three staff and a single chartered aircraft.[11] The company, theoretically independent, but actually a tool of the Abwehr, soon began covert missions over the Soviet Union and Western Europe using Junkers F 13, and later Heinkel He 111 aircraft. It grew in importance throughout the 1930s and eventually split into two new units, which became part of the Luftwaffe:

- *Versuchsstelle fur Hohenflug* (Experimental High-Altitude Unit)
- *Fernaufklarungsgruppe ObdL* (Long-range reconnaissance for the C-in-C of the Luftwaffe).[12]

First World War cameras were modified in cooperation with the Zeiss Optical Works at Jena. In 1935, the agency moved to Berlin and increased its strength to five aircraft. When the new Luftwaffe command structure was formed in 1936, Rowehl's unit had matured sufficiently to be incorporated into the Intelligence Division of the Luftwaffe Operations Staff, as part of the 5th Abteiluing, in the Reich Ministry, giving it greater access to the latest aircraft and photographic apparatus.

January 1939 saw the creation of the *Aufklärungsgruppe Oberbefehlshaber der Luftwaffe* (Luftwaffe Reconnaissance Units) and the setting up of *Stab/Aufkl.Gr. Ob.d.L.* at Berlin-Tempelhof from the commander and staff officers of the former *Fliegerstaffel z.b.V.* Operating directly under the Commander-in-Chief and Headquarters of the Luftwaffe, the *Stab* was responsible for carrying out high-altitude photo reconnaissance for the production of target maps used by the Luftwaffe to plan and conduct war. The missions were disguised as commercial or research flights and executed in great secrecy. The *Stab* also directed the testing of new aerial photography equipment and the operational evaluation of specially modified high-altitude aircraft. The *Stab* moved from Berlin-Tempelhof to Werder-Havel south-west of Berlin by 1 September 1939, to Fritzlar-Hesse in December 1939 and then briefly to Stavanger-Sola-Norway during the second half of April 1940. Following the occupation of France, the *Stab* transferred to Paris-Orly for a few months before returning to Berlin in October or November 1940.

The first *Staffel, 1.(F)/Aufkl.Gr. Ob.d.L.*, was set up under Major Erich Keienburg at the same time as the *Stab* at Berlin-Tempelhof initially equipped with Dornier Do 17s, Junkers Ju 86s and Heinkel He 111s. It moved to Seerappen, near Königsberg in East Prussia, in November 1940 to carry out clandestine photo reconnaissance of Soviet airfields and other objectives in North Russia and Belorussia, and then just before the launch of Barbarossa, on 16 July 1941, it transferred to Minsk-South for assignment to Luftflotte 2. Three more *Staffeln* were set up on 10 October 1939.

The second *staffel, 2.(F)/Aufkl.Gr. Ob.d.L.*, was created at Prenzlau-Brandenburg from *2.(F)/Aufkl.Gr.121* and equipped with Dornier 17 Fs and Ps, which were replaced by Dornier Do 215s at the beginning of 1940. Initially under the command of Major Alfred Wenz, it was transferred to Norkitten-Moritzfelde in East Prussia in June 1941 for assignment to Luftflotte 1 for the attack on the Soviet Union when command was transferred to Major Friedrich-Karl Prager.

The third *staffel, 3.(F)/Aufkl.Gr. Ob.d.L.*, was established under Hauptman Karl-Edmund Gartenfeld at Werder-Havel south-west of Berlin from *(F)/Lehrgeschwader 2* and initially equipped with Dornier Do 17 Ps, but did not see service over the Soviet Union until 10 August 1942.

The fourth *staffel, 4.(F)/Aufkl.Gr. Ob.d.L.* was made up of various units under Oblteutnant Josef Bisping at Berlin-Tempelhof and equipped with Dornier Do 17 Ps. The *Staffel* moved east at the end of 1940 to photograph Soviet airfields and drop agents in the area between Minsk and Kiev.

Once Barbarossa was launched great importance was attached to conducting aerial reconnaissance, using specially developed high-quality optics, film and photography, but, crucially, much attention was paid to the technical aspects including the rapid processing of film and the transmitting of intelligence directly from the Luftwaffe to ground forces. The Germans had conducted extensive aerial reconnaissance of the Soviet Union and its armed forces on the eve of Operation Barbarossa, paying special attention to the tactical and operational depth of the Soviet military formations. In December 1940, short-range reconnaissance squadrons had been set up for each of the armies and Panzer groups.

Deployment of specially designed reconnaissance and observation aircraft such as the Focke-Wulf Fw-189 (Owl) with its high performance and low vulnerability, played a significant role alongside the more than 250 long-range Dornier Do 17s and over 300 other reconnaissance aircraft, including the Henschel Hs-45, Henschel Hs-46 and Henschel Hs-128. In his memoirs, General Field Marshal Albert Kesselring stated that the Luftwaffe won air supremacy in the early days of the war thanks largely to 'great aerial photography' and 'continuous aerial reconnaissance'. It was this reconnaissance, according to Kesselring, that allowed the Germans to destroy Soviet aircraft in large numbers on the ground. One of the most important factors contributing to the degradation of German intelligence over the course of the war would be the slow erosion of aerial reconnaissance capability. By 1942, reconnaissance aircraft came under increasing attack and were obliged to carry extra defensive weaponry and crews. Technical developments in infra-red photography were curtailed and trained personnel were transferred to combat squadrons. There was simply nobody of sufficient rank at army headquarters to champion the cause against more pressing needs. The shortage of trained photographic analysts was bad enough but when responsibility was transferred from the Wehrmacht to the Luftwaffe all coordination between reconnaissance and strategy was lost.

Kinzel was 'efficient [and] operationally gifted' and by no means a total incompetent as his later war record shows but the FHO's performance before Barbarossa was heavily criticised.[13] With its paucity of staff and wide-ranging responsibilities, it was quick to point a finger at the Abwehr for its lack of support and deflect criticism from its own intelligence gathering operations, the results of which could not claim to be 'absolutely correct [and were simply the result of] an evaluation of more or less probable pieces of information'.[14] What was significant, however, was the changing appraisal of the Soviet soldier who was now considered to be much more technically proficient and capable of being trained to a significantly higher degree than was formerly the case. The reverse was true of the officer class, however, where it was accepted that the recent purges had decisively weakened the Red Army. Many of those who were felled, such as Mikhail Tukhachevsky who had a long history of liaison with the Germans, had been held in very high esteem but the new younger men drafted in to fill the leadership gaps were thought to lack skills and experience required of their positions and would, of necessity, be too wedded to political correctness to act decisively and with initiative in a battlefield scenario. Underlying all, however, Kinzel optimistically assumed that what the Germans considered to be the typical Soviet characteristics of sluggishness, schematicism, fear of decision-making and responsibility remained unchanged.[15] In the face of an attack, the Red Army would be forced to look to its 'natural ally' in the vastness and impassibility of its territory. Lacking any feasible alternative, the OKW was content to rely on its traditional image of the Soviet Union as a *Koloss auf tönernen Füßen* (Colossus with feet of clay).

Schellenberg clashed with Canaris concerning estimates of the Soviet military and industrial capabilities. In his memoirs, he claimed to have found Canaris far too relaxed about tank production, for instance, but such allegations must be weighed against the fact that Schellenberg was, to some extent, trying to rehabilitate his reputation after the war and that Canaris would not survive to give his version. It should also be remembered that, at that time, Schellenberg, as Heydrich's amanuensis, was pursuing an agenda designed to undermine the Abwehr and capture many of its resources.

On 11 April 1941, FHO reported that Soviet forces were deployed in purely defensive formations. Halder was sceptical. His own view was that the Soviets could 'pass over to the offensive' at short notice although he thought it was unlikely that they would do so.[16]

The university-educated lawyer Heinz Maria Karl Jost had been an early recruit to the Nazi Party and when he was 30 years old, he was appointed to the party's foreign intelligence agency, the SD, on 28 July 1934. At the same time, he had signed up with the paramilitary *Schutzstaffel* (SS) with the rank of major. Two years later, Heydrich appointed him head of Department III with, amongst other duties, a counterespionage brief. As with other Nazi organisations, Jost found himself distracted with internal and inter-agency feuds. This, naturally, restricted the amount of time he had to spend on spying on other countries.

After the German invasion of Poland, Jost served as a civil administrator in the occupied regions, but was soon to suffer a humiliation when Heydrich accused Department III of intelligence failures even though it had been Heydrich himself who had kept Jost and his assistant, Dr Alfred Filbert, short of anything like adequate resources or time to carry out extensive operations. Jost was removed from his SD post and saw his department absorbed into Himmler's RSHA, along with the German State Police, but he still retained *Amt VI* with responsibility for espionage against enemy and potential enemy countries. Department *Amt IV* of the RSHA became better known as the Gestapo, run at that time by SS Lieutenant General Heinrich Müller, and comprised the SD, the Security Police, the Criminal Investigation Police and the Secret State Police.

The function of *Amt IV* was the 'investigation and liquidation of opposition [to the Reich]'. It was divided into six sections (I-VI) – IV A was further subdivided – with responsibilities as follows:

- IV A1 – communists and underground groups
- IV A2 – anti-sabotage, active sabotage and sedition
- IV A3 – reactionary, monarchist or liberal opposition
- IV A4 – protective services for senior Nazi officials
- IV B – churches, sects and Jews
- IV C – administration of concentration camps
- IV D – German-occupied territories and foreign workers in Germany
- IV E – counterespionage in German industries
- IV F – passports and aliens

Jost's Amt VI was also subdivided, the most important sections being as follows:

- VI A – administration
- VI C – Soviet Union and Japan
- VI F – technical support for agents of Amt IV
- VI G – economic study group set up by Schellenberg
- VI S – sabotage under Otto Skorzeny

Of course, Jost was powerless to stand up against Gestapo influence especially in regard to the recruitment of agents. Qualifications for that role had been stipulated by Himmler himself. Recruits had to be of German blood, German citizens, politically sound and, if that wasn't enough, had to be trained to acquire 'an SS attitude in word and deed' in preference to skills appropriate to their role.[17] It was no surprise when

Heydrich' frustration with Jost's weak and ineffective leadership led him to humiliate the unfortunate man by cutting of his funding entirely and embarking on a pitiless propaganda war against him. Coordinating the timing of his action with the launch of Barbarossa, Heydrich had his protégé, Walter Schellenberg, promoted to Obersturmbannführer and catapulted in as Jost's assistant with special responsibilities for the Soviet Union. With Schellenberg breathing down his neck, Jost would soon quietly fade from the scene to let him take full control.

Schellenberg had graduated in Law from the University of Bonn in 1933 at which time he had joined the SS and the Nazi Party. Heydrich, whose SD was generally populated by people whose main attribute was brawn rather than brain, had been impressed by Schellenberg's background and education and took to him instantly. Rising through the ranks by way of a series of assignments carried out with aplomb, Schellenberg showed industry and initiative and was chosen by Heydrich to reorganising the RSHA, which he did by creating six departments with himself as head of IV E (Gestapo foreign intelligence). Part of his appeal to Heydrich was that, unlike many Nazis, Schellenberg did not involve himself in internecine feuds. He was ambitious but unassuming in manner and never channelled that ambition in ways that posed a threat to others. Heydrich grew to trust him implicitly and favoured him as someone who would not interfere with his own obsession, which was the acquisition of personal power and authority within the Reich.

It was the multiplicity of German intelligence agencies that would prove to be most detrimental to their effectiveness during the following years. Apart from the inter-department squabbles, most of the agencies were weakened by having elements dispersed across a number of countries whereas their imminent foe could focus its entire resources on a single enemy in a specific space.

Chapter 7

OPERATION BARBAROSSA

Day and night smoke belched from the chimneys of the NKVD,
the Supreme Court, the Commissariat of Foreign Affairs,
various other institutions and Party headquarters. Our leaders
were hastily destroying records, wiping out the clues to their
decades of official crimes. The government, evidently under
orders from the top, was covering up its traces. The first snows
of October were sooty with burnt paper.[1]

In the days immediately prior to 22 June 1941 neither the Abwehr
nor FHO had a precise picture of the enemy's situation. As a result
of agent penetration and aerial reconnaissance, German intelligence
concerning Soviet border forces was good, but there was very little
understanding of what lay in reserve. This was not a cause of concern
for OKW, however. There was an overwhelming expectation that the
Soviet army would be destroyed within weeks. The Red Army would
be denied orders to fall back, since that would expose the Soviet
industrial areas that Stalin was expected to defend at all costs. The
border force would stay and fight and all available reserves would be
hastily and chaotically sucked in. The inevitable consequence would
be the annihilation of the Red Army by vastly superior, efficiently
organised and expertly led German forces within weeks. The talk at
OKW headquarters was of a short war and a rapid march to Moscow.
Troops were given no winter clothing and provisioned with fuel for
only three months.

The intelligence agencies were affected by this mood of supreme
confidence to the point that they felt somewhat superfluous, not least
because OKW hardly called on them at all for their input and paid them
little heed when they reported. The overarching mood of confidence
saw no requirement for large-scale information gathering once battle
was commenced. Nothing would be allowed to threaten German

morale ahead of the attack. Nobody at OKH headquarters wanted to know about Soviet military industrial potential. They did not want to question their estimates of Soviet manpower. Kinzel's FHO reports did nothing to disabuse them. The Red Army, he said, lacked mobility and sophisticated coordination; 'Ponderous' was the word he used to describe them. He added that the senior Soviet officer corps lacked experience and their troops were poorly trained and resourced. This arrogance was to cost them the war.

What did the Germans know or think they knew about the Soviet forces that would be facing them? The only country that had any experience of facing the Red Army was Finland but they had little incentive to collaborate with the Germans after they had stood by, as an ally of the Soviet Union, and done nothing to help them during the Winter War. What the Finns had done, however, was expose the shortcomings and deficiencies of the Red Army during that short conflict. Radio intercepts were the only reliable source of intelligence upon which to make an assessment. Intercept stations had been set up in Bulgaria, Romania, Hungary, Bohemia, Moravia, western Poland, East Prussia and Finland, but because there were insufficient personnel to man what was, anyway, inadequate equipment these stations did not give much information about what the Soviet forces were beyond Desna and Dnepr, the Baltic States and some of the border areas close to Finland. Based on this somewhat flimsy intelligence and estimated population figures, Kinzel calculated that the Soviets had the potential to create more than 350 'large formations' but on 20 June 1941, his estimate was that there were no more than 179 rifle divisions, 33 cavalry divisions, 10 armoured divisions, 42 motorised brigades and 7 paratroop brigades extant.[2]

Estimates of Soviet Air Force strength was 8,000 aircraft in total of which 6,000 were in Europe. The composition was believed to be 800 obsolete close reconnaissance planes, 2,000 fighters – including 250–300 modern types – 1,800 bombers – including approximately 800 up-to-date aircraft – 700 fighter-bombers – consisting of Stormoviks and obsolete planes – and 700 naval planes of obsolete designs. In a bid to further persuade Hitler of Soviet friendship and possibly warn him of Soviet capabilities, in spring 1941, a few Luftwaffe experts had received permission to visit some aircraft factories in the Urals where they saw evidence of large-scale aircraft production. They reported this to Berlin but it had no effect on OKW plans and preparations.

In his book, *Operation Barbarossa: Strategy and Tactics on the Eastern Front, 1941*, Bryan Fugate proposed the startling hypothesis that Stalin and Zhukov had harboured no illusions about German intentions with its military build-up on the border.[3] According to Fugate, Stalin would certainly have been happier to wait another two years before the great encounter, but accepted the inevitability of an attack during summer 1941 and had prepared for it meticulously. It was Stalin, Fugate assets, who had outperformed Hitler in the field of deception by giving the impression that he was dismissing all German manoeuvres as strategic deception and appeared to be leaving the Soviet Union in a pitifully vulnerable state defensively.

According to the theory, Stalin had deliberately deprived his forces on the border areas, far from being the best available, of modern equipment, particularly tanks and aircraft. Much heavy artillery was withdrawn some 500 kilometres to the rear where the real strength of the Red Army was being concentrated. He had studied the Blitzkrieg of *Fall Gelb* and clearly saw, as Churchill had at the time, that the Panzers forging way ahead of their infantry support were particularly open to dislocation, encirclement and destruction; what Churchill called 'cutting off the turtle's head. The British and French had failed to take advantage despite a valiant attempt by the British 1st Army Tank Brigade to cut off the German 7th Panzer Division at Arras on 21 May 1940, but the lesson had not been lost on Stalin.

The border divisions were never intended to halt the German attack. They were far from the best that Stalin had at his disposal and while it had been argued that he did not deploy more and better defences on the border to avoid provoking the Germans, it might have been a less disastrous outcome during the first few weeks of the actual German attack had he done so. When General Dmitry Pavlov's Western Front collapsed within days of the attack, he was charged with military incompetence and executed to 'serve the fiction', as Fugate puts it, that he was personally responsible for the stunning German breakthrough. What Stalin had in mind all along, according to Fugate, was to draw the German mobile units deep into Soviet territory beyond infantry and logistical support, cut through their supply lines then encircle and destroy them with his modern T-34 and KV tanks and MiG-3 fighter aircraft. Fugate's arguments are based entirely on German sources. There are no documents or testimonies in the public domain from the Soviet side to support Fugate's argument, but his thesis is fortified by ex-GRU officer Viktor Suvorov in his book *Ledokol: Kto nachal vtoruiu mirovuiu voinu? (Icebreaker: Who Started the Second World War?)* published in 1992.

According to Suvorov, it was Stalin's long-term ambition to see Germany enter into a series of wars with its neighbours, preferably on more than one front, that would exhaust it and prepare that country for a communist uprising. This, says Suvorov, was the rationale behind the Molotov-Ribbentrop Pact encouraging Germany to attack Poland and draw in Britain and France. It was, in effect, an up-to date version of the Brest-Litovsk Treaty of 1918. When the German attack went in on 1 September 1939, Stalin held off occupying that part of Poland that had been agreed was his until German victory was certain and so sustained rather less casualties than the Germans. Another important reason for Stalin's hesitation was that had he joined Germany in the attack, Britain and France would have been duty bound to declare war against the Soviets or refrain from getting involved altogether, neither of which was part of Stalin's strategy. Suvorov addresses the question of why the Soviet Air Force failed in June 1941 and claims that it was because pilots had been trained primarily for ground attack, which is an offensive strategy, rather than defensive air-to-air combat.

The main argument against Fugate's thesis is that in June 1941, the Soviets only had 967 T-34s and 508 KVs and the operating and maintenance crews were only just beginning to get to grips with them.[4] The fact that the mass production of military equipment and ammunition had not yet gone into overdrive was a further piece of evidence contradicting it. The Soviets were still dependent upon huge orders of military equipment from the Germans that had been promised in exchange for the raw materials of ore and timber pouring across the border in the opposite direction. It was a bone of contention, and had been almost from the start, that supplies of these were much slower to materialise than had been expected but this had not caused Stalin to read into it a more sinister intent.[5]

Right up until the moment of the attack, Stalin had continued to supply Germany with raw materials to supply Hitler's war industries as had been agreed in August at the time of the Molotov-Ribbentrop Pact and Stalin believed that Germany had become reliant on this trade, which further reinforced his conviction that there would be no attack in 1941. From the German perspective, which Stalin had not foreseen, this was irrelevant because they anticipated a swift conclusion to the war with the Soviets after which all the trade goods would be theirs for the taking. It remains a moot point as to whether Stalin invited an attack or whether he genuinely believed that one was not forthcoming before 1942.

Another point made by Suvorov in support of his contention that Stalin was planning to attack Germany is one that would have consequences in light of what actually happened in 1941. As early as 1920, the Soviets had set up partisan units who would be extensively trained and equipped to operate behind enemy lines during any future war. Between 1924 and 1936 special schools were set up and arms dumps were established on Soviet soil for use in the event of a foreign invasion but in 1937, the whole partisan strategy was abandoned apparently on Stalin's orders as a gesture towards Germany implying that the Soviet Union would not need such a force since the country would not come under attack within the foreseeable future. It may have had more to do with Stalin's fear of internal opposition, however, because not only was the whole partisan structure disbanded, many of the leaders and experts in the field were eliminated during the purges.

Two days after Barbarossa was launched, the head of the British Secret Intelligence Service (SIS) Stewart Menzies was authorised by Churchill to deliver to the Soviets all Enigma intelligence Britain had accumulated over recent months about German strategy and tactics in the war on the Eastern Front. While Stalin's response was muted, all this historic intelligence was rushed through to front line Soviet commanders along with real-time intelligence as it came in.

Before 22 June, the Abwehr had sent waves of agents into the Soviet Union, many of whom had some connection with Soviet intelligence. Their objective was to acquire up-to-date information about the location of NKVD offices and the places where their files were kept. Up to three months into the war, only one had returned with information. It was a hazardous enterprise given the strict border controls and the extremely hostile environment beyond. In what amounted to a state where 'every citizen [was] an employee of the NKVD' informants were thick on the ground wherever you looked.

As the German forces rapidly advanced further into the Soviet Union, operational groups of the SD, including *Einsatzgruppen* murder squads moved with them into all occupied areas from the Baltics to the Black Sea hoping to capture masses of documents, but they found that most had been removed or destroyed. They did, however, make a large number of arrests and executed Soviet intelligence personnel wherever they were found. To counter this loss of assets, the Soviets parachuted around 500 agents from the 212th Soviet Parachute Brigade behind German lines knowing that the vast majority would be rounded up but hoping that a small number might survive and return with vital information.

Many local political groups that had been suppressed by the communists rose up in revolt in anticipation of a German occupation, which they hoped would liberate them. The Soviets responded with mass executions of activists. Under German occupation, they fared little better as stringent controls were introduced with the aim of combatting Soviet intelligence activity. Local populations were reluctant to cooperate with the occupying forces fearing that the Soviets might return, and they knew what that would mean. They were also wary of partisan groups who terrorised the villages and whom the Germans hunted down by offering bounties of 100 roubles for Soviet soldiers and 1,000 roubles for each partisan turned in.

The NKGB response to invasion was a directive issued by its head Vsevolod Merkulov to take operational measures against the civilian populations to 'interdict any attempts on the part of hostile elements to inflict damage on the Soviet Union' by which he meant internal threats as well as that from the invading armies.[6] Specifically, he mentioned espionage, terrorism, sabotage, uprisings, banditry, and calls for strikes and counterrevolutionary sabotage, and indeed all and any manifestations of anti-Soviet behaviour. For those arrested under these terms, their family members were also indicted as a collective punishment. All military units were to strictly maintain their positions unless ordered to do fall back and to crush all signs of panic and confusion within their ranks. Anyone spreading rumours about German advances were to be arrested and brought before a military tribunal. If occupants of penal institutions in Belorussia, Ukraine and the Baltic states could not be evacuated to the east they were to be executed on the spot. On 25 June, a Politburo resolution called for the confiscation of all radio receivers and transmitters to ensure that only the official news could be heard.

By 26 November 1941, there were 490,000 Russian dead, 1,112,000 wounded, 520,000 missing and 3,806,867 captured by the Germans. The Soviet Union was at the point of capitulation and Stalin faced a disastrous situation. After the first catastrophic onslaught, in July 1941, the NKGB had become the GUGB and merged with the NKVD with the OOs being subordinated to it. This regrouping of the special departments enabled them to re-establish the framework within which to carry out offensive counterintelligence and political security operations. They were made up of elements from the Border Guards and the Internal Troops whose mission was not simply one of combatting desertion, but of capturing enemy agents, setting up roadblocks, arresting suspicious persons in the operational area of the Red Army. Not only had the OOs been designed as an instrument of political repression they were also a counterintelligence organisation charged with combatting espionage and sabotage in the Red Army, but crucially OO officers were no longer answerable to the regular army and could concentrate more on state security work. This had a marked influence on their effectiveness and would lead to further radical security developments especially when the tide of war turned in the Soviet Union's favour.

The German army's order of 28 July 1941 was based on an intelligence summary of the day before which had concluded that the bulk of the regular Red Army forces had been destroyed. The 150 infantry, 25 armoured and 5 cavalry divisions that had been identified along the German front were believed to have suffered a reduction in strength of 50 per cent. The Red Army command was making every effort to stabilise the situation, but the twenty-five newly Soviet divisions hurriedly deployed were poorly equipped, inadequately trained and short of heavy weapons. Morale remained high, however, and there were no signs of internal disintegration.

All available intelligence pointed towards the bulk of Soviet forces being deployed to the defence of Moscow. It was with some dismay that Halder noted in his diary on 11 August that 'the colossus Russia ... has been underestimated by us'. Hitler was quick to point a finger at German military intelligence when he told Benito Mussolini that it 'had failed'.[7] Whereas original estimates of Soviet strength were put at 200 divisions, some 360 had already been identified. The Soviets seemed to have limitless reserves, albeit poorly equipped and led, which were severely impeding German advances and taking advantage of gaps in the increasingly extended German front line.

Chapter 8

GERMAN FIELD INTELLIGENCE

'A large proportion of the intelligence received during
times of war is contradictory, an even greater proportion
is wrong and the greatest proportion by far is subject to
considerable uncertainty. Here officers can be expected
to show a certain ability for discernment.'

Carl von Clausewitz,
Vom Kriege (*On War*)

The Polish campaign had revealed that the Abwehr knew almost
nothing about Soviet Russia and urgent measures were taken to remedy
that situation. It was hoped and expected that things would improve
once the attack went in, and agents would be able to enter Soviet
territory and establish networks, conduct sabotage and reconnaissance
behind Soviet lines, but this would require much closer cooperation
between the Abwehr and the Wehrmacht in the field. An arrangement
was formalised on 9 June 1941, under which the Abwehr created
Dienststelle Walli (Office Walli) sometimes called *Befehlstelle Walli*
(Command Walli). *Stab Walli* (Walli Staff), Field post number 57219,
was set up in Sulejowek, but it apparently exercised no command
authority, being merely assigned to coordinate activities in the east.
It was a special agency of the Abwehr Foreign Directorate created on
the Soviet-German front to coordinate reconnaissance, sabotage and
counterintelligence activities against the Soviet Union and to speed up
the flow of intelligence.

On 18 June 1941, the 'Front Line Reconnaissance Detachment I
East' was established. This operated under the code name of *Walli I*,
sometimes referred to as the Baun Agency, and handled military and
economic intelligence. It was always located in close proximity to the

Foreign Armies Department of the High Command of the German army on the Eastern Front. Its chief was Major Hermann Baun, a 'short, thin, chain-smoking ex-infantryman', who had been born in the Black Sea port of Odesa. He had grown up speaking Ukrainian, Russian, English and French and was considered to be Canaris's foremost Russian expert.[1] Baun had been an intelligence officer on the Eastern Front during the First World War and later worked for the *Auswärtiges Amt* repatriating German PoWs from Russia. Working for the consular service, he later claimed to have operated as a spy collecting economic, political and military documents for the local military attaché at the Moscow embassy. It was a characteristic trait of Baun that he rejected the idea of keeping files on his agents considering that to be the height of insecurity.

The instructions given to *Walli I* stipulated that

> While the group leader will remain within our own lines, his subordinates and their agents will penetrate deep into the enemy formations in accordance with their assignments. Transmission from and to group leaders will take place by radio. Groups will be formed from members of the indigenous populations.[2]

To accomplish this, under the control of *Walli I* were reconnaissance teams and groups attached to the headquarters of army groups and armies to conduct reconnaissance work in the relevant sectors of the front, as well as economic intelligence teams and groups that collected intelligence data in prisoner of war camps.

Within *Walli I*, Baun created subdivisions with specific responsibilities:

- I X – reconnaissance of ground forces
- I L – air force reconnaissance
- I G – production of fictitious documents
- I Vi – economic intelligence
- I I – provision of radio equipment, ciphers, codes
- Personnel department
- Secretariat

A special team of engravers, graphic artists and Soviet PoWs who understood about the paperwork in the Soviet army and Soviet institutions were assembled as part of I G to produce fictitious documents. Their output was impressive, including such items as the following:

- Identification cards
- Travel orders
- Pay and kit books
- Food certificates
- Orders for transfer from one unit to another
- Powers of attorney to receive various types of property from warehouses certificates of medical examination with the conclusion of a medical commission
- Certificates of discharge from the hospital and permission to leave after injury
- Red Army books
- Certificates of exemption from military service due to illness
- Passports with appropriate registration marks
- Work books
- Certificates of evacuation from settlements occupied by the Germans
- Party tickets and candidate cards of the All-Union Communist Party Komsomol tickets
- Award books
- Temporary award certificates

The 1G team supplied the *Abwehrkommandos* (operating units), which also had their own 1G groups, with the prepared documents, and instructed them regarding changes in the procedure for issuing and processing documents on the territory of the Soviet Union. To provide the deployed agents with military uniforms, equipment and civilian clothing, *Walli I* had warehouses of Soviet uniforms and equipment that had been captured by the Finns during the Winter War, a tailor's and shoemaker's workshops.

Subordinate to *Walli I* were *Frontaufklärungsleitstellen I, II,* and *III* (Forward Abwehr Command Posts I, II and III), three *Frontaufklärungskommandos* (Front Reconnaissance Units – FAKs) and the twelve *Frontaufklärungstruppen* (Front Reconnaissance Troops – FATs). FAKs and FATs were subdivided into FAK I (FAT I), operational intelligence, FAK II (FAT II), sabotage and FAK III (FAT III) counterintelligence. FAKs and FATs would be highly mobile and never stay in one location for very long. A typical FAT might include two intelligence officers commanding between 50 and 200 men with 2 or 3 trucks, maybe 5 motorcars and 6 light machine guns. Money and valuables were available for bribes but tightly controlled as was the alcohol and treats such as warm clothing that were kept for payment to informers. Units would carry out reconnaissance in occupied Russian territory as far as 200 kilometres ahead of the advancing German army and up until mid-1942 proved to be one of the best sources of operational intelligence. They were primarily tasked with discovering the location of enemy regional headquarters, transportation hubs and airdromes, but were quickly dragooned into anti-partisan counterintelligence roles. By 1944, some 9,200 men would be assigned to FAKs and FATs, but they were significantly outnumbered by Soviet counterintelligence personnel.[3] As a result of this disparity, FAK units of *Walli III* suffered around a 30 per cent casualty rate. Neither FAKs nor FATs were universally welcomed by army commanders in the field, however. They preferred to rely on their own army intelligence. Field Marshall Küchler in particular complained that FAT units delegated to his personal security, impeded him while he was out 'Elk hunting'. Historian Magnus Pahl says that 'Baun himself considered them only to be the extended arm of an infantry reconnaissance patrol.'[4]

Selection of FAT agents was carefully monitored. Special schools were established for advanced training for the best recruits who became very valuable intelligence assets. Although a knowledge of the Russian language was a prerequisite, special schools were set up to teach language skills, especially dialects, local geography and customs. Particular attention was paid to agents who then underwent training with combat units before being sent on missions. When the Battle of Stalingrad was reaching its fateful conclusion, FAT agents were the last Germans to be evacuated on special aircraft. *Walli I* was connected to Berlin with radio and all its staff were provided with transport. Each army group had its own sabotage and reconnaissance section, which were all subordinated to *Stab Walli*.

FAT III agents were primarily engaged in apprehending Soviet agents and interrogating them to discover their mission. Senior officers would then correlate all this intelligence to try and determine what the Soviets were planning based on what they were trying to find out about their enemy. The number of Soviet agents caught was taken as an indication of the level of Soviet military activity facing that part of the front. It would be a serious error when, later, the OKH ignored intelligence from FAT III at Stalingrad and Orel.

Other FAT III duties covered security against partisan activity of vital facilities such as fuel dumps and places where Soviet personnel might congregate for relaxation. Where partisan groups were known to be operating, FAT III agents would be assigned to make contact with them and infiltrate their ranks. This would, by its very nature, be an extremely hazardous assignment but where operations were successful, they proved invaluable in the war against partisans.

Sometimes, against normal protocol, a FAT III team would be sent into an area without the local Wehrmacht commander being informed.

As an example, a group of FAT 318 agents assigned to the Third Panzer Army were assigned to a mission against the Sokolov partisan brigade at Vibetsk. Two officers with twenty agents arrived posing as inspectors of poultry in surrounding farms with a mission to confiscate all the eggs. Once there, they ensconced themselves in woods and staged a successful attack on the partisans.

Baun, however, was unable to recruit sufficient indigenous personnel to cover the whole front and was obliged to call on the services of *Walli II* run by Major Seeliger, an 'irregular warfare' specialist who would be killed by Soviet partisans in 1943. *Walli II* would send *Abwehrkommandos* and *Abwehrgruppen* (motorised columns) deep behind Soviet lines to carry out sabotage, subversion and reconnaissance missions. Actions might include securing bridges just before the German attack, sabotaging telephone and telegraph cables, electricity and water supplies, and reporting the locations, operations and movements of Soviet troops. *Walli II* was the main body of German military intelligence and counterintelligence operating on the Soviet-German front.

Special *Jagdkommando* fighter units made up of various nationalities were employed to capture and hold strategically important objects in the rear of the Soviet troops until the main forces of the German army arrived. They were dressed in Red Army uniforms and provided with false documents. Assignments included the bombing of trains, railway tracks, bridges and other structures on railways leading to the front, destruction of military and food warehouses and strategically important objects and assassination of Soviet officers and political leaders. An OKW directive to *Walli II* demanded that they 'promote rivalries and hatred between the various peoples of the Soviet Union'. The broken nature of the front line made infiltration comparatively easy. In addition to the work of ASTs, KOs and *Walli*, Abwehr activities against the Soviet Union were supported by non-German agencies such as the Polish *Deuxième Bureau*, the Bulgarian Intelligence Service and the Romanian *Service Speciel de Information*.

Each army group command on the Soviet front would be assigned one Abwehr Group Command, which contained three *Abwehrkommandos* (Kdo) attached to each of *Abwehr I, II* and *III*. In turn, each Kdo included *Abwehrtruppen* (Trupps) composed of V-men, Soviet PoWs or volunteers and took their orders from army intelligence. Kdo 1 B (later Kdo 103) was assigned to the German Army Group Centre at Minsk. Its commander was Lieutenant Colonel Felix Görlitz. Its Field mail number was N09358B and its call sign 'Saturn'. Görlitz recruited agents from among Russian White emigrants and members of Ukrainian and

Belarusian nationalist organisations but after June 1941, agents were recruited mainly in PoW camps in Borisov, Smolensk, Minsk and Frankfurt am Main. Later in 1944, recruitment of agents was carried out mainly from police officers and personnel of the 'Cossack units' who fled with the Germans. Kdo 304 was formed shortly before the German attack on the Soviet Union and was assigned to the Army Group North. It was located at Kaunas and Riga, then moved to the Pskov region in June 1942. Its Field mail number was N10805 and its call sign 'Sperling' All counterintelligence activities of the Kdos and Trupps, and the partisan movement in occupied Soviet territory in the zone of front line, army, corps and divisional rear areas was supervised by *Walli Z* whose teams operated on the Soviet-German front in the rear of German army groups and the armies to which they were assigned, carrying out active intelligence work to identify Soviet intelligence officers, partisans and underground workers, and also collecting and processing captured documents. They attempted to create a network of local resident agents who would later keep in touch with *Abwehrgruppen* when the Germans began their retreat. These teams and groups also used captured Soviet intelligence officers to send misinformation back to their units. Some were also sent back into Soviet lines and identify other Soviet agents who were being sent behind the German lines.

Training establishments for agents were set up in Köninsberg, Stettin, Vienna and Kraków teaching reconnaissance and sabotage techniques a few months before the German attack. Initially, they recruited from White Russian emigrant communities and various Ukrainian, Polish and Belarusian anti-Soviet nationalist organisations. Conscription to the espionage service was thought unsound because agents taken on in this way could not be relied upon. Volunteers were encouraged to believe that they were fighting not for Germany but for their own nations whose independence would be restored after the defeat of the communists. Once the war with the Soviet Union began, the network of schools was expanded and recruitment reached out to PoWs and Red Army defectors with preference given to radio operators. The training period for agents varied according to the nature of their future activities. For intelligence officers in the near rear, two weeks to a month was considered adequate but for deep penetration agents, saboteurs and radio operators, up to six months was needed. Deep penetration agents would often operate under the guise of wounded soldiers discharged for medical reasons and civilians who carried documentation exempting them from military service. A typical example was the Borisov School, created in August 1941 by Kdo 103.

It trained intelligence agents and radio operators of Polish nationality who were sent behind Soviet lines in groups of two to three people to the Moscow, Kalinin, Ryazan and Tula regions. Transfers were carried out by aircraft from Minsk airfield or on foot from Petrikovo, Mogilev, Pinsk and Luninets.

Agents were given contracts stipulating their obedience to Abwehr control and describing the summary justice that would be handed out if they failed to comply with their commitments. To encourage cooperation, the contract might also contain personal information about the agent that might cause them embarrassment or imprisonment if it became widely known. The contract would be dictated and written in the agent's own hand. A photograph was attached, and the whole was then sent to *Walli* headquarters at Sulejowek. The agent would then be given a code name for communications and a cover name as an alias when on mission.

Agents were recruited from a variety of backgrounds. One of the most widely used sources was captured Soviet officers, many of whom had not been particularly fervent communists in the first place, who were bitter critics of Stalin whom they believed had sacrificed the border troops through his stubborn refusal to prepare an adequate defence. They had seen NKGB and party members flee the front after the German attack while they had been required to stand and face the onslaught without the means to resist it. Having seen what happened to their leaders who had been cut down in the purges, it was not hard for them to believe that they would be the sacrificial lambs who would pay for Stalin's failure for the Soviet debacle.

NKVD men had been captured also. They had good reason to cooperate with the Germans and get out of the camps where they would have suffered brutal recriminations if their identities were uncovered. Of course, these men were already trained in the dark arts and were particularly useful but there were few of them.

Of all the victims of Stalin's rule, none had suffered more than the Kulaks in terms of numbers. Some 4 million had died of deliberate state-engineered famine in 1932–1933 and those who survived nurtured deep hatred for the regime. Whilst not particularly suitable for espionage work these former peasants were fanatical opponents of communism and would undertake the most dangerous tasks in order to strike any sort of blow to the Soviet system.

Sometimes informers would offer themselves as recruits to become agents, but they were treated with extreme care. They might have a number of reasons for putting themselves forward for promotion not least of which was that they were working on behalf of the NKVD. The

Abwehr might also recruit from prisons where criminals could earn commutation of their sentence by agreeing to act as agents. Again this was fraught with hazards since they might well simply use their cover as agents to perpetuate their criminal career.

Operational demand made on Kdo agents were considerable. Only the toughest would survive. For agents, just existing covertly in enemy territory and unable to relax their guard even for a moment had its own pressures and that was before carrying out missions in which they would carry out sabotage or executions. For Kdo German officers, the conditions were harsh also. Generally isolated from other ground units in an unforgiving Soviet landscape, surrounded by the alien languages and mentalities of their V-men, they had to inspire confidence and maintain morale both for themselves and for their charges. The question for them was who to trust, especially V-men returning from missions. It was also their responsibility to interrogate captured Soviet partisans and soldiers, which took a toll on many.

One such man recorded his experiences in a diary. He wrote about having to interrogate a 17-year-old Soviet girl called Barisov. She had been coerced into her role through threats to her family. He called her 'a helpless human being, a child ... and I am responsible for her life and death'. In his diary he described conditions in the field as they hunted down partisans. 'Horribly dark and the roads knee-deep in mud', he wrote, 'the batteries of our pocket lamps gave out'. They searched a 'tumbledown hovel surrounded by 'all the stenches of the east'. When the interrogation of a detainee was complete, he wrote of seeing the person 'vacant and apathetic' and asked himself 'is there nothing else in this human being, no love, no self-respect, personality or faith?' They seemed to him to meet death 'apathetic and dull'. Writing about his relationship with one of his agents, he describes how he saved the man from a firing squad for which, he believed, the man would 'never cease to be grateful'. Now he was a tool in German hands and looked on as simply an informant working for money and not at all a 'real man'. For his own part, he writes of having to adapt to circumstances so as not to 'sacrifice the smallest of the treasures of [his own] soul'. One had to 'think like a Bolshevik and [still] have a German heart', he wrote, 'to understand Slavic feelings yet not injure [one's] German honour, be hard and yet sometimes be able to pray like a child.'[5]

Schmalschäger's *Walli III* was an *Einsatzkommando* unit operating behind enemy lines concentrating on scouring government, Communist Party and Soviet intelligence abandoned offices as well as military facilities for Soviet documents. Numbering some 500 men, they were subdivided into 5 groups. In small units which included

Abwehr officers, translators, radio operators, they moved with the troops, often even ahead of them with the forward tank units. *Stab Walli* received intelligence and counterintelligence materials from these operational units in the field and, after a preliminary evaluation, sent the materials to Abwehr headquarters in Berlin and to the FHO. The most important success of *Walli III* in 1941 was the acquisition of a relatively complete picture of the Soviet intelligence and security services based on captured documents, and the interrogation of captured Soviet agents and intelligence officers. It was they who produced one of the first important reports in spring 1942 uncovering the extent of Soviet partisan activity but it was largely ignored by OKH whose Barbarossa plans had anticipated a swift victory and who, even now, chastened by experience seemed incapable of conceiving such a thing as a resistance movement. Schmalschläger, however, recognised the threat from this quarter and beefed up his FAT and FAK units with his best men and expanded his informant network. It was this early failure of OKH to take partisans seriously that allowed these somewhat disparate groups to orient themselves strategically and tactically and develop operational cohesion.

The greatest burden under which the Abwehr operated was the lack of total trust between its officers in the field and many of those who they relied on for information. Had those agents of Russian heritage who chose to work against the Soviet Union fully understood the Nazi's fundamental concept of Slavs as *Untermenschen* (sub-humans) they might well have refused to cooperate. Their handlers had been conditioned by propaganda to the concept of *Lebensraum* (the concept of German conquest of Russian soil) and the idea that Slavs were fundamentally deceitful and devious and could not be trusted. Forced to adopt a duplicitous attitude, as part of the deal struck, handlers promised their sources that victory in the war would result in the destruction of Soviet control in a Russia freed from the yoke of communism. It became harder and harder to retain credibility for this promise when all around them agents were seeing what horrendous destruction the German *Einsatzgruppen* were inflicting on the Soviet population. It is doubtful if Baun's operations could ever have made a contribution to German strategic decisions given the nature of intelligence it produced. It tended to be an accumulation of individual tactical intelligence rather than providing anything about Soviet operational intentions.

While *Walli* operated in Soviet held areas, counterintelligence was taken care of in the German occupied regions by *Residenturas* (local permanent cells). There were as many as a thousand Soviets, male and female, working under the various German commands each of which was assigned to a particular *Residentura*. These *Residenturas* were located at strategic locations in large villages and towns in German-occupied territory from where agents carried out reconnaissance and security details. Intelligence from these agents was fed to the Abwehr who financed them and might assign new missions but who were not allowed to interfere with their implementation.

The head of each *Residentura* was a local person with a good knowledge of the people and surroundings. Although responsible for local operations, they would keep contact with other agents in the vicinity down to an absolute minimum. A small *Residentura* might have only two agents assigned, one to maintain records and send reports and the other to act as bodyguard. The number of agents was generally in proportion to the population of the area covered. They would be paid 'in kind' with cigarettes, vodka and extra food rations. Falso identities were backed up with appropriate documentation, which also might give them privileges to avoid labour detachments and, on occasion, to carry weapons. If they were assigned to go behind Soviet lines, all documentation was left behind and special passwords were given to facilitate passage through German checkpoints.

When the German armies swept across the Soviet Union, they occupied vast territories inhabited be a variety of nationalities. Nazi doctrine meant that there was no attempt to generate goodwill amongst them or to set up any sort of self-governing administrations under German control. What the Wehrmacht would have liked to control the population was a well-organised counterintelligence system, but what they had was a patchwork of improvised organisations that showed little enthusiasm to work together. At first, there was little need for punitive measures of control since the occupied populations showed no inclination to resist the Germans, especially in rural areas, and they were not coerced into working for the occupation forces apart from snow clearing to keep roads open. Horses captured from the retreating Red Army were handed over to the peasants who fed and sheltered them through the winter but were understandably enraged when the German commandeered them for their own use in spring 1942. An additional burden for the peasants was the demands placed upon them by Soviet partisans who took the young men into their ranks and generally took what food and clothing from the population as they wanted. Urban residents had been much more hostile from the start of the occupation. For them living standards plummeted from what they had before and whereas the peasants had access to food resources, townspeople relied on supplies from the countryside, which had virtually dried up. German propaganda and the disdain with which the people were treated as sub-human Slavs not to mention wholesale executions of Jews and other marginalised groups engendered a general state of fear, which turned to loathing.

In January 1942 information received at Abwehr headquarters indicated that there was a distinct anti-Soviet sentiment amongst a large number of prisoners in a Soviet concentration camp holding some 20,000 men near Kolpino just outside Leningrad (St Petersburg). Canaris saw an opportunity to incite the inmates in a positive way. Conditions in the camp were atrocious with heavy labour duties imposed on the prisoners resulting in a high mortality rate, which made him think that they might easily be persuaded to act in support of the German army if given the opportunity. A plan was drawn up by FAT II attached to the Eighteenth Army to drop German agents into the camp to stir up revolt. The first group of twenty to thirty parachutists would overpower the NKVD guards, then weapons would be dropped into the camp from aircraft and distributed to prisoners. A second group would then drop to consolidate the position at which point significantly more weapons would be dropped. Prisoners would then be liberated from the camp and, armed with their weapons would go out into the countryside and organise revolt against the Soviet administration. When all preparations had been made, Hitler refused to sanction the operation fearing that the armed men could not be relied on to act in support of Germany once they had been set free. Although the operation was aborted, it had given the Abwehr the idea of using Soviets against their own country's forces and it would be revisited at a later time.

Under German occupation, Soviet citizens were faced with death, deportation or starvation. Many chose to work with the occupation forces by enlisting in fighting units or working as espionage agents. The German approach was based on the expendability of such a resource. Deployment was fraught with hazards so, where possible, mission objectives were kept simple. Missions were often duplicated in anticipation of a high attrition rate. Often women were chosen and sent out in pairs but little effort was put into sound preparation. Combat companies of local men were formed, which was strictly against National Socialist doctrine, but when their usefulness became apparent, restrictions were relaxed. Armed with rifles these companies of up to 100 men would be used as security details to protect German troops against partisan activity. After a while, the groups grew in size, augmented by volunteers from PoW camps and eventually were assigned to German army units to take part in combat against partisans and Soviet forces.

At first, German counterintelligence had no particular regulations to govern its activities. They were forced to learn quickly and to formulate procedures as they went along. Little of their experience in the west was applicable to their operations in the Soviet Union. It was agents themselves who devised protocols and tactics. Their missions would be primarily to identify Soviet saboteurs, counterintelligence agents and anyone engaged in propaganda to incite resistance to the German forces. All Soviet citizens who worked for the Germans in any capacity, be it as secretarial clerks, cleaners, police, informers or interpreters and translators were kept under constant surveillance.

The Abwehr were aware that infiltration of their offices was a main objective of Soviet agents. Soviet espionage agents posing as deserters or *Besprisorniki* were encountered everywhere along the 'endless Russian highways or rough country roads … tramping along with a bundle on their back'. An Abwehr report of November 1942 claimed that many of these tramps had attended espionage schools. When questioned many were carrying currency notes marked 'in an unobtrusive manner and put together in definite arrangements or playing cards with markings all representing intelligence that is impossible to decipher.'[6]

The same report describes a youth arrested for making notes outside a building where German troops were billeted. A paper confiscated showed that he had been recording the number of men coming and going in the house. Under questioning he refused to give serious answers and so, to concentrate his mind he was told that he would be shot and he was taken to a place where seven others were executed in front of him. He was put up against a wall and the firing squad took aim. At the last minute, he was told that if he gave the names of his contacts his life would be spared. 'I know very well that when I've told you I'll be shot anyway', he replied and died without telling.[7]

Special watch was kept on Soviet girls and women who struck up relationships with German officers. Agents had the power of arrest and, in some cases, interrogation but could not detain suspects who had to be handed over straight away to the GFP. In cases where an arrestee was suspected of a serious offence, such as communicating with the Soviets or engaging in blackmail or sexual exploitation, the *Residentura* might be ordered to liquidate them but only after receiving a specific order to do so from a senior Abwehr officer.

Special German agents would, from time to time, check up on *Residenturas* to ensure that they were not abusing their privileges for personal gain and those found to be doing so were subjected to peremptory justice. Either by removal to another location if it was a minor infraction, or by execution if it had involved blackmail or endangerment of other agents.

Chapter 9

OPERATION KREMLIN

'If the enemy does not know where to expect an attack then he
must make defensive preparations in many different places.
Thus, he will be weakened wherever he is engaged.'

Sun Tzu,
The Art of War

By the end of October 1941, a combination of factors had resulted in
the first major Wehrmacht reversal of the Second World War. Faulty
intelligence, poor logistical planning, atrocious weather and the
unexpected tenacity of the Red Army soldiers had halted the Germans
all along the entire front and especially at the gates of Moscow. Losses
of men and material could not be replaced in full meaning that any
1942 offensive would be conducted along a single axis as opposed to
three in the original attack. There were only 2,847,000 German troops in
the east and they were plagued by shortages of tanks, motor vehicles,
horses, ammunition and fuel.[1] Renewing the offensive against Moscow
would have made strategic sense given that there were forces in place
to execute it and the morale-boosting effect of taking the city would
be considerable both in the field and back home but Hitler decided
that an attack against the most heavily defended sector of the whole
eastern front would be too costly and, instead, initiated *Fall Blau*
(Operation Blue). This was a plan to secure the Caucasus oilfields and,
as a secondary objective, occupy the city of Stalingrad thus controlling
armament supply centres and economic resources of the Volga region,
which would, in the longer term, be more beneficial to the whole
German war effort. Intelligence reported that the Caucasus supplied
more than 90 per cent of all Soviet oil requirements.[2]

It was important, however, to convince the Soviets that Moscow
would indeed be the target of the 1942 summer offensive and so a strategy
of deception was begun under the code name of *Fall Kreml* (Operation

Kremlin). On 12 February 1942, OKW chief Field Marshal Wilhelm Keitel, issued a directive entitled *Richtlinien für die Feindtäuschung* (Guidelines for Enemy Deception). German counterintelligence agents were given the job of convincing the Soviets that Moscow and the industrial areas of the middle Volga region would be the primary targets of the renewed German offensive. Members of the recently formed *Russkaia Natsional'naia Narodnaia Armiia* (Russian Nationalist People's Army – RNNA), made up of former Red Army PoWs, were trained as spies and saboteurs and transferred to the Soviet rear. Operation Kreml was kept secret even from Germany's other Axis partners.

Importantly, preparations for Operation Blue would be made well to the German rear and would be largely hidden from Soviet intelligence but could not remain secret forever and so, in May, efforts were made to convince the Soviets that the German Army Group South had inherent weaknesses. German units were withdrawn from that front, ostensibly for transfer to Army Group North and they were replaced by those of satellite armies. Army Group North, meanwhile, intensified reconnaissance on the Moscow front and spread misinformation through increased radio traffic, which they knew would be picked up by the Soviets. At home, military journals and the German press reported on the vital importance of Moscow as the focal point of Soviet resistance and suggested that the city's capture was Germany's priority.

On 29 May, the commander-in-chief of Army Group Centre, Field Marshal Günther von Kluge, finally signed the order that supposedly made Moscow the target of the German summer offensive and copies of the order were deliberately allowed to fall into Soviet hands. The order stated that the armies were to be ready to begin their attack no later than the end of June.

Soon afterwards the intelligence department of Army Group Centre reported a concentration of Soviet armour and a strengthening of defences near Belëv (Belyov) apparently in 'nervous' preparation for a German attack. It was understandable that the Soviets expected a renewal of the German offensive against Moscow and they prioritised reinforcement of the Bolkhov-Belëv and Orël-Mtsensk sectors. The British, however, cast doubt on the Soviet strategy by passing on Enigma intelligence showing that the German *VIII Fliegerkorps* was being transferred from the central sector to the Crimea, indicating that a German offensive was imminent there. Again, Stalin was sceptical and refused to accord sufficient importance to British intelligence reports. The Soviets also misinterpreted the movement of German Panzer units from Bryansk to Orël as part of the build up to a Moscow offensive when, in fact, these units were in transit to Army Group South.

On 5 June 1942, to the north of Kirov, the German 4th Army issued an order detailing plans for an attack in the Sukhinichi salient and another north of Bolkhov towards the Oka river. A 1:300,000 scale map together with a detailed list of requests for additional reserves was issued. It called for air support concentrated in the sector of LVI Panzer Corps. XXXXVII Panzer Corps would try to take the important town of Tula. A particularly strong contingent was concentrated along a short front of the Sukhinichi salient. Increased numbers of agents were sent across the lines and the fact that most did not return indicated that Soviet intelligence was clearly aware of intensification of activity. On 13 June, the chief intelligence officer of Army Group Centre reported his opinion that the deception had been a complete success. The Soviets had fallen into a defensive posture and had commenced attacks in the Bolkhov-Belëv sector and other places along the front to impede German preparations and gain some intelligence about German dispositions. The object was to allow various pieces of the puzzle to fall into Soviet hands and let them put the jigsaw together themselves.

By now, the armies involved were working hard together to try to give the impression that they were preparing for a genuine operation but still, only the chiefs of staff of the headquarters in question knew that the whole operation was merely an elaborate ruse. Then with only days to go before Operation Blue was to start, the chief of operations of XXIII Panzer Division, Major Joachim Reichel, crash-landed behind Soviet lines while on a reconnaissance mission. Against all of Hitler's strict protocols for the operation, he had been carrying orders, maps and details of deployments for the first stage of Operation Blue that the Soviet's recovered from the wreckage. When this was reported to Stalin, he interpreted it as yet more misinformation to disguise the German attack against Moscow.

The German Army Group South began Operation Blue on 28 June by smashing through the almost 2 million Soviet Red Army forces and advancing almost 50 kilometres on the first day. The Soviets had twenty-eight armies between Leningrad and Tula, but only eighteen in the southern sector between Tula and the Caucasus. The Soviet collapse allowed the Germans to capture the western part of Voronezh on 6 July and wheel south towards Stalingrad. At the same time, the Germans finally started winding down Operation Kremlin, but the Soviets were still deceived and they continued to attempt to make a breakthroughs along the Orël-Briansk line. The Chief of Staff of Army Group Centre, Major General Otto Wöhler, was sure that the Soviets had transferred only very few units south and had clearly strengthened their defences before Moscow. Only weeks after the major Soviet defeat at Kharkiv in May, Stalin and *Stavka* (the Soviet High Command) were still anchored to the view that Moscow was the real target despite Soviet intelligence identifying the large concentration of German forces and their preparations for an offensive on the southern strategic axis. Stalin and Molotov also continued to ignore British intelligence pointing to the Caucasus still suspected that, at some point, Britain and the United States would strike a deal with Germany to cease hostilities, leaving the German and Soviet armies to destroy each other on the Steppes. The Soviet Lieutenant General Ivan Bagramian, who was the Chief of Staff of South-Western Direction at the time, later refused to admit that the destruction of his forces had anything to do with Operation Kremlin, but it is clear that he was in denial.

Molotov and Ribbentrop, architects of the Nazi–Soviet Pact

Reinhard Gehlen head of FHO

Hermann Baun, head of Walli I

German radio detection van

German field radio operators

Operation Zeppelin radio communications centre

Red Army troops following a Soviet T-34 tank at the battle of Kursk

German soldier's despair at the Battle of Kursk

Soviet partisans attacking a rail depot

Soviet partisans laying mines after killing a German guard

General Andrei A. Vlasov head of the Russian liberation Army

Rudolf Roessler who ran
the Lucy spy ring

Heinrich Scherhorn who was
coerced into taking part in the Soviet
deception Operation Berezino

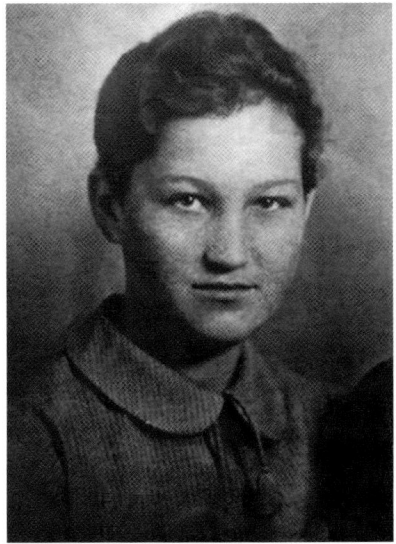

Zoya Kosmodemyanskaya

Zoya Kosmodemyanskaya walking towards her palce of execution

Zoya Kosmodemyanskaya hangs lifeless after being executed by the Germans in reprisal for partisan attacks.

Chapter 10

STALINGRAD

'While it is so far not possible to investigate the tactical situation
in the breakthrough locations in detail, it appears probable
that a major crisis is now upon us [at Stalingrad].'
Reinhard Gehlen[1]

The Red Army had been quick to appreciate the effectiveness of
German deception techniques employed in Operation Kremlin. The
strategy of deception, known in Russian as *maskirovka*, was not new to
them, however, it had been part of the Imperial Russian Army strategy
since before the First World War. The experiences of that war and
the Russian Civil War that followed in its wake clearly indicated that
surprise was an essential factor in achieving success on the battlefield
and led the Red Army to place great emphasis on *maskirovka* in military
doctrine. This was defined as

> the means of securing combat operations and the daily activities of forces;
> a complexity of measures, directed to mislead the enemy regarding the
> presence and disposition of forces, various military objectives, their
> condition, combat readiness and operations, and also the plans of the
> command ... *maskirovka* contributes to the achievement of surprise for
> the actions of forces, the preservation of combat readiness, and the
> increased survivability of objectives.[2]

It became an integral part of *Obespechenie Boevykh Deistvii* (Protective
Combat Action – PCA) along with *razvedka* (see page 135).[3] There were
four fundamental guidelines in the planning and implementation
of deception. The first incorporated the idea of 'activeness' to
aggressively intrude in the enemy's decision making. It is important
here to emphasise that any misdirection had to be plausible to
the enemy. The objective was to create doubt and confusion and

thereby cause him to make mistakes. Theory calls for rapid tactical and strategic exploitation of any opportunities emanating from this. Secondly, *maskirovka* measures must not be half hearted and must be adequately resourced. Thirdly, deception must be planned to the same high level as genuine aggressive operations with careful attention given to timing and integration. Finally, deception measures had to be diverse pointing to a single conclusion from many different angles. This demanded coordination across a number of perspectives to create a 'three-dimensional' impression that did not rely on any one facet. *Maskirovka* could not be an afterthought. Some actions such as Operation Bagration in June 1944 concealed the movement of reinforcements and supplies required the time and efforts of hundreds of thousands of men to execute properly.

The Red Army 1929 Field Regulations had stated that commanders must achieved surprise by carrying out operations 'with the greatest concealment and speed' to distract and deceive the enemy's perception of where the offensive would fall. The objective was to camouflaging troop deployments and prevent the enemy from learning of an offensive in time to reposition forces and prepare for it. The 1936 Provisional Field Regulations emphasised the importance of surprise through speed, concealment, and the introduction of new weapons and tactics. Misdirection was essential to hide the main focus of the attack and at the same time attacks are to be carried out attacks against enemy units on each side of the actual attack direction and center of gravity.

Regulations emphasised the movement of troops at night, especially river crossings combined with multiple fake crossings to disguise the intended bridgehead locations. Other methods included fake radio transmissions, fabricating documents to be captured by enemy patrols, the creation of false encampments and supply depots. Important also was the prevention of enemy aerial reconnaissance. Overall, any deception strategy required careful integration and commanders were to accord it consideration on a par with actual operations. The way in which it was employed by the Germans in 1941–1942, however, was a clear indication that the Soviets needed to revisit the doctrine and make it fit for purpose under the prevailing circumstances.

After the initial phase of Operation Barbarossa, the Red Army found itself surrounded at Brest-Litovsk, Bialystok, Kiev and Minsk but in November an operational pause in the German advance before Moscow gave *Stavka* time to stabilise their situation and offer up the opportunity to begin one of its first deception efforts in a desperate gamble to protect Moscow. They were helped by seriously flawed German assessments of the situation. On 18 November, Halder had written in his diary, '[the Red Army] is throwing in the last ounce of strength. [they have] nothing left in the rear'. Two weeks later he added, 'Enemy defence has reached its peak. No more reinforcement available.'[4] That was far from the truth.

The Soviet 1st Shock, 10th and 20th armies were part of a counteroffensive planned for 6 December 1941, designed to push German forces back from the gates of Moscow. They had been held in reserve behind the front and moved up to their assembly positions in night stages, observing strict light and camouflage discipline, and absolute radio silence. The three Red Army commanders themselves were unaware of their objective until a few days before the counteroffensive began. The deception was helped by poor weather conditions, which severely hampered Luftwaffe reconnaissance activity. Halder had noted the appearance of new Red Army forces along the Oka river, but he did not think their numbers were great and, overall, his mood was still upbeat. Neither did Army Group Centre intelligence consider that the Soviets were in any position to launch a major counteroffensive. When they presented their position maps on 4 December, they showed only seven Soviet armies operating within the Soviet Western Front and no sign at all of the 1st Shock, 10th or 20th armies.

Completely unaware that Soviet forces had been significantly augmented, the Germans were unprepared for the forceful counteroffensive and were forced to withdraw but the Soviets were poorly equipped for mobility and soon found their supply lines over extended. The harsh winter conditions also took their toll. The Soviets could not sustain the pressure and as soon as the Germans were able to shore up their positions with reserves, the counteroffensive petered out at the end of December, but it had been a warning for them and, although it had been a makeshift and somewhat disjointed effort, it was an example to the Soviets of what tactical *maskirovka* might achieve with better management. Where they could identify German weaknesses, concealed offensive preparations were indeed possible especially in regions which the Germans considered unsuited to combat operations.

A sobering FHO intelligence report of 1 December 1941 had made it clear that the road ahead for the Wehrmacht promised to be long and hard. Of particular concern was the sheer volume of tanks and guns available to the Soviets, which indicated a production capacity way beyond anything previously known. The Soviets had launched their first coordinated offensive to retake Rostov in November, which had alerted FHO to a hitherto underappreciated logistical capability to resupply units and to the way in which civilian labour had contributed to construction of rear area defensive lines. It was about this time also that German intelligence began to take note of the highly efficient and speedy transfer of Soviet troops using the rail network, which remained functional despite Luftwaffe attempts to disrupt it. It was also the first time that a report stated what the Wehrmacht already knew. Rather than just 'canon-fodder', the Red Army soldiers were extremely adept at utilising natural terrain, creating makeshift defences and employing camouflage and when put under extreme pressure, seemed willing to hold their ground to the bitter end. Nevertheless, the Army High Command Order of 8 December struck a glaringly unrealistic note by describing the shortage of heavy weapons as severely affecting Soviet morale. This was the day that the Red Army launched a counteroffensive, which came as a complete surprise to German intelligence. Unbeknown to them, the Soviets had transferred 18 divisions, 1,700 tanks and over 1,500 aircraft from the Far East having learned from their spy Richard Sorge that Japan was not about to attack Soviet forces there. Hitler responded with a slew of dismissals as Brauchitsch, Guderian, Hoepner, Strauss and Bock were sent packing and he took on the role of Supreme Commander himself in order to 'educate' the army in the ways of national Socialism.[5] Halder heeded the warning and decided to restructure FHO by bringing in a new man to run it. Halder had given Kinzel the benefit of the doubt after his underestimation of Soviet strength in 1941, but his time was up and Halder declared that he 'does not satisfy my demands'. On 1 April 1942, he was replaced by Lieutenant Colonel Reinhard Gehlen.

Gehlen was a highly-valued protégé of Halder. Before elevation to FHO, He had been a very well-respected officer in the General Staff Operations where he had played a significant part in the planning of Operation Barbarossa. Gehlen, however, had no background in intelligence and little knowledge of the Soviet Union, but Halder believed that his experience in operations was exactly what was required to delve into the minds of Soviet military planners. Gehlen would later say of his appointment,

> My appointment resulted from the chief of staff's desire to see a change in the leadership of the branch. He was dissatisfied with my predecessor, and we were on the threshold of launching a major offensive in Russia toward the Volga and the Caucasus. Part of General Halder's motive for selecting me may have been that I had served as his personal staff officer from the end of 1939 until early 1940 and that I had subsequently worked on the planning for the new Caucasus offensive in the operations branch right up to the date of my new appointment … I was therefore familiar with our objectives and military dispositions and with our intermediate and long-term aims on the eastern front.[6]

Gehlen's inexperience shone through his first report of 4 April 1942, in which he relied heavily on the work of his predecessor Kinzel. He said, 'Russian forces at the front have suffered so severely from battle wastage and the weather that scarcely a single formation can be described as fully battle-worthy.'[7] It was not long before this assessment was proved wrong, and he was quick to learn his lesson. Thereafter, he resorted to a careful and pragmatic approach to analysis tending towards the over cautious when writing reports, which were characterised by an array of options in any given situation. He rarely presented any one assessment as having priority over others and was usually able, after the event, to show that at least one of his analyses had been accurate. This hedging of his bets allowed him, to some extent, to avoid repercussions but his ambiguity was rarely of any great value to OKH operational planners.

FHO was responsible for the evaluation and analysis of any intelligence concerning the foreign armies in the east but this proved to be beyond its structural capabilities. In 1942, it lacked manpower having no more than 50 officers, around 100 NCOs and some 50 female assistants, many of whom were family members. Crucially, the FHO had no personnel for the actual procurement of intelligence and had to rely on the Abwehr, the RSHA, the *Auswärtiges Amt*, and signals and army intelligence to provide it. In particular, Gehlen could rely on *Walli I* and *Walli II* with their FAT and FAK units (see Chapter 14 – German Field Intelligence). It also relied upon Luftwaffe intelligence to an appreciable extent and this proved to be a dwindling resource as air supremacy was inexorably lost as time went on. Radio intelligence was useful, but only on the tactical level and this also diminished as the Red Army tightened up on radio discipline.

In his usual efficient and focussed approach, Gehlen immediately set about reorganising the FHO by making it more relevant to the OKH. Kinzel's main problem had been the lack of real intelligence, so Gehlen now demanded of troops at the front that they submit reports every ten days recording the strength and location of enemy artillery which was indicative of Soviet ambitions. He also wanted up-to-date numbers of German agents who failed to return, again because it showed where Soviet forces were grouping and tightening up security. Amended questionnaires were distributed to PoW interrogation centres to elicit more information.

FHO itself was reorganised into six sections:

- Group I – responsible for producing daily situation reports.
- Group II – conducted detailed research into all aspects of the Soviet

military effort including its military industrial potential. A subgroup maintained a card index of the Soviet order of battle, which included biographical information about its commanders.

- Group III – monitored Soviet publications, radio broadcasts and captured documents.
- Group IV – covered Scandinavia.
- Group V – prepared the situation maps.
- Group VI – looked after administration.

Having expanded his sources of intelligence, Gehlen now concentrated on the way in which his findings were reported to OKH. He started making extensive use of maps and charts to encapsulate information and make it simpler to understand. The use of colour to identify friend or foe was quite revolutionary in the way that it showed the position and strength of opposing forces along the front. Hitler, in particular, was impressed by the simplicity of this innovation.

Administratively, he imposed a rigorous routine at FHO headquarters at Angersberg close to Hitler's 'Wolf's Lair' headquarters in East Prussia. The daily intelligence digest, 'Enemy Situation Report East', was delivered to the Chiefs of the General Staff for their meeting at 22.00 hours. FHO was primarily responsible for determining the structure of the enemy's defensive forces, their distribution and their order of battle, which it did quite successfully in the early days of Gehlen's tenure. This was acquired through interrogation of Soviet PoWs who had been captured or who had surrendered but the sheer volume of PoWs in 1941 meant that there was never enough time or staff to conduct a comprehensive programme, so Gehlen filtered out all high-ranking prisoners and had them transferred to a VIP camp. Many were only too happy to cooperate in the hope of seeing the eradication of the oppressive Soviet state, which they had been forced to endure. Targeted questioning produced results that proved valuable in calculating Soviet military potential. Then, together with experts the Abwehr and the *Feldwirtschaftsamt* (Field Economics Department), Gehlen built up a picture of Soviet military production capacity. Many of these experts were civilians, often Baltic Germans, with special knowledge or skills in economics or foreign policy. Some had been in the pre-revolutionary Tsarist army, but bitterness and prejudice often clouded their judgement. Despite its shortcomings, the FHO was the only General Staff division that still demonstrated a high degree of 'personal unity, internal co-ordination, and exemplary trust in each other'.[8]

On 28 June 1942, the Germans launched Operation Blue designed to take control of the Caucasus oilfields. The Army Group South's

IV Panzer Army crossed the Donets river, and advanced quickly to Voronezh, catching *Stavka* unawares and this time Stalin, as part of a deliberate Soviet strategy of mobile defence, allowing the Red Army to fall back and avoiding the catastrophic encirclements of the previous year. The German advance was so rapid that by 12 July, *Stavka* was resigned to establishing a defensive front at Stalingrad. By late August 1942, the Luftwaffe was pounding the city and von Paulus's Sixth Army was closing fast despite Hitler's vacillations about the extent to which he allocated support to it. At this point, it is fair to say that, not for the first time in the campaign, OKW was optimistic almost to the point of complacency.

Far from being despondent, *Stavka* realised that they now had some freedom of manoeuvre. It had always been their contention that the Germans did not have sufficient resources to attack on two fronts in 1942 and now that they had shown their hand it was clear to *Stavka* that there would be no concerted attack on the capital. The Soviet reserves that had been built up during the first part of the year could now be safely deployed in the south, which would greatly widen *Stavka's* strategic options, but it was vital to do this by employing *maskirovka*. By this time both sides were employing deception to confuse enemy intelligence, but the Soviets were arguably becoming the more adept at its implementation. The Red Army devised *Operatsiya Uran* (Operation Uranus) to retake Stalingrad a crucial part of which was a series of deception and intelligence operations in order to conceal troop redeployments and confuse German intelligence about their intentions.

The first part of the plan involved Soviet posturing on the Kalinin front to divert German attention from Stalingrad and the Caucasus. From 30 July to 23 August, in the Battle of Rzhev, also known as the first Rzhev-Sychevka Offensive, the Red Army employed a large and elaborate feint, which was to cost them massive casualties, but which prevented German divisions from transferring to Army Group South to contain the new salient. Zhukov implemented a variety of measures to deceive the Germans, including the simulation of a false troop concentration to distract German attention from the main attack sector.

Special units constructed 833 mock-up tanks, vehicles, guns, fuel tanks and mobile field kitchens. They simulated rail unloading and movement, and concentration of tank and motorised rifle columns into the assembly and concentration areas, and passed false radio messages between fictitious units to and from higher headquarters. To deceive Luftwaffe reconnaissance, real tanks and vehicles laid multiple tracks to simulate actual column movements. When Luftwaffe bombers attacked these false positions, fires were started to simulate damage.[9] The level of success was demonstrated when German air strikes intensified against the false region of concentration and against the railhead where the false columns simulated unloading. This allowed the real troop movements to continue unhindered while the Germans moved critical reserves up to the false region in expectation of an attack.

Despite all Soviet efforts, by the end of August, German forces were on the outskirts of Grozny and engaging Soviet troops on the outskirts of Stalingrad but the operation was beginning to feel the effects of fuel and transport shortages. Then later, in September, Soviet troop movements in and out of the Western Front confused German intelligence who still believed that the main Soviet offensive would be against the Rzhev-Sychevka salient. Gehlen confidently predicted, in a speech to the German War Academy in September that 'the area around Stalingrad and the oil-producing region in the Caucasus would be firmly in German hands before the onset of winter.'[10]

Stavka saw the coming battle for the Caucasus as a defining moment and pulled together its best military minds to make their plans. Zhukov was made coordinator and brought in General A.I. Antonov, one of the architects of successful *maskirovka* at Rostov, and General Aleksandr Vasilevsky to his team. They began by undertaking a thorough analysis of Soviet strategy and tactics to date especially in terms of the application of *maskirovka*, which was now included in all orders at every level of command. It was steep learning curve and a number of glaring errors were identified. Where false concentrations had been attempted, they had lacked sophistication by, for instance, failing to create a sufficiently varied array of dummy equipment.

Elaborate arrangements were made to conceal the movement of Soviet forces to the Stalingrad front with the purpose of launching a double envelopment of von Paulus's Sixth Army at the same time as misleading German intelligence about the time, place and scale of their counteroffensive. By this time, to guarantee any measure of success it was clear that a formal approach was required when preparing operational and tactical *maskirovka* plans, which were now an integral part of all Soviet operational planning and had been placed under the control of special staff, resulting in a marked improvement in technique and application. It was still a constant struggle to keep Luftwaffe reconnaissance at bay and this became the most significant weakness in Soviet operations until such time as the Soviet air force could effectively interdict.

On the Voronezh front, to the north-west of Stalingrad, the Soviets organised large-scale training exercises of river crossings and manoeuvring concentrations of armoured and artillery formations to grab the attention of the German Army Group Centre. Then from 29 September to 4 October, the Stalingrad front launched attacks to maintain bridgeheads on the western bank of the Volga south of the city to draw German forces away from the fighting inside the city itself, This gave time and space for the 62nd Army to integrate reinforcements into the Stalingrad defences.

In his assessment, 'Thoughts regarding the Further Development of the Enemy Situation in the Autumn and Winter', Gehlen anticipated that there were three possible Soviet responses to von Paulus's occupation of Stalingrad in September 1942. They could either launch a direct counterattack to retake the city, strike towards Rostov to prevent a German move into the Caucasus or counterattack against the weaker Axis positions at Serafimovitch and Korotoyak, at the juncture of the Romanian and Italian armies. However, because of insufficient Soviet manpower, Gehlen believed that none of these would actually materialise. In his report, 'Estimate of the Enemy Situation in Front of Army Group Centre', he made it clear that the Red Army would counterattack further north against Army Group Centre. His evidence for this was the large amount of recently captured documentation, PoW interrogations and intercepted radio traffic available to him. Even when the Luftwaffe reported a comprehensive regrouping of Soviet forces between the Don and Volga in September together with the establishment of a new Soviet field headquarters, it was interpreted as 'defensive enemy behaviour'. Then, when short-range radio reconnaissance came up with compelling evidence of new, large Soviet troop concentrations behind the Don front, FHO saw this as no more than preparations for a possible attack against the 3rd Romanian Army, but concluded that the available Soviet forces would be too weak for 'far-reaching operations'.

Once the Volga bridgehead was established, the Soviets gradually moved two mechanised corps, one tank brigade, two rifle divisions, and seven artillery divisions across the river under cover of darkness. Both concealed and false night river crossings were made over the Don accompanied by false concentrations of artillery and vehicles to mislead German reconnaissance. In this way, three tank corps were able to assume assault positions undetected across from German lines. Simultaneously, Soviet troops all across the Stalingrad front were openly deployed in a defensive posture that was reinforced in depth to convince the Germans that they posed no immediate offensive threat. It would now be seen whether *maskirovka* could be successful on the biggest stage and, crucially, how it would integrate into large-scale offensive operations.

Great efforts had been made to make *maskirovka* measures effective and confound German intelligence assessments. It was necessary to disguise the forward deployment of the 300,000 men, 1,000 tanks and 5,000 guns along with huge amounts of ammunition, fuel and other supplies needed to conduct a successful offensive and all using a limited transportation network and operating in limited bridgeheads south and west of the Don river at Serafimovich and Kletskaya.[11]

Soviet intelligence played a crucial part in Operation Uranus by identifying weaknesses in the Axis lines for the counteroffensive to exploit. This was accomplished primarily by aerial reconnaissance and an effective, complex system for intelligence collection and processing, which they called *razvedka*. This is a single generic term which covers 'all actions necessary to achieve a better understanding of the enemy' and refers to every possible means of intelligence collection and analysis.[12] It also involved securing the area of operations to establish intelligence superiority over the enemy and preventing, or at least limiting, the infiltration of German spies and collaborators to the area of operations. NKVD, Smersh and Red Army counterintelligence were all involved in this process. Because *razvedka* contributed to gathering intelligence about the German dispositions, it helped to ascertain how the enemy reacted to *maskirovka*.

Reconnaissance diversionary forces were controlled by the NKVD and GRU. The *Otdelnaia Moto-strelkovaia Brigada Osobogo Naznachenia* (Separate Motorized Rifle Brigade of Special Designation – OMSBON) was created in late 1941 subordinate to the NKVD, providing a nucleus for reconnaissance diversionary activities controlled by national intelligence organs. These specially selected and trained forces provided specialised reconnaissance diversionary groups, detachments and teams, which were employed under direct NKVD control or assigned to control by individual Soviet fronts. In essence their role was to

> cooperation with the development of a massive partisan movement; assistance to the party-soviet underground; deep reconnaissance; ascertaining plans of the German command; assistance to the Red Army by means of reconnaissance, diversionary activities and combat actions; disorganisation of the German rear area; counter-intelligence operations; and acts of retribution against Hitlerite butchers or traitors to the Soviet Motherland.[13]

During the Battle for Moscow in the winter of 1941–1942, special OMSBON ski detachments had been used for a variety of missions covering distances up to 60 kilometres per night. They reported on locations of German reserve units, airfields and ammunition dumps. They also conducted raids on several corps and division level headquarters, destroyed stretches of railway line and ambushed vehicle columns.

The NKVD also operated *istrebitel'nie batal'oni* (destroyer battalions) initially formed, in subordination to the NKVD, from NKVD border units and other regular forces bypassed by advancing German forces early in the war. They were transformed into diversionary detachments for operations in the German rear maintaining, in many cases, radio contact with the army or front in whose sector they found themselves. In some instances, these units formed the nuclei for evolving partisan detachments made up of local patriots and Red Army soldiers who found themselves isolated in the German rear areas. In all cases, their leaders were NKVD officers. In this way, the Soviets were able to establish politically reliable special operations forces in the German rear very early in the war.

The basic concepts of radio *razvedka* had been established in the 1930s and came into their own during the Second World War by demonstrating a considerable capability for the use of radio to collect intelligence data. Its purpose was to obtain information about the enemy by means of interception and analysis of his radio transmissions. Specifically, by the use of radio direction finding equipment to determine the type, designation and location of enemy radio stations using radio reception apparatus designed to intercept and analyse enemy radio transmissions. They employed techniques like triangulation to determine type of enemy radio, the nature and location of the transmitter, and the identity of transmitting units.

In the Stalingrad area, aerial *razvedka* probed up to 40 kilometres behind German lines monitoring railway lines and hard-surfaced roads for German operational and tactical reserve movements. On the ground, raids brought back documents and personnel, which, on 1 October 1942, included the capture of Operation Blue documents near Sadavoe confirming the order of battle and timetable for the advance. Then, on 9 November, more captured documents revealed how poor morale and readiness was affecting the German troops. The time between reconnaissance and operations was of the highest importance. Any delay could very quickly render intelligence redundant in the case of mobile forces.

It was not possible to maintain total deception but when Soviet tactics were identified, they did not always suffer consequences. When the Romanian Third Army commander, General Dumitrescu, reported to the German Sixth Army Command that he observed an increase in the number of Soviet penetrations of his lines and that his own reconnaissance confirmed a general buildup of Soviet forces, German commanders and staff officers contemptuously dismissed his concerns.

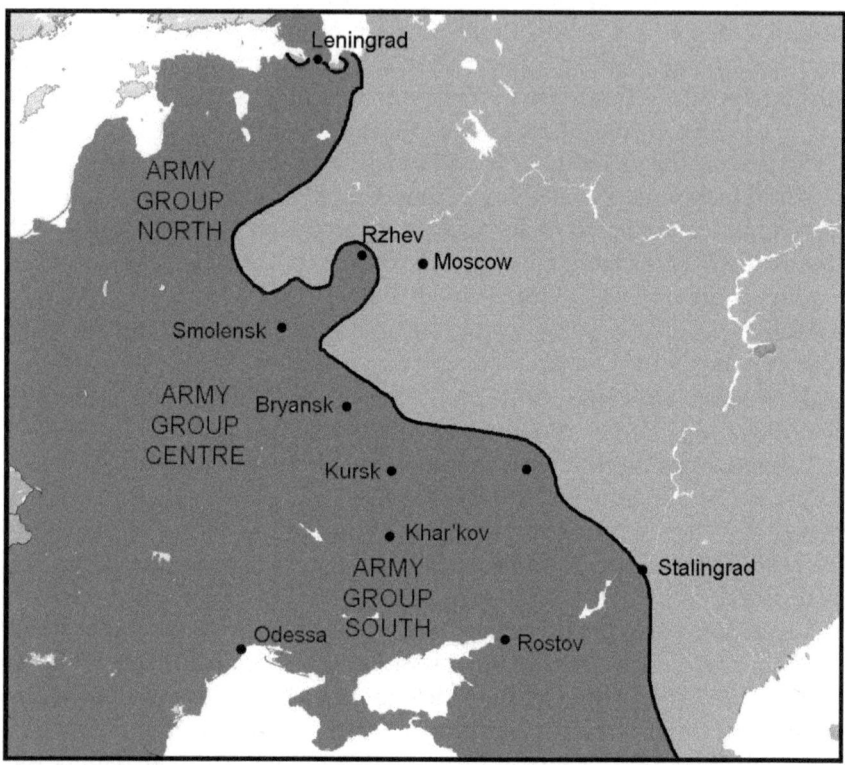

The Eastern Front November 1942.

The Soviets launched Operation Uranus and Operation Mars on 19 November achieving complete tactical and operational surprise, striking against the Romanian units south of Stalingrad and driving into the German flank, while XIII and IV Mechanized Corps advanced deeper into the German rear. In line with the assessment that they could expect only local attacks, the Romanians had received only the understrength XXXXVIII Panzer Corps in reserve. Within four days, Soviet forces joined up at Kalach-on-Don encircling von Paulus's Sixth Army and part of Hoth's 4th Panzer Army but it was not immediately clear to the Soviets just how great a haul they had made but the Germans knew straight away that they faced a disaster if they could not break the encirclement. Field Marshal Erich von Manstein's Army Group Don, with Romanian support, may well have succeeded had they been better prepared and acted immediately, but they had temporarily withdrawn. This gave the Soviets time to rapidly tighten the noose around the Sixth Army's neck by piling in reserves to back up the cordon and interdict Luftwaffe attempts to resupply the enclave. Even before Operation Uranus, OKH had cut von Paulus's supplies from 700 tons a day to 300, but even 300 was now no more than a dream. Hope of relief for the 250,000 Germans dwindled as Romanian forces broke up in disarray. Other weaknesses in the German front that had been identified by Soviet intelligence were targeted by Red Army forces the existence of which OKH had been hitherto quite unaware. The German 6th Army along with elements of the 4th Panzer Army were trapped in an enclave 50 kilometres across and 40 kilometres deep.

FHO passed over this intelligence failure in silence. Not until 9 December, did Gehlen modify his stated conviction that Soviet preparation for the attack in the south had not proceeded far enough to expect that a large operation would be conducted in the near future simultaneously with the expected offensive against Army Group Centre. He was now forced to admit the possibility that the Soviets could have shifted their main effort from Army Group Centre more toward the southern section of the front, but even as late as 10 December, in his report, 'Possible Indications for a Beginning Russian Shift of Main Effort from the Middle Front Section of the Don Front', he was still stubbornly insisting that there was insufficient evidence to say that the main Soviet winter offensive would be anywhere other than in the direction of Smolensk against Army Group Centre.[14]

Still the FHO could not say whether a large-scale offensive should be expected across the Don against the Italian Eighth Army and the Second Hungarian Army with the objective of Rostov. When the attack came against the Italian sector of the front, it surprised FHO, which was still under the impression that the Red Army was taking up a defensive position to prepare for a German counterattack to relieve von Paulus.

FHO must bear the final responsibility for the intelligence failure at Stalingrad in November. Its failure to make a correct assessment of Soviet intentions on the Don-Volga front was not down to a lack of tactical and operational intelligence. Army Group B intelligence had come up with a much more accurate picture of Soviet strategy based on the same intelligence as was available to FHO and concluded that a Soviet counterattack was to be expected.

The defeat of Stalingrad essentially resulted from poor intelligence performance by the German General Staff, its Operations Division and FHO. They completely underestimated the Soviet military resources in the area and the Soviet commanders' ability to carry out large-scale sophisticated coordinated pincer operations. The fact is that the Soviets understood the terrain and were able both to overcome the Romanian forces who seemed to have strong defensive positions and to manoeuvre efficiently and rapidly south of Stalingrad on terrain the Germans considered unsuitable to tank warfare. It was this failure to anticipate the southern 'claw' of the pincer, above all else, which doomed von Paulus's Sixth Army.

Little of substance was produced by FHO as von Paulus's Sixth Army was decimated in the freezing horror of Stalingrad but the mood lifted somewhat after von Manstein's counteroffensive had halted and destroyed four Soviet armies at Kharkiv and Belogrod in early spring. Gehlen's report of 23 March 1943 titled '*Beurteilung der Feindabsichten vor der deutschen Ostfront im grossen,* adjudged, of 23 March, adjudged that 'the Red Army had decided to revert to the defensive on the southern front in the face of German counterattacks; on the basis of the high Russian losses during the winter' and doubted whether the Red Army was in any position to a major summer offensive in 1943. This again proved to be a seriously flawed assessment of Soviet capabilities.[15] Hitler, never given to taking intelligence seriously at the best of times, was paying even less attention to FHO reports after Stalingrad. The General Staff had also had their confidence in German intelligence severely dented.

Gehlen relied heavily on intelligence provided by the *Walli* groups and in early 1943 poached Baun's *Walli I* from the Abwehr and had it transferred to FHO. He could see that Baun had become frustrated at having to rely so much on *Walli II* and *Walli III* for agents. Canaris took little persuading, in fact he was glad to see the back of Baun. He had developed a reputation within front line Wehrmacht units for somewhat fanciful reports, which often bore little relation to reality and which did nothing for the prestige of the Abwehr already struggling to be taken seriously by OKH. Despite Baun's shortcomings of which Gehlen was very well aware, *Walli I* did offer a modicum of intelligence gathering potential, which had previously been altogether missing from FHO and which Gehlen could harness and improve, but it was never much more than an accumulation of individual tactical intelligence rather than providing any valuable information about Soviet operational intentions.

Gehlen was pleased with his acquisition, however, and encouraged Baun to intensify his recruitment and training of agents by showering him with increased resources. Baun was quick to respond but the inevitable outcome was that he was forced to recruit from the lowest ranks after other intelligence agencies had taken their pick and despite improvements in facilities, most of the agents he sent behind enemy lines failed to return. It is doubtful if Baun's operations could ever have made a significant contribution to German strategic decisions given the nature of intelligence it produced.

There were exceptions, however. In July 1941, the German Army Group North established the 1st Russian Foreign Educational Battalion of Russian émigrés under the former White Russian army officer Boris Smyslowsky. Born in St Petersburg, Smyslowsky moved to Poland after the Russian Revolution and then to Germany where he undertook military training. In 1939, after the German occupation of Poland, he became head of the Warsaw office of the White Russian military organisation ROVS, which was called the Association of Russian Military Unions in Nazi Germany.

He later joined the Abwehr under the alias von Regenau and set up *Sonderstab R* (Special Staff Russia) made up of twenty high-ranking White Russian officers and a few hundred young men from Abwehr schools and intelligence groups, and attached to Baun's *Walli I*. It collected intelligence mostly on partisans and the NKVD through a network of informants recruited among local Communist Party members, members of the Komsomol and former Soviet functionaries, who were usually forced to work for the *Sonderstab R* under threat of being arrested or sent to Germany as slave labourers.

In 1943, Smyslowsky's intelligence net was renamed *Sonderdivision R* (Division for Special Task Russia) and became part of the Wehrmacht with Russian, Ukrainian and Belorussian departments consisting of intelligence and partisan sections. Then, at the end of 1943, the Gestapo arrested Smyslowsky on charges of alleged support of the anti-Nazi Polish Home Army and the Ukrainian Insurgent Army. He was acquitted but the *Sonderdivision R* was disbanded and the Germans lost the best intelligence net they had ever had at the Eastern Front.

Chapter 11

GERMAN SIGNALS INTELLIGENCE

'This was the only field of intelligence in which the Germans
came near to an adequate personnel and technical solution.'[1]

Following the successes scored by *Nachrichtenaufklärung* (signals
intelligence) during the First World War, the quantity of information
obtained pertaining to tactical operations increased to the extent that
large organisations were required to handle it. On the other hand,
extensive arrangements were made to shield military communications
from enemy scrutiny. This required secret codes, or ciphers and a strict
radio discipline.

The Spanish Civil War had provided both the Germans and the
Soviets with a classroom in which to develop their own techniques
and equipment and also examine those of the other side. The Polish
campaign, however, showed the Germans just how much more
needed to be done. The most glaring problem was that radio intercept
companies lacked mobility, and, in a dynamic military environment,
they were poorly integrated with the fighting units.

The training of German intercept companies was modified according
to the lessons learned in both campaigns and personnel became
highly competent in the field. They were now deployed to intercept
radio traffic emanating from Soviet units stationed in occupied
Poland and later traffic from Soviet troops engaged in the Winter
War with Finland. While Soviet radio security had been efficient and
secure under peacetime conditions, in time of war, it proved to be
spectacularly vulnerable to enemy intercept services and became the
single most valuable source of *Walli* intelligence on the Soviet order
of battle. It was variously described as 'the most important means for

clarifying the enemy picture', 'the darling of all intelligence' and 'the most copious and best source of intelligence'.[2] This was vital for the understanding of grouping of Soviet forces and the interrelationships within the Soviet chain of command but as with much intelligence that was collected outside the individual army commands, insufficient attention was paid to it within the German High Command. History would show how inept this was.

During 1941 and 1942, German radio intelligence was assigned to the Commander of Intercept Troops in Posen and concentrated mainly on long-range operations, which had the potential to provide the German command with important information about the enemy. There were three permanent intercept stations at Warsaw, Königsberg and Breslau all under Army Group Centre. The functions of intercept units were as follows:

- Analysis of enemy operating techniques
- Analysis of radio net structure
- Cryptanalysis
- Evaluation

The Soviets had a serious problem when it came down to communications due simply to the vastness of its lands and the huge distance between population centres. It lacked the sort of high-capacity long-distance commercial teletype circuits and military telephone links that were common within the highly industrialised Western countries, forcing them to rely to a much greater extent on radio communication.

The equipment available to the Wehrmacht, however, was simply no match for the vastness of the areas it was asked to cover. Stations on the border were unable to reach very far into the Soviet interior and *Funkpeilung* (radio direction finding) operations with shortwave equipment were not effective until 1942.

During the first stage of Barbarossa, German signals intelligence meticulously monitored the deployment and structure of Soviet air force units and formations, and collected information even on the tactical and technical characteristics of Soviet military aircraft. In particular, the Wehrmacht was able to identify the combat dispositions of the Soviet air force, its supply system and movement of its units, which fed into its process of target, identification. Crucially, however, they were unable to acquire information about Red Army reserves located deep inside Soviet territory.

Generally, German radio operators, especially at the divisional level, were much better trained and technically more proficient than their

Soviet counterparts and Soviet radio security had been shattered by the initial Barbarossa assault, allowing the Germans to extensively monitor Soviet communications. This allowed Wilhelm Flicke, the senior cryptologist in German signals, to report in October 1941 that the Soviets were training forty new army divisions to be brought into the reserve. The composition and strength of each unit was detailed, but when Flicke's superior, General Erich Fellgiebel, submitted it to Hitler, the Führer dismissed it out of hand.

Colonel Randeweg commanded German intercept units covering the southern Soviet Union in the weeks before June 1941 and confidently reported that the Soviets had around 10,000 aircraft of all types available and production facilities would ensure that figure continued to grow. OKW rejected this as a gross overestimation and preferred their own figure of 3,000. After the first weeks of the Barbarossa offensive the OKW folly was exposed when verifiable estimates of Soviet aircraft destroyed proved to be close to 6,000.

Soviet radio security had been notoriously lax up to the invasion and they lost vast numbers of radio transmitters and operators during the first weeks. It was months before the equipment could be replaced, although much of that lost was antiquated and had already been scheduled for modernisation. Replacing operators was rather more difficult but, as with other aspects of the war, the Soviets were quick to learn from their mistakes and take urgent measures to rectify the situation.

The war had seen a vast increase in Soviet radio traffic, which the Germans had not been equipped to handle. They struggled to provide sufficient radio operators and translators to deal with the extra load. New men were drafted in but they did not have time to acquire the experience that would allow them to operate the radio direction finding equipment and make best use of that intelligence even when vital breakthroughs were made by unbuttoning the Soviet ciphers. German cryptanalysts were also able to break some NKVD, railways and shipping codes but Soviet signals security was significantly improved after 1942 restricting the scope of surveillance. The Red Army also quickly learned to impose strict radio silence before major offensives. Nevertheless, signals intelligence remained the basic source of all FHO estimates of the enemy situation. Then came *Funkaufklärung* (radio reconnaissance) and *Drahtaufklärung* (telephone reconnaissance) for tactical intelligence. As many as 1,600 agents, many of whom were members of nationalist organisations, were active collecting human intelligence (HUMINT) within a zone up to 200 kilometres behind Soviet the border especially in cities such as Kiev, Minsk and Leningrad.[3]

When Barbarossa was launched, Army Group South had the unenviable task of intercepting Soviet radio communications over an area that stretched from the Pripyat marshes in the north and as far east as the Dnepr river including the Odesa and Kiev military districts. On the first day, Soviet radio security collapsed under the weight of a massive volume of transmissions, but so much was passed uncoded that the Germans could very quickly sketch a rough estimate of the identity, strength and position of all forces opposing them. Where coding was employed, many of the codes had already been broken by the Germans and it was on these lower-grade communications that they directed their main effort rather than tying up resources in trying to break the high-grade ciphers. This bore fruit because the problem for the Soviets was that their generally poorly educated radio operators at division level and below could handle only simple ciphers.

The Germans had realised early in the campaign that the greatest benefits came from centralised evaluation of intelligence coming in from a widely dispersed array of intercept stations. Experience showed that a correct picture could be obtained only by assembling all the intercepted messages at higher headquarters and by disseminating intelligence from the top down, rather than from lower echelons up. In this way each piece of intelligence received its proper place in the over-all picture and was not allowed to skew perceptions by overestimation of the value of any single message.

The German 3rd, 7th and 57th Intercept Companies in the Kasatkin-Delaya Tserkov-Uman area monitored the area ahead of the advancing German Seventeenth and Sixth armies. An exceptionally high yield of clear-text messages across a confused Soviet radio net strongly suggested that the Soviet Twelfth Army was on the point of collapse, but also suggested that the Soviets were carrying out a reorganisation that OKH found difficult to believe. It seemed as if tank and infantry brigades were being combined, which would be an incredible feat to bring off quickly under the circumstances. Time would show that the radio intelligence had been correct. One tactic that took the Germans by surprise and puzzled them for a while was the use of radio controlled detonations, but even when it was exposed, because of manpower constraints, OKH refused to allow the creation of a special unit to detect and neutralise the signals.[4]

Having reached the Dnepr, the three intercept companies set up extreme long-range intelligence operations against the western and southern regions of the Caucasus adjacent to Turkey and Iran. With a much expanded area to cover, they requested – but were denied – a fourth company be assigned to protect the First Panzer Army. A regularisation of Soviet radio traffic and a tightening of security was a clear indicator that the Red Army was finding its feet after its initial demoralisation. Soviet fronts were established, but the Germans continued their advance from the Dnepr to the Donets with radio direction finding tactics mapping out the disposition of Soviet forces ahead of them. Radio interceptions detected several Soviet divisions south-east of Rostov, which was at variance with other intelligence sources that predicted only weak forces there. Again, the German generals chose to see the radio intelligence as Soviet deception, but were soon to regret it when the Soviets attacked Rostov in November 1941.

The Germans planned to employ their own radio deception in January 1942 by boosting radio traffic all along the front, but in doing so failed, at first, to detect a build-up of Soviet forces south of Kharkiv. When they brought in extra short-range detection units to work alongside the long-range units, laborious analysis of Soviet signals allowed them to plot the locations of three enemy forces in the region near Voltschansk, Lozovaya-Balakleya and Slavyansk under the command of General Ivan Koniev. Having deduced that these forces included a large proportion of mobile units, an attack was predicted but it was not possible to say when.

The German cryptanalysts suffered a major setback in April 1942, which lasted for several weeks, when the Soviets introduced new codes and call signs. German radio intelligence operations against Soviet communications were proving to be less and less productive as the German armies advanced and spread out into ever more expansive regions. Equipment and personnel were not increased in proportion, which diluted the effectiveness of the facility. The huge expanses over which the armies now ranged was also a hindrance to the Soviets who had few wire communications and were forced to rely on radio which might not have been such a problem if their security had been tighter. Only when they imposed strict radio silence, were they successful in restricting German radio intelligence to a few meagre scraps during the German attack across the Donets in July 1942.

Radio security within Soviet tank forces, however, was particularly lax as demonstrate by an incident in July when the 82nd Tank Brigade found itself encircled by the German Ninth Army. On an open radio link, the Soviet commander frantically asked for orders and was told to attempt a breakout along the same line that had taken him into the trap. The Germans intercepted the signal and lined the escape route with their 88mm anti-tank guns. The T-34s that survived the ambush fled into the swamps and got stuck. The Germans now transmitted on the Soviet wavelength purporting to be a Soviet rescue mission requesting the position of the tanks. Now their thick frontal armour that was able to deflect even a 40-pound shell was of little use as the German assault guns could be sited to strike at will at the thinner flanks with the result that the whole brigade was wiped out.

Overall, it was clear that the Soviets were tightening up on radio security, however, and the early German successes in this area would become increasingly difficult to replicate but the breaking of a large number of the Soviet codes in August enabled the Germans to plot the dispositions of the Russian forces on the east bank of the Don between the mouth of the Khoper and Voronezh. A month later, the shortage of land lines forced the Soviets to rely more on radio and the Germans, with their customary painstakingly systematic thoroughness, were able to identify Soviet forces along the Don-Volga Corridor in front of Stalingrad, which was something that could not have been foreseen a few weeks earlier. The Germans were also to learn that the Soviets had gauged the weakness of the Romanian and Italian Armies and the vulnerability of the boundaries separating them, but Gehlen told OKH that the Red Army was massing further north and he did not recognise the danger to von Paulus's Sixth Army until it was too late.

While Soviet radio security was tightened up especially before a major operation, much everyday communication was still by low grade cipher or uncoded. The Germans were able to pick up a huge amount of intelligence on a tactical level but this was gradually and inexorably reduced as more and more listening posts were overwhelmed by the Soviet advance westward after Stalingrad. One thing they did discover was a Soviet practice that had the effect of bolstering German resolve in combat. On several occasions Soviet regimental staff officers were heard complaining that they were not being given access to German PoWs for interrogation. Could at least one be spared for questioning before being shot, they asked.

The last major achievement of German radio intelligence on the Eastern Front was the coverage of the gigantic preparations for the Vistula-Oder offensive of January 1945. German communication intelligence had detected all the unmistakable signs of an impending Soviet offensive. Gehlen amassed intelligence covering the deployment of artillery and rocket launchers indicating where the concentrations of fire could be expected. The transfer of several divisions, corps and armies indicated where the main attack would land. All this he presented to Guderian who was by now Chief of the German General

Staff. Guderian duly took it into Hitler who reacted furiously when told that Soviet forces outnumbered the Germans by more than three to one, which was actually an underestimation. At the focal points of the attack, the Soviets would outnumber the Germans by a ratio of ten to one. Hitler dismissed Gehlen's numbers as Soviet deception and described his report as the ravings of a madman. He refused Guderian's request for reinforcements and a few months later the Red Army was in Berlin.

An overview will conclude that up until the invasion of Poland in September 1939, Soviet radio communications had been poorly secured by the widespread use of primitive codes but the service had a reputation for high standards of application. These began to slip during the Winter War with Finland when discipline faltered under the pressure of combat and had hardly had time to recover before the German invasion of June 1941 when they suffered huge losses of equipment and personnel during the first few months. The Germans soon broke the Soviet codes and call signs and had what amounted to free access to Soviet communications until the Soviets tightened up their procedures and resupplied their troops with modern equipment in the spring of 1942. After this and especially after the tide of war turned against them the Germans found it increasingly difficult to gain significant advantage from radio intercepts. This was also hampered by the application of Soviet deception techniques when much disinformation went out over the airwaves. As time went on, the Soviets methodically corrected the deficiencies in their use of radio by strict disciplinary measures against defaulters. It was only when Soviet forces failed to follow the correct procedure, and there were plenty of instances of this, that the Germans could continue to benefit from radio intercepts.

German counterintelligence relied on radio intercepts in their fight against partisan groups who were in communication with the Red Army. The ever-increasing levels of partisan activity made it vital for OKH to determine the extent to which they were working with the Red Army and the role they played in preparing the ground for major Soviet attacks. Identifying radio nets set up by enemy agents and partisans bled radio intercept units of personnel but the Germans had little choice but to pursue the partisans as their operations became more and more disruptive. The task of locating these groups, however, was daunting. Their radio communication with the army group headquarters and Moscow adhered to standing procedures. Discipline was far superior to those of the ordinary Red Army field radio operator. Their messages tended to be brief, and they were very mobile, which made it difficult to pin down their transmissions. In some few instances, the Germans had some success in deceiving Russian aircraft loaded with supplies for the partisans using fake radio and lighting signals making them drop their cargoes or land at the wrong place.

Neither was the German army innocent of security breaches. In cases of extreme urgency, they would not hesitate to communicate in plain text but only after written authorisation from the tactical commander. Later the service had to cope with inexperienced replacements when they suffered losses of personnel and equipment. These new operatives had little chance to get acclimatised to conditions because the Chief of Army Signal Communication clamped down on security by refusing them permission to practice and hone their skills at the front. They had to learn the hard way. German radio nets were consistently closed down immediately before an operation and where telephone lines could be used instead. The main deficiency in German signals was the way in which political control by Himmler's SS constantly prevented the formation of a unified agency to impose standardised practice. Despite all its difficulties, German radio intelligence provided accurate tactical intelligence throughout the war, but its efficiency progressively diminished alongside that of aerial reconnaissance, PoW interrogation and defections.

Chapter 12

SOVIET PARTISANS

'The Soviet Partisan Movement which was established in
the wake of the German armies invading the USSR in 1941
was, in both conception and scope, the greatest irregular
resistance movement in the history of warfare.'[1]

Before July 1941, the Soviet had given little thought to partisan warfare
but when it became apparent that the German advance was swift and
overwhelming, they were forced to revisit that omission. There had
been no stockpiling of food and weapons, and the swift advance of
the Wehrmacht through western Russia made last minute attempts
to form partisan groups virtually impossible. At first, the Kremlin
suspected that Soviet citizens in the occupied areas would be unlikely
to risk life and limb for the Soviet regime that had done little for them
and so would not be amenable to supporting partisan activity against
the German forces. The rapid German advance, however, had resulted
in large numbers of Red Army troops cut off with their heavy guns
and vehicles after bridges had been demolished as part of the Soviet
'scorched earth' strategy. Many of these then hid in surrounding
woods and formed *ad hoc* partisan units terrorising farms and villages
for food. They became active within the first weeks of occupation
attacking German supply routes and field hospitals. OKH was soon
very concerned about the large numbers of what Halder called
'stragglers and guerillas' harassing German infantry.[2]

Before long, the Soviets realised that these partisan groups could
play a vital role in the war and set about creating a support network not
only for them but also for groups of saboteurs, many of them refugees
who were familiar with the terrain of their home ground, parachuted
behind German lines to demolish infrastructure and cut telephone
lines. More than 1,000 Communist Party members had remained

behind German lines in Belorussia, and more were ordered to stay –
as the Wehrmacht rolled over them – and organise communications
networks, and find safe houses and other hiding places in which build
up caches of weapons for future use.

These groups were led by Red Army officers and regularly supplied
by air drops of food and ammunition. Partisan training schools had
been set up in cities such as Leningrad, Odesa, Cuipaiov, Nikolayev
and Moscow, recruiting fit young people to train in the use of radio
and explosives. While left-behind Red Army regular troops were a real
menace for the German forces, these parachuted partisans, who had
been given scant training were generally ineffective initially and had a
low mission success rate. Many men were scattered far and wide often
far from their target. When they were rounded up by the Germans
they were seen as little more than a nuisance and certainly did not look
like the forerunner of the formidable resistance movement that was to
come.

With rather more preparation and training, other agents, usually
Communist Party functionaries, were infiltrated through the lines
to organise and directing partisan activity and political work in the
occupied areas. They linked up with local communist groups forming
loosely knit guerrilla organisations. Their general mission was to foment
rebellion and commit acts of sabotage whilst, at the same time, terrorise
the local population to deter collaborate with the occupying forces. They
were backed up by *Istrebki* – 'annihilation' or 'destruction' – battalions
of which some 1,755 were created by the NKVD during July 1941 alone.
They comprised volunteers, party members and regular troops. The
main qualification was ideological reliability. Their primary mission,
initially, was internal security in the Soviet rear and defence against
German parachute attack, but they were to allow themselves to be
bypassed by the German advance and operate clandestinely behind
the lines living off the land. Although armed they were not trained for
formal combat and were not expected to be used in the line. By August
1941 these three types of group began to show a definite pattern of
insurgent activity and started to look like a definite movement on the
part of the Soviets to set up and sustain a centrally directed irregular
movement.

Stalin set up a new State Committee of Defence to improve the morale
and combat initiative of the Red Army, but also to reassert control over
Soviet territories occupied by the Germans where the populations
were at risk from German propaganda against the communist state.
This required tight party control of the nascent partisan movement
to bring all the irregular units under the central control of Moscow

at the earliest possible date. Committees were formed from the top levels of government down to local levels to regulate guerrilla activities. Powerful figures in the party, the NKVD and the Red Army competed for control of the partisans but it was the head of the Main Administration of Political Propaganda of the Army and NKVD, Lev Mekhlis, who won out.

The Partisan Movement was officially created and placed under the control of the Tenth Department of the Political Administration of the Army, and ultimately responsible to the Central Committee of the Communist Party. Well-armed partisan combat battalions were established in the main zone of operations where the principal units of the enemy troops were located. One of the earliest partisan units was a Belorussian detachment formed in Surazh, north of Vitebsk, Called *Shmyrev Otryad* and led by Mihay Filipovich Shmyrev, this group of fifty men would evolve into the 1st Belorussian Partisan Brigade, one of the premier partisan units of the war. It was typical of what the Germans called *Ortsansaessig* – a detachments operating out of a fixed base and within limited boundaries. Shmyrev's first significant action was to surprise a group of Wehrmacht soldiers bathing in a river when his men killed or wounded twenty-five of the party. Also typical of the problems faced by all partisan units, *Shmyrev Otryad* saw its numbers fluctuate wildly through recruiting, desertions, expulsions and disputes, but by the end of September it numbered almost seventy. The unit was soon recognised by Soviet officials, who sent 12 Red Army soldiers to reinforce it along with 4 heavy machine guns with 15,000 rounds of ammunition and a light and a heavy mortar. Soviet directives tried to bring some sort of organisation to the disparate partisan groups and *podpolya* (recruiters and propagandists) and establish operating guidelines in July 1941. The outstanding success of 1941 was probably the destruction of the Kiev railway freight station, railway workshops and two factories.

The emergence of partisan warfare had been anticipated even by Hitler who said on 16 July, 'The Russians have now ordered partisan warfare behind our front. This also has its advantages: it gives us the opportunity to exterminate all who oppose us.' Two weeks later he issued a cold-blooded order to deal with offenders saying, 'The troops available for security in the conquered territories will not be [restricted to] legal means [and must] inspire sufficient terror among the population to stamp out the will to resist.'[3] He had earlier given the troops immunity from prosecution for atrocities committed during the campaign.

A prime example of what this permitted was the case of a young girl named Zoya Kosmodemyanskaya. Aged 18, she had joined a partisan unit in autumn 1941 and quickly adapted to the life. In November, she was captured by the Germans while carrying out reconnaissance around the village of Petrischevo. After interrogation and beatings, during which she refused to speak, she was marched through the village half naked and hanged. Her body was left on the gallows for more than a month until the village was recaptured by the Red Army. Many young Soviet soldiers carried a photo of her, and the words 'For Zoya' were also written on Soviet tanks and aircraft heading to Berlin. Streets, *kolkhozes* (collective farms), pioneer organisations, a mountain and a minor planet were all named after Zoya.

Right from the start, the task of eliminating these pockets of resistance prove to be beyond the capabilities of the German security divisions and police battalions that were given the job as the fighting moved further to the east. The expanse of territory within which the partisans operated was too great. By the end of August, the Germans had realised that some of the partisans were in more than casual communication with the Russian rear and had established an embryonic radio net, but could not do much about it. In December 1941, Army Group Centre reported that,

> As the Russians have become more active on the front, partisan activity has increased. The troops left to this command are just sufficient to protect the most important installations and, to a certain extent, the railroads and highways. For active anti-partisan operations there are no longer any troops on hand. Therefore, it is expected that soon the partisans will join together into larger bands and carry out attacks on our guard posts. Their increased freedom of movement will also lead to the partisans' spreading terror among the people, who will be forced to stop supporting us and will then no longer carry out the orders of the military government authorities.[4]

The reality was that, in the early stages, the lack of foresight and hasty planning for guerilla warfare had initially condemned the partisan movement to play a minor role and morale amongst them was low. Attacks were generally against 'soft' targets, which, though annoying, caused little harm but that changed. The Red Army had fallen back in disarray so quickly in the Vitebsk-Orsha-Smolensk triangle that most bridges and culverts remained relatively intact and so in the lower reaches of the Pripyat marshes it was partisan action that accounted for the large number of blown bridges and long sections of destroyed railway track.[5]

Stavka saw the need to quickly assert strict control over the numerous partisan organisations operating in the German rear to ensure that they were directed toward specific political and military goals. To this end they established a Central Staff of the Partisan Movement under the direct command of Voroshilov. Trained personnel were parachuted into the German rear areas to make contact with partisan units and establish an organisational infrastructure. Groups of between ten and twenty-five members would normally have a politically reliable commander, commissar, deputy commander for reconnaissance, radio operator, medic, demolitions instructor and others. Representatives of partisan organisations sat on the respective military councils of the fronts and armies in whose areas they operated and over time, *Osobykh Otdeli* (Special Sections – OO) of NKVD personnel were set up at all levels bringing a higher level of sophistication and communications with Red Army units and the Central Staff. Operations were then carried out against deep targets either inaccessible to partisans or requiring special skills to eliminate.

Some special sections were used to gather intelligence on anti-Soviet partisans operating in the Ukraine while others were dispatched to infiltrate the German Abwehr training schools or otherwise conduct deep reconnaissance. These groups also specialised in 'black operations' to assassinate German officers and eliminate 'enemies of the state' who were otherwise beyond the reach of Soviet authority. These unilateral operations were controlled by the 4th Department of the NKVD, and as a rule involved no contact with local partisan organisations but were an integral part of Soviet counterintelligence.

One 'black' operator was Nikolai Ivanovich Kuznetsov, a member of a *Pobediteli* (composite special operations group) called 'The Victors' under the command of NKVD Colonel Dmitrii Nikolaevich Medvedev. This particular group was designated as *otriad spetsial'nogo Naznacheniia* (detachment of special designation or Spetsnaz) and operated independently in the German rear. Fluent in German, Kuznetzov volunteered in 1941 to operate behind German lines and worked there for almost two years in and around Rovno and Lvov using the pseudonym, Paul Siebert, a lieutenant in the German army. Officially he is credited with six assassinations of members of the German hierarchy in the Ukraine. In addition, he seriously wounded the Gauleiter of the Ukraine with an antitank grenade and kidnapped General Hermann Knut whom the Soviets tried and executed. Ukrainian nationalists eventually tracked down and surrounded Kuznetzov in a forest outside of Lvov. He killed himself with a hand grenade. He was posthumously awarded the highest Soviet honour, Hero of the Soviet Union.

Partisans seldom launched a raid without previous reconnaissance and tried to avoid direct confrontation with German troops. Operating in areas they knew well, they established bases on swamp islands and in deep forests, marching only by night over prearranged routes. Some partisan groups grew to the size of small armies. The German *Einsatzgruppe B* encountered one such force in Byelorussia and engaged it in a firefight killing over 1,500 of them but that did little to diminish the overall numbers deployed.

The difference between the Germans and the Soviets in the way that agents were able to operate behind enemy lines was stark. Unless Soviet partisans were encountered in action, identification and apprehension was far from easy. German rear area commands had the job of keeping supply lines open to the field armies and exploiting the occupied areas for provisioning and military use. It fell to security divisions within the army commands to crush the partisan movement who threatened to agitate the population and disrupt communications and supply lines in these areas. *Landesschuetzen* units patrolled roads and rail lines and guarded important bridges and supply dumps. Other regiments were employed to clear up pockets of partisans while the general maintenance of order and control of traffic on the roads was in the hands of the police units. Deficiencies of the security units were soon exposed, however. OKH had anticipated a short campaign in which partisan activity was never considered. The units had not been prepared to operate in such a vast area and, short of vehicles and fuel, were not equipped for this sort of mobile combat against a guerilla force.

Again, because of the overconfident attitude and failure of the OKH to prepare for a long war, provisions for security in the occupied areas was woefully lacking. Even when partisans were captured, they were able to confound the security services by claiming to be Soviet deserters of whom there were a great number. The immense numbers of Soviet prisoners taken in the first few months of war meant that many could not be processed and were left to roam the countryside as vagabonds. Sometimes they were even given official German identification papers. Naturally, some joined partisan groups. There was no census of local populations, which made identification of non-residents difficult, and many more remote villages were barely touched. Weapons were handed out to local community leaders ostensibly for protection against partisans but more often than not they ended up being handed over to them.

Very soon, measures were taken to rectify the situation. Unauthorised possession of weapons was taken as proof of partisan activity and those caught were shot. Where villages were found to have aided partisans, they were burned to the ground. In some areas all the adult male populations were rounded up and held in detention camps. Then when many security units were drawn into front line action as the German advance faltered and security came more and more under the control of the SS who recruited local volunteers.

In the countryside, crops remained unharvested and food became scarce in the cities. Any hope that local populations would settle down to accepting German occupation was vanishing and the Germans realised that conditions created fertile ground for partisan activity. Public morale was further eroded by partisans themselves who launched terror attacks on small rural communities. Farms were destroyed along with machinery. Livestock was killed and food stores were looted both to deny them to the German forces, and to remind the population that the Soviets might have been driven back, but there would be a reckoning when they returned for those who aided and abetted the Germans. Local leaders who cooperated with the occupying forces became targets for assassination. Soviet propaganda leaflets were dropped from aircraft. One such entitled 'Directive for Partisans in the German Zone of Communications', predicted a Soviet resurgence at which point 'The enemy who has trodden on our soil shall perish on it!'[6]

The Germans tried to adapt to circumstances and drew up a sort of blueprint for all anti-partisan units to follow. The 'Directive for Anti-Partisan Warfare' was distributed to all units on the Eastern Front in October 1941. This first example of anti-partisan doctrine was really just a formalisation of measures that had gradually already been adopted in practice. First of all, priority was given to discovering the location and strength of partisan groups and to this end a network of informants was established. Counterintelligence tactics were toughened to the point of brutality. SS brigades were formed into highly mobile task forces of several companies each and held in constant readiness at strategic points. Patrols along roads and rail lines were stepped up. Villages were given extra support against terror raids and once an area was considered pacified, it was regularly patrolled. Local volunteers were taken on for reconnaissance and guard duty. Not the least important measure was that the Germans started making a complete record of all partisan actions and countermeasures along with transcripts of prisoner interrogations. The penetration of radio nets was of the highest importance and all captured equipment, along with operators, was sent directly to army headquarters. Military supply convoys were grouped together for better security and often included empty trucks so that anyone found wandering in the countryside could be picked up along the way. Reprisal executions were carried out in the ratio of two inhabitants for every German soldier killed by partisans. Where important installations were attacked, three inhabitants were shot and anyone found outside at night risked being shot on sight. Such measures hardly disincentivised the partisans and in fact played into their hands by further alienating the local populations against the Germans.

On 5 June 1942, the Germans launched *Vogelsang*, a large-scale anti-partisan operation, to clear the forests around Bryansk and secure the rail line supplying the Second Panzer Army. Although 1,200 partisans were killed, 500 captured, and large quantities of supplies and materiel taken, in no way did it approach a permanent solution. The majority of the partisans had withdrawn from the area in an orderly manner leaving specialists behind to reorganise the region once the Germans had moved on. On the whole, however, the partisans continued to display a distinct lack of aggressive intent. Although there were some spectacular successes. In October 1943, a large partisan raid destroyed an entire 12-mile section of the Bryansk-Dmitryev rail line and tore down several miles of telegraph wires.

For a year and a half, the Soviet partisan movement had been operating from a defensive perspective, but after Stalingrad it prepared to strike at a weakened enemy. Small bands of partisans were able to have effects way beyond what their numbers might suggest. One partisan demolition group led by A. Andrianov destroyed one of the few remaining bridges across the Sestra river, creating a massive bottleneck on the east side of the river. The Soviet air force quickly homed in on this and, in a large-scale attack, destroyed over 100 vehicles before the Germans could find alternate routes. The partisan movement was now effectively a fourth armed service, standing on a level with the Red Army, the Red Air Force, and the Red Navy but, unlike the other three, under direct political control of the Central Committee of the Communist Party. It had a structure similar to that of the Red Army with the addition of a political security section under NKVD control. Each front command had a partisan staff, but the partisan chain of command ensured that they did not allow themselves to he absorbed by the Red Army. Central Staff retained the authority to alter the partisan organisation or insert special task groups into the enemy rear without reference to any military agency. Despite this leadership of the partisan groups was essentially in the hands of Red Army officers who had been trained in special partisan schools and whose primary task was to ensure political security.

As the movement expanded, its ranks were filled mostly from the native populations, not always on a voluntary basis, who saw the tide of war turning against the Germans. Experts in the fields of demolition and communications were regularly flown in to train partisan groups, especially in the use of radio at which the partisans, out of necessity, became much more proficient and security conscious than their Red Army counterparts. A priority list of targets included roads, railway lines and rolling stock, bridges, telephone and telegraph lines and supply depots with information gathering of lesser importance at this time. That was very much in the hands of informer nets in the occupied areas, often wives or relatives of Red Army personnel who worked as railway employees, servants and workers in German installations, members of the local administration, and local native police.

An important aspect of partisan activity under the new structure was the regeneration of the Communist Party in the occupied regions. The bands, greatly increased in numbers and operationally much improved were now ready to take over with some authority the clearly defined role assigned them in the Soviet war effort. Infiltrating through gaps in the German line, there were large groups forming a solid block from Bryansk-Orel to Gomel and Bobruysk to Orsha and Vitebsk. By March 1943, the Germans had identified thirty-four separate units between Orel and Gomel totalling more than 25,000 men. In the Pripyat, west of Gomel, were another 7,500 men, and in the Orsha-Vitebsk-Nevel region another 21,000. In total, there were an estimated 78,000 partisans operating behind German lines. It is interesting, therefore, to note that during the first half of 1943, partisan groups showed little aggression and appeared to be simply building their strength. Much time and effort were expended on recruiting and training.

The German *Landesschuetzen* security units around whom the anti-partisan movement was built had been depleted through transfers to the front line leaving mostly personnel of low combat value who were often too old to carry out exhausting all-weather operations in forests and swamps and where there were losses, through death injury or defection to the Soviets, no replacements arrived to fill the gaps. To rectify this shortage, they turned to a mix of *Ostbataillone* (native security units), *Einwohner Kampf Abteulungen EAK* (local volunteers), *Hilfswillige* (foreign labour units) and *Volkswehr* (anti Soviet groupings) most of which were not up to the task. There were exceptions such as in the Lokot region of Bryansk where an anti-Soviet Russian engineer of Polish extraction, Bronislav Kaminski, had organised a force of nearly 1,500 anti-Soviet volunteers, who became infamous for their extreme brutality. Within months, the group had grown to some 9,000 and the

Germans recognise it by creating a *Selbstverwaltungsbezirk* (autonomous district) around Lokot and handing over security to Kaminski.[7] Kaminski and his men were known for their extreme cruelty and ruthlessness. Partisan and non-partisan villages alike were destroyed. Rape, plunder and massacre were the order of the day for this small army whose actions matched the worst excesses of the *Einsatzgruppen*. In June 1944, the Kaminski's brigade was absorbed into the SS and renamed Waffen-Sturm-Brigade RONA, with Kaminski being given the rank of *Waffen-Brigadeführer der SS*. Soon afterwards, Kaminski's brigade took part in the suppression of the Warsaw Uprising in which they focused entirely on looting and murder. This was too much even for Himmler who saw Kaminski now as completely out of control. Having been tried by a court martial and found guilty of stealing 'property of the Reich', the renegade commander ended his days in front of an SS firing squad on 28 August 1944.

In August 1942, based on experience of the previous twelve months, a new 'Directive for Anti-Partisan Warfare in the East' was issued that showed a much better understanding of what the Germans were up against in this area. New political, economic and propaganda measures were brought into play. Under Himmler's authority, such military, SS and police units as could be released for the purpose, were to take vigorous offensive action employing 'the harshest measures' against partisans and those who nurtured them.[8] Use of the term *Partisanen* (freedom fighter) was forbidden, and replaced in all documents and communications by *banditen* (bandits). In glaringly uncharacteristic manner, Himmler also emphasised the importance of the population regaining a feeling of security and receiving fair treatment from the occupation administration. Where possible and where supported by regular troops, the anti-partisan units carried out large-scale sweeps of the countryside but with little success. That, however, did have the effect of maintaining a level of security for the movement of army supplies and of keeping the partisans off balance preventing them from establishing centres of resistance. They also probed constantly with smaller units for evidence of activity within the local community. Dummy partisan groups were set up to tempt anti-German elements into joining them before deporting them to labour battalions. The aim was not to drive the partisans out but to eliminate them.

By early 1943, focussing on their priorities, the partisans stepped up their attacks. There were 5 partisan brigades, totalling some 7,000 men, that harassed the Roslavl-Bryansk railway line, while another 6 brigades of more than 6,000 men maintained pressure on the Bryansk-Lgov line. Another 10,000 partisans were concentrated along the

Minsk-Gomel line, which carried much of the supply traffic for Army Group South, the Second Army and Second Panzer Army. This was an entirely different challenge than the Germans had faced from partisan groups in 1942. The offensive capabilities had improved considerably under tight-knit commands and well-developed communications systems. The forests and swamps behind the two most vulnerable German fronts offered ideal cover for guerilla operations. Local populations were badly demoralised by German occupation and, influenced by partisan propaganda predicting a return of Soviet forces, either abetted partisans or turned a blind eye to their activities.

These bands were now in positions where they could make significant military contributions on a strategic level. In the event of a Soviet offensive, they could disrupt railway communications to shut off supplies and hinder the relocation of forces leaving them to travel on the available roads. *Stavka* had conceived a major role for them at Kursk after they blunted the German Operation Citadel. During the German withdrawal, the partisans were to strike at the rail network forcing the Second Panzer and Ninth armies in the forward areas to hold ground without prepared defences so that they might be cut off and destroyed. On a signal from Moscow, railways were to be attacked simultaneously, continuously and systematically. Special manuals on rail demolition technique were distributed and mines and bulk explosives were air-landed well in advance.[9]

The Germans meanwhile had made plans to implement two operations, *Unternehmen Freischuetz* and the smaller *Unternehmen Osterei*, to clear the Bryansk region of partisans. The carefully planned 10-day *Freischuetz* operation was conducted during a spell of particularly heavy and persistent rain with inadequate forces and rather than encircle and destroy the 4,000 to 6,000 partisans it targeted succeeded only in driving them to another location and they simply returned later. Two more attempts to clear areas of partisans followed. *Unternehmen Zigeunerbaron* and *Nachbarhilfe* swept the deeply wooded area trying to pin 6,000 partisans against the Desna river. The Germans recorded 1,584 partisans killed and 1,568 captured but within a few short weeks, partisan strength was restored to previous levels. Fighting a guerilla war for which they had been completely unprepared, the Wehrmacht were not the first and would not be the last Leviathan to be outmanoeuvred and outthought by irregular forces.

With the Germans in retreat after the Battle of Kursk on 22 July partisans hit them hard on the Bryansk-Konotop railway line, blocking the transfer of troops between the central and southern sectors for forty-eight hours. On the same day, an explosion destroyed two ammunition trains and a trainload of Tiger tanks in the station at Osipovichi, on the main line between Minsk and Gomel. Then early in August with the German withdrawal from Orel well under way, Moscow ordered the simultaneous detonation of 8,422 demolition charges damaging or demolishing 266 locomotives and 1,378 trucks alongside extensive stocks of railroad construction and maintenance material.[10] This forced the Germans to interrupt their policy of committing security battalions to the front line after which partisan raids on the railways were reduced but attacks on roads continued unabated, especially in the Pripyat marshes where truck convoys, German-occupied towns and supply depots were raided. The partisans continued their twin policies of disrupting German communications and committing acts of terror against the families of local railway employees and those serving in the locally recruited security battalions, which, alongside news of further German military setbacks, accelerated the number of local desertions. Indigenous populations were much less inclined to report partisan activity out of fear of later Soviet reprisals. Although the space in which they were operating was being compressed, it was becoming increasingly difficult for the Germans to get any clear control of partisan activities.

The SS response was to take vicious reprisals with the burning of villages, destruction of farm animals and in many cases, forcible evacuation of adults leaving their children to fend for themselves. Morale of local populations plummeted to new depths in September, when 150,000 men, women and children were evacuated on foot from the area between Lake Ilmen and Lake Peipus ahead of Soviet advances despite there being no facilities for caring for the evacuees on the march and no camps suitable for housing. Rather than go west, large numbers absconded and went over to the partisans threatening an intensification of partisan activity. Indigenous *Osttruppen* security forces were weakened by widespread defections.

Partisan raids continued with undiluted ferocity against German communications all through autumn 1943. The Orsha-Minsk-Brest-Litovsk signals cable was cut more than a hundred times during October alone, but operations were curtailed as the partisans concentrated in making preparations to survive the coming winter. They resorted to widespread looting of civilian food sources which became so troubling to Moscow that *Stavka* issued a directive that food could be requisitioned through negotiation with the village elders, and anyone caught pillaging by night was to be shot.

German forces now under severe pressure from Red Army advances made extraordinary efforts to protect themselves against partisan activity. Security of the Minsk-Brest-Litovsk railway line was boosted by 3,000 men of the 1st Ski Brigade but little that was done elsewhere made much difference as more and more security troops were drawn off for transfer to the front line. Two *Kampfgruppen* of police and SS units were transferred from Army Group Centre to take part in the anti-partisan *Unternehmen Heinrich* in Lithuania. This was at a time when so many of the indigenous population was flocking to join the partisans that there were not sufficient arms to go round and surplus volunteers were slipped through the lines for service in the Red Army. German supply and troop movements were not entirely paralysed, however. Partisan activities failed to cut off all axes of retreat as *Stavka* hoped. Despite constant harassment, traditional German efficiency and organisation saw troop withdrawals proceeding in an orderly fashion and almost on schedule with a manageable loss of men and supply trains. While demolition attacks had been effective, they were not continuous as Moscow had ordered. With no follow-up attacks, the space between gave the Germans time to repair the damage. It was also noticeable that many of the demolition charges were of low quality or were inexpertly laid, which meant that detonations resulted in less damage than might have been otherwise expected. Often attacks were carried out in areas most convenient for the saboteurs, i.e. where there was extensive cover, or on small feeder lines with little security rather than on those locations where they could have done most damage.

The partisans, under strict Moscow control were biding their time, reserving their strength and facilitating the return of communist control to the countryside. Despite the harsh winter weather, they were far from totally inactive, however. The Army Group North War Diary for January 1944 includes numerous entries describing their actions:

- Strong partisan bands on line Bateskaya-Soltsy north and south of station at Utorgozh [11 miles north of Soltsy]. About 140 demolitions.
- Arrival of 8th Jaeger Division cannot be predicted due to numerous demolitions.
- 8th Jaeger Division much delayed by railroad demolitions. Numerous demolitions on other rail lines.
- 8th Jaeger Division has to detrain in Utorgozh due to railroad demolitions.
- The rail-road is completely paralyzed.
- Numerous demolitions by partisans, especially on all supply routes of Eighteenth Army. Partisans attacked railroad stations and installations.
- Many partisan attacks against railroads, especially the Dno-Soltsy Line.[11]

The role of the NKVD grew in January 1944 when the 4th Department of the NKVD assumed many of the functions originally attributed to the Central Staff after the disbanding of the Central Staff of the Partisan Movement. As a result, intelligence operations assumed a significance at least equal to combat operations and the partisan movement started to have an appreciable impact on the course of the war. By the end of January, partisans were working much more closely with the Red Army and operating almost exclusively according to specific directives from the NKVD, scouting for advancing Russian units informing them of German movements and dispositions. Aa a result, the German transport situation continued to deteriorate with restricted supplies getting to the front. Large sections of railway track were out of commission for up to forty-eight hours and the few roads capable of handling heavy traffic were continuously mined and attacked. By early February, telephone lines were extensively targeted forcing the Germans to depend on radio communications that were, more often than not, monitored by Soviet intelligence.

Red Army and NKVD officers were now being dropped behind German lines in the Baltics where, apart from Lithuania, there had been little partisan activity due to the antipathy of the locals to Soviet rule after their brutal occupation of 1940–1941. Well aware of the hostility towards Moscow, the Germans here hastily drafted locals into security units for anti-partisan operations. Elsewhere, experienced Red Army officers were brought in to lead partisan groups in a more aggressive and professional manner and more fully integrate them with Red Army operations. By March, there was hardly any part the immediate German rear areas where partisans were not either dominant militarily or poised to take control of roads and railways not yet under Communist Party administration. With their backs up against the forest and marshlands, the German were now almost totally reliant on one double track heavy duty railway line and five of lesser capacity all of which became the focus of partisan attacks.

At no time can it be said that the partisan contribution to the Soviet war effort was decisive. Only in the north did they come anywhere close to realising their potential in this regard. Where they came into direct contact with German forces, they were shown to be a 'third-rate militia [of] poor and unenthusiastic soldiers in ill-disciplined units' and markedly inferior and so suffered accordingly.[12] It was never a problem for the Soviets to deploy large numbers of partisans and quickly replace losses, but it meant that training was perfunctory since they were seen as expendable. The problem of effectively controlling such a large and irregulars force operating up to 100 miles behind enemy lines was one that was never adequately addressed.

Chapter 13

OPERATION CITADEL

'From July through August [1943]
Soviet forces had fired off 42,105,000 shells.'[1]

The Soviets now took steps to put their earlier intelligence failures firmly behind them. Even Stalin was starting to realise the value of *razvedka* and was more inclined to defer to his generals when formulating military strategy. By November 1942, things had improved to the extent that they had the capacity to monitor German tactical defences to a depth of some 20 kilometres. This had proved crucial at Stalingrad when they were able to predict the general pattern of German movements as they tried to relieve their encircled forces. Based on these developments, in spring 1943 a new much more robust and complex Soviet intelligence capability emerged with a centralised structure for assessment and exploitation all coordinated through the GRU. This revitalised service included the following:

- Special OO and KRO departments coming under one centralised control.
- Establishment of a partisan network.
- Creation of aerial *razvedka* and photo reconnaissance squadrons.
- Creation of the first radio intercept and interference units.
- Introduction of routine troop *razvedka* in Red Army units for reconnaissance in force.
- Introduction of artillery *razvedka* to improve target selection.
- Introduction of engineer *razvedka* for enemy defence reconnaissance.

The GRU was the hub through which all intelligence passed. It was responsible for the training of agents, their deployment and processing the product of their endeavours. Subordinate to the GRU were front intelligence departments who conducted troop *razvedka*. Studies have shown that German intelligence in 1943 had little appreciation of the complexity and capabilities of the multi-faceted Soviet intelligence system.

The most effective intelligence gathering operations were carried out by short-range troop, artillery and engineer *razvedka*. Reconnaissance 'destroyer' battalions and partisans operating in the German rear were closely integrated with the GRU and played an important part at all levels. Along with more sophisticated reconnaissance in force, the sheer volume of material they provided allowed the Soviets to build up a comprehensive picture of German positions.

Following the fall of Stalingrad, the entire course of the war in the east changed abruptly as the Germans attempted to set up their defences along the line of the Donets river. The Red Army went onto the offensive and

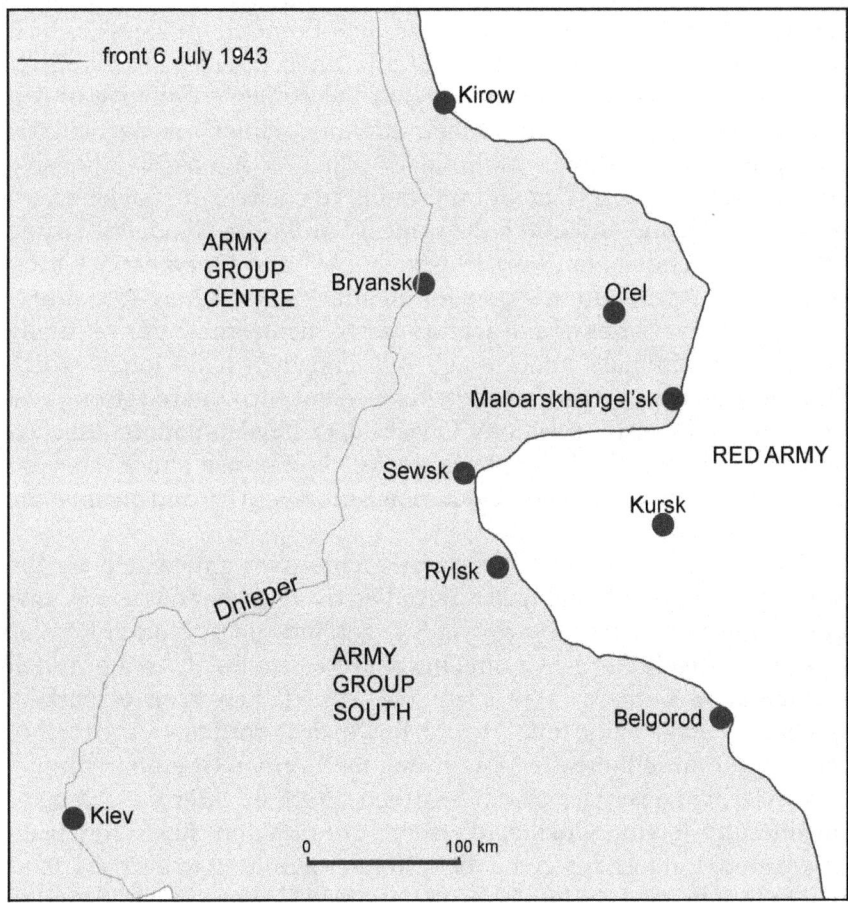

The Kursk/Orel Front on 6 July 1943.

gained the initiative along almost the whole front. They attacked across the Don and quickly routed the Italians at Rossosh and Valuiki capturing Voronezh on 23 January 1943 opening the road to Kursk. Maintaining the initiative, they continued the attack both north and south-east of Kharkiv. On 5 February, General Nikolai Vatutin crossed the Donets captured Kursk on two days later and then swung to the south and took Belgorod disrupting the entire German position on the upper Donets. At this point, however, the Soviet attack slowed with communications lines badly overstretched since their front in the south had almost doubled in length. A sudden thaw saw the ice turn to *rasputitza*, the mud season, giving the Germans a breathing space to consolidate their defensive positions and reorganise. By the end of March, they established a line roughly the same as they had held in spring 1942.

The German capture of Orel in October 1941 had resulted in a German salient sitting directly above a Soviet salient centred on Kursk, which became a worry for the Wehrmacht after their disaster of Stalingrad. German planners were keen to regain the strategic initiative and it was to Kursk that they turned their attention. Hitler was particularly enthusiastic when shown preliminary plans for a massive offensive *Unternehmen Zitadelle* (Operation Citadel) to encircle the Soviet forces around Kursk and straighten the front. To authorise Citadel he issued Operational Order No. 5 on 13 March 1943 and Operational Order No. 6 on 15 April, with the date for an attack set at 3 May 1943, but it was subject to a series of at least four postponements. They eventually launched preliminary attacks on 4 July and their main forces struck with close air support on the following day, but encountered strong and deep Soviet defensive positions. On 6 July, the Soviets counterattacked and four days later had completely halted the German attack. Then on 12 July, the Soviets launched Operation Kutuzov to try and encircle the German forces around Orel.

Evidence suggests that Operation Citadel was anticipated by the Soviets as a result of intelligence supplied by a number of sources, one of which was the Lucy spy ring in Switzerland run by Rudolf Rössler. Lucy had already furnished vital information leading up to the launch of Operation Barbarossa in early 1941, but it had been essentially ignored by Stalin at the time. He did, however, accord the source rather more importance thereafter concerning the German Operation Blue.

Rössler had a contact whom he called 'Werther' after the character invented by Johann Goethe. Werther's true identity has never been discovered, but just before he died, Rössler admitted to a close friend that four of his sources had been an unnamed German major (believed to be Canaris's deputy, Hans Oster), the Abwehr officer, Hans Bernd

Gisevius, Carl Goerdeler, the ex-Lord Mayor of Leipzig, and someone he called General Bölitz, of whom no trace has ever been found. Of the four, Oster is generally considered to have been the most likely candidate.[2]

The Lucy spy ring was a small part of the much larger *Die Rote Drei* Soviet espionage network run by Dora (Sándor Radó) in Switzerland. Moscow had been receiving intelligence in Lucy's name through Dora since late 1942, but by March 1943, they were still trying to ascertain Rössler's credentials. They knew that his source, Werther, had come up with valuable intelligence about the movements and objectives of Army Group Centre and Army Group South during the winter and spring of 1943 but Dora, to some extent, contradicted it in April when a source, believed to be Gisevius, reported that 'only modest' operations were planned for early May.[3] It is widely believed that Werther's intelligence was flawed since it corresponds to orders and dates issued by OKW especially designed to misdirect and, in the event, it was disregarded by Moscow. It might be argued that if Werther was embedded in OKW then it would be an understandable mistake because, in reality, OKW at this time was not privy to the detailed plans of OKH in the east being preoccupied with events further west in Italy meaning that OKW might have been under the impression that Citadel was indeed scheduled for May as Werther predicted.

By 23 June, Werther was actually telling Moscow that Citadel had been delayed indefinitely when he reported,

> OKW does not wish to provoke a large-scale Russian offensive in the central sector under any circumstances. Therefore, one considers the German preventive attack in the southern sector no longer serves a purpose [because] Soviet build-up in the Kursk area since early June is now so great that German superiority there no longer exists.[4]

Even in early July, after the Battle of Kursk had begun, Werther was telling Moscow that the German action was just a response to a massive Soviet attack apparently triggered by German reconnaissance efforts on 4 July and was still being viewed by OKW as a defensive action. If taken at face value this can only mean that Lucy intelligence had little influence on the Soviet preparations to meet Operation Citadel and the intelligence that informed their extensive countermeasures must have originated elsewhere. It also casts doubt on whether Lucy was a genuine source or a 'plant' but other Soviet sources show that in other circumstances, the Lucy group provided valuable intelligence.

The British contribution was again based on ULTRA intelligence. On 22 March 1943, Bletchley Park had discovered that the Germans planned an offensive to eliminate the salient at Kursk but were struggling to gather sufficient armour to support it. A month later, they had decoded Luftwaffe signals transmitted using 'hedgehog' codes indicating a build-up of air strength for an operation they called *Zitadelle* and also read an OKH document prepared by Army Group South intelligence discussing possible Soviet responses to a German attack at Kursk. When this information was passed to the Soviets they were more inclined to accept it as an indication of a much bigger operation than the one predicted in the Lucy reports because of intelligence they were also receiving from their 'mole', John Cairncross, who worked in the British Government Code and Cypher School at the time and who was privy to ULTRA intercepts pertaining to the Luftwaffe. The British had also cracked the *Geheimschreiber* (fish) cipher and were reading traffic between OKH and Army Group South, which uncovered more details of Citadel.

There was now a danger that British help would dry up. Two things were causing them to think twice about continuing to furnish the Soviets with ULTRA intelligence. First of all, it was clear that the Soviets were not making good use of it and secondly, the British were increasingly worried about Soviet cipher security. The risk was growing that the Germans might break Soviet codes and become aware of high-value intelligence passing between Britain and the Soviets and start asking questions about where the British were getting their information from.

Meanwhile, ULTRA intercepts in May indicated that Luftwaffe units were being relocated from the Soviet Union to Germany and Italy to counter Allied gains in North Africa. It was now the British view that there was no way that Army Group Centre would get enough aircraft to launch a concerted attack before the autumn. By the end of June, at the time that German forces were getting their final orders and gearing up for the attack, MI6 had even concluded that the whole operation had been postponed indefinitely and the Germans would settle into an 'active defence' posture, at least in the centre. Winston Churchill, however, was more forthright. In a terse note to Stalin, on 13 June, he had warned that 'On the balance I think Hitler will attack you again, probably in the Kursk Salient'.[5]

The discrepancies between Lucy and ULTRA can probably be explained by the lack of cohesion in German planning and the differences between the generals and Hitler when it came down to the conduct of the war. Not only did OKW and OKH differ in their assessments of strategy, but both in turn were confounded by a Führer, firmly ensconced in the space between them, who would not adhere to sound military principles and a consistent policy. The fact that the Soviets were well informed about Citadel and made extensive plans to counter it owes much more to other sources of intelligence.

They issued warnings of an impending German attack three times during May and once at the beginning of July just days before it actually took place. On each occasion the warning was triggered by a burst of movement of Panzer Corps to the south. These movements had been carried out at night but were reported by agents and detected by radio intercepts.

Two years of war had made the Germans and the Soviets very aware of each other's strengths and weaknesses. Having, in some instances, been confronted by the same strategic and tactical challenges over that time, each had, in fact, learned from and copied the other. When they turned to their intelligence for answers their questions were almost identical. For FHO, the Battle of Kursk was probably the high point of its performance and one of the few occasions when Gehlen was able to congratulate his staff on a sound prognosis. They had identified the deep Soviet defensive measures that had been put in place particularly thanks to the fine spring weather and relative air supremacy that facilitated Luftwaffe reconnaissance. 'The course of the fighting on the Eastern Front', he told his staff, 'has once again confirmed precisely every detail of the intelligence picture of the enemy we produced.'[6] He had, however, somewhat varnished the truth. His assessment of Soviet strength had been essentially correct, but he had failed to see that two Soviet armies had been brought into the reserves undetected.

Nevertheless, Gehlen's reputation within OKH soared. His reports, liberally sprinkled with diagrams and coloured maps, were highly praised and, up to that point, his performance far outshone that of Kinzel, which, to be fair, had not been difficult. For the first time, OKH started to take FHO reports seriously. His standing was also enhanced by his habit of issuing a booklet noting how each of his predictions since taking office had successfully recognised the enemy's intentions; a vitally important factor now that the German advance had stalled and the Wehrmacht was being thrown onto the defensive. This was blatant propaganda on Gehlen's part, however. He may well have been a good and efficient intelligence officer and performed well under difficult circumstances, but he was far from perfect.

His reports were carefully crafted to include competing scenarios and predictions, which, in any given situation, described a range of possible actions the Soviets might take. The liberal use of words such as 'probably' and 'not excluded' ensured that that at least one prediction would prove correct and it was this that allowed Gehlen to say that his prescience was vindicated. His report of 18 November, which was the day before the 250,000 men of von Paulus's Sixth Army had marched into the 'meat-grinder' of Stalingrad that saw no more than 5,000 survive Soviet captivity, was a prime example. 'Expected attacks ... may possibly exceed local proportions', he wrote, and 'Simultaneous attacks ... do not appear excluded'.[7] It was a far cry from sending up warning flares anticipating what was the single most debilitating German defeat of the whole war.

Soviet front-line positions at Kursk were susceptible to German fighter aircraft of Luftflotte 6 and VIII Fliegerkorps who were, at this point, still able to overfly at low level and take photographs. Long-range reconnaissance monitored road and rail arteries for any increase in normal logistics traffic. Intelligence units of the Second Panzer Army had been reporting a build-up of Soviet forces north of Orel since the middle of May. All units on the front line between Kirow and Belgorod were collecting intelligence through physical observation, infantry raids, captured documents and from interrogation of captured Soviet soldiers, many of whom tended to respond positively to encouragement being generally less than enamoured of the Soviet regime. A German campaign of *Silberstreif* (silver lining) employed intensive propaganda and encouraged Red Army PoWs to enlist in the 'Russian Army of Liberation' under Soviet defector General Andrei A. Vlasov. Intelligence derived from PoW interrogations proved to be particularly productive all through the Battle of Kursk, but it was signals intelligence that was undoubtedly the primary source of tactical and operational intelligence both before and during the battle. The Soviets never really recovered from the huge losses of trained radio operators during 1941–1942, which resulted in poor security allowing German short-range reconnaissance units to read most of the Soviet signals traffic, much of which was not even encoded.

On 8 March 1943, von Manstein took into consideration the shortage of German forces when he proposed to Hitler that the Kursk bulge be cut in half with strikes from the west and from the south, which were to converge near Kursk. This was not sufficiently ambitious for Hitler who craved a much larger scale initiative. Three days later Hitler issued Operations Order No. 5, which was an amended plan to cut of the Kurst salient completely and pre-empt any possible Soviet attack in the centre.

In the three months during which Citadel was being planned, key Soviet dispositions were identified along with many new units brought to the front. The task of FHO was to provide OKH with continuously updated intelligence about Red Army positions and strength around Kursk. Despite the large volume of intelligence, Gehlen was covering himself by suggesting that the Soviets had tightened up on radio security meaning that FHO was unable to give assurances that reinforcements had not been moved into the salient.

The level of uncertainty displayed by the German is clear from the fact that the date set for the attack on the Kursk salient was postponed at least four times not least because of negative reports coming from the front describing the conditions to be unfavourable for a major offensive. Few German army group intelligence assessments from the early planning stages survive but Gehlen's assessment of 21 May predicted a Soviet attack against German Army Group South in the direction of Dnepr at the same time as attacking the Orel salient in the direction of Bryansk. Whilst the intelligence on Orel proved to be correct, nowhere does Gehlen indicate that he anticipated the full dimension of the Soviet effort and the length of time they were able to sustain their aggression.

Chief of the German Army General Staff, Kurt Zeitler demanded of Gehlen that he address the question of whether the Red Army had sufficient forces to defend the Kursk salient or whether they would launch a pre-emptive strike to forestall the one the Germans were planning. On 19 April, Gehlen came back with a report, 'Likely Behaviour of the Enemy in the Face of [German] Army Groups South and Centre', based on the data from all the German intelligence agencies, which concluded that 'We must count on the intention of the Russians to hold the Kursk area in the event of a possible German offensive against the encirclement [and therefore] we must count on the retaining of a large [Soviet] reserve group behind the front line.'[8] He warned that large forces were to be expected to the near and east of Miropol'e, Korocha-Volokonovka-Novyi Oskol and Izyum–Starobelsk threatening a counterstroke against the northern flank of Army Group South.

This was accompanied by another report of the same date, which threatened to have a major influence on the timing of Citadel. This report entitled 'Regarding Statements on Planning a Large Defensive Campaign by the Soviet Union for the Summer of 1943' expressed the view that the Soviets had decided to go on the defensive and prepare for a German assault while building up reserves in preparation for a Soviet offensive in Ukraine and Belarus after the Allies had opened a second front in the west. Gehlen made it clear that he did not agree with the conclusions of this second report. The current pattern of distribution of Soviet forces, he said, did not meet the requirement of defensive warfare. Furthermore, from the distribution and regrouping of the Soviet forces and the concentration of the tactical and strategic strike groups in their rear, he concluded that the Soviets were planning large-scale operations with far-reaching goals for summer 1943. This was based on FHO understanding of the rules and criteria of operational warfare rather than intelligence received from on agents and diplomatic circles. He did believe, however, that an opportunity existed for the Wehrmacht to conduct their own large-scale offensive operations in several key areas.

Gehlen had to balance reports of varying reliability. Indeed, it was probably the most difficult of all FHO tasks to rate intelligence they were receiving and the sources from which it was emanating according to how much confidence they had in its relation to the truth. One agent reported

> Very low combat effectiveness of the untrained poorly equipped [Red Army] units [who were] mostly recovered wounded; their mood depressed. The supplies for this group are coming through Kuibyshev from East Asia. The losses in manpower and equipment in winter were much heavier than was previously thought.

Another report that purported to be an appreciation of the Red Army's view of the situation said that the Soviets had insufficient forces in the south to repel a large German offensive. A Soviet headquarters report had apparently stated that 'substantial movements' of German forces had been detected behind Balakleya under cover of Luftwaffe protection which suggested a substantial operation at a time when a major German offensive was expected. A German military attaché reported to FHO that some forty or fifty divisions were concentrated around Moscow in anticipation of a German offensive on the capital. Another 'reliable' agent reported on a meeting in the Kremlin, on 23 April, between Stalin and all the commanders of the fronts and commanders of the armies to discuss, amongst other things, signs of a German offensive and the morale of troops on the front line. There is no evidence that such a meeting ever took place. To say that Gehlen was struggling to get a clear picture was an understatement. Rather than evaluate contradictory intelligence he would attach them to his reports to Zeitler to indicate the sort of material he was having to contend with. Of course, it was Gehlen's job to find out which reports could be relied on, but, for the most part, that was impossible.

In early May, he followed up with a report that the Red Army was preparing to defend the Kursk salient and doing so on a large scale meaning that it would be extremely difficult and costly to dislodge them. In customary fashion, he tried to appeal to differing viewpoints, favouring neither. He agreed with Zeitler that a stubborn defence where Soviet forces refused to give ground would offer the opportunity to destroy a large group of Red Army forces, but the attack would have to go in without delay. On the other hand, he saw merit in the views of OKW chief, General Alfred Jodl, and the Chief Inspection of Armoured Troops, General Heinz Guderian, who doubted the feasibility of the whole operation.

The commander of the German 9th Army to the north of the Kursk salient, Colonel General Walter Model, had actually sent a report to OKH, which he requested they forward to Hitler expressing grave misgivings about going ahead with Citadel at all. His troops were ill-prepared, he said. The enemy was rapidly strengthening their positions in front of him with both engineering fortifications and increased reserves. Evidence was included in the shape of aerial reconnaissance photographs. If *Zitadelle* was to go ahead as planned, he would need everything he had been promised and even then he would require more time to make a breakthrough than had been allocated to him in the plan. If neither was agreed to, he strongly urged cancellation.

Hitler was impressed by this report from a man for whose opinion he had a great deal of respect. He reacted by suspending the attack and called for a conference in Munich on 4 May of Army Group Centre and Army Group South Chiefs of Staff. Gehlen was called on to submit a report to the conference on the issued raised by Model. 'As in our previous assessments, we believe that the command of the Red Army has begun preparations for a large offensive operation in front of the northern wing of Army Group South towards the Dnieper', he wrote making it clear that he had little new intelligence to add to his report of two weeks previously. No date would be set for the German offensive until they have accumulated a sufficient tactical, mobile reserve probably in the area of Kupyansk-Starobelsk-Valuiki and Korocha-Volokonovka-Novyi Oskol as well as near Kursk and in the Livny-Yelets. The Soviets had been constantly 'pulling up new forces from the depths' since March, Gehlen said, but their locations were unknown due to complete Soviet radio silence. Ominously, he wrote 'Therefore, we must expect a constant increase in enemy units and forces as well as high defensive capabilities of the Russian units located in the zone of the planned German offensive.' It cannot be discounted, he continued, that the Soviets were preparing both to repel a large German offensive at the same time as planning an offensive of their own. If this was the case, the enemy would concentrate initially on defence before bringing up reserves for the counteroffensive. He concluded by saying that there were indications from Soviet activity around Kursk that they had previous knowledge of German plans.[9]

Gehlen's report of 3 May shows the extent of FHO's undercover network capabilities but its tentative nature is indicative of the lack of information available to tackle such a complex and wide-ranging issue. However, in general, during April and early May, FHO reports were notable for their 'objective appreciations and accurate predictions', which were by no means overly optimistic.[10]

The question arises as to what attention OKW and Hitler paid to FHO reports. Manstein's plan had been to hit the weakened troops on the Voronez front from the centre and south before they had time to recover from three months of constant bombardment. By mid-April, however, reserves had been brought up under marshals Konstantin Konstantinovich Rokossovsky and Nikolai Vatutin to shore up the Soviet positions and by early May, even before Hitler's Munich conference, this was well known to OKH. Caution demanded a postponement of the attack, but that only gave the Soviets more time to prepare. It was well known in Berlin, by this time, that Moscow had been forewarned of Citadel, which had accelerated its strengthening of the Kursk salient. Hitler, however, refused to alter the focus of the attack, which had been stipulated in Manstein's original presentation. He considered much of the intelligence surrounding Soviet capabilities to be exaggerated. This was despite aerial intelligence indicating that these were the precise areas that were being fortified. It was almost as if Hitler was saying to Stalin, 'Do your worst but you will still not stop us.'

False reports continued to flow into FHO. One report of 18 June from what was tagged as a 'reliable' source said that Stalin would be returning to Moscow after a short trip to Voronezh. Stalin, in fact, never left Moscow at all during the month of June. Another report said that, on 7 July, 'Marshal Zhukov and Marshal Vasilevskii with their headquarters [staff] arrived in Valuiki on two heavy bombers'. This was also quite wrong; the two men had been in the Kursk salient at the time.[11]

Agent 'Olaf', again thought to be 'reliable', reported that 140 tanks, 50 of which were American built, of the 5th Guards Tank army had gone by rail to Staryi Oskol Skorodnoe and the 4th Motorised and Strike Army had moved into Tim just south of Kursk. In fact, the tank force had numbered some 700 and had gone by road through Staryi Oskol on its way to Prokhorovka. The 4th Motorised and Strike Army did not exist at all.

It was only because Gehlen's staff was composed of agents with experience of serving in combat units and at the headquarters of large formations and well knew the nature of warfare and the fact that they were able to compare reports from a variety of sources that they were able to function as efficiently as they did.

Gehlen later claimed that he had done everything he reasonably could through his reports to get Hitler to abandon Citadel. On 3 July 1943, he went as far as to submit a report entitled 'Appreciation of the Enemy's Moves if Operation Citadel is Carried Out', which laid out two scenarios.[12] The first one assumed that the Soviets would concentrate all their efforts on defence by drawing in reserves from other neighbouring fronts. The second predicted that they would simultaneously put up a strong defence and launch strong diversionary attacks and counterattacks in the Orel area and the lower Dnieper with the aim of striking towards Kharkiv in an attempt to penetrate deeply into the flank of the advancing German troops. This second scenario turned out to be exactly what the Soviets did but at the time it was submitted Hitler disputed its conclusions and the report had no significant impact on the decision-making process.

One day later, in the last of a series of reports emphasising caution over Operation Citadel Gehlen wrote,

> From the point of view of the general war situation, there is not one ground that could justify launching Operation Citadel at the present juncture. The prerequisite for victory in the offensive is twofold – we should have numerical superiority and the advantage of surprise. At the time originally planned for the launching of the offensive, both conditions were met. But now, from what we see of the enemy situation, neither is met. For weeks the Russians have been just waiting for our attack in the very sector that we have picked for the offensive. And with their customary energy they have done everything in their power constructing line upon line of fortifications one behind the other and moving up the necessary forces to halt our offensive as soon as it begins. Thus, there is little likelihood that the German offensive will achieve a strategic breakthrough. Taking into account the total reserves available to the Russians, we are not even entitled to assume that Citadel will cost them so much in strength that they will later be incapable of carrying out their general plan at the time they choose. On the German side, our reserves, which will become so desperately necessary as the war situation develops (particularly in the Mediterranean!), will be tied down and thrown away uselessly. I consider the operation that has been planned a particularly grave error, for which we shall suffer later.[13]

He was clearly right but it was far too late to make any difference.

German efforts to discover exactly what the Soviets were doing during the build-up to Citadel were, for the most part, confounded by Red Army *maskirovka*, which was being incorporated into their strategic planning at a high level. This involved strict measures to blanket the assembly and deployment of reserves in secrecy and also required other sectors to carry out diversionary attacks to draw German forces away from the Orel / Kursk sectors and tie down their reserves. The Germans were misled into thinking that a major Soviet counteroffensive was being prepared in the Izyum and Mius river regions. In this area, Soviet lack of *maskirovka* was, in itself, a master stroke of *maskirovka*. By deliberately neglecting tactical and operational deceptive measures they contributed to the overall success of a strategic plan.

Where *maskirovka* was employed, it included the concealment of preparations, creation of false troop concentrations, simulation of false radio nets and communications centres, construction of false air facilities and false aircraft, and the spreading of false rumours along the front and in the enemy rear area.[14] At least fifteen false airfields were set up complete with mock-up aircraft, runways, control towers and aircraft shelters, along with numerous mock-up tanks to simulate armoured assembly areas. Success was measured by the number of times that false airfields were bombed by the Luftwaffe (nine). Strict communications security was introduced, which saw all radio call signs changed daily and frequencies changed as much as five times a month. All movement of troops was carried out at night or during poor weather conditions and supply depots were stablished in thickly forested areas.

A meticulously prepared plan called for in-depth defensive measures to contain the first German assault followed by two counteroffensives, one to coincide with the German attack and the second to follow a few days later. The Soviets started their defensive operations hours before the German attack was launched with an artillery and Katyushka rocket barrage over a broad front. Some reaction had been expected after the preliminary reconnaissance operations of 4 July but the ferocity of the Soviet action was quite unexpected and it caused serious damage to German artillery positions, communications and observation posts. Then when the German attack went in, they were further surprised by the depth of Soviet second-echelon defences, especially the extensive minefields and were shaken by what General F. von Mellenthin called 'The horrible counterattacks, in which huge masses of manpower and equipment took part'. Keitel commented that 'We in no way expected that the Red Army was not only prepared for the repulse of our attack, but itself possessed sufficient reserves to switch to a mighty counter-offensive'.[15]

By 12 July, The German offensive had exhausted itself on the Soviet defences and the Red Army went onto the attack at Orel. Soviet intelligence had kept a close eye on German operational reserves that had moved to counter the diversionary attack in the south. On the South-Western Front they attacked across the Northern Donets river at Barvenkovo, and the Southern front across the Mius river toward Stalino. The Orel counteroffensive, Operation Kututzov, had been in the planning since late April. Adherence to strict *maskirovka* strategy meant that German intelligence completely failed to detect Soviet preparations for offensive action and were unaware of the forward deployment of Soviet armoured units. Gehlen, for one, seemed unable to abandon his prejudiced view that the Soviets were incapable of sophisticated strategic deception. Even tactical radio deception, he said, had only ever been of 'limited importance'.[16] The natural heavily forested environment especially along the northern Donets river was perfect for concealment. Soviet radio transmissions and operational documents had been forbidden to make any mention of the word 'offensive'.

By the time Zhukov launched his Belgorod-Kharkiv operation in August, German operational reserves were exhausted. They were no longer able to defend any position forward of the Dnepr river. Subsequently, in mid- and late August the Soviet counteroffensive swelled to include the bulk of their forces on the Eastern Front.

Immediately after the German failure at Kursk, Gehlen predicted that the Soviets would continue their summer offensive 'beyond the local areas' then dig-in ahead of a winter offensive. It is indicative of the greater difficulties now faced in the area of intelligence gathering that FHO was unable to gather sufficient intelligence to foresee massive attacks in the south and centre that pushed the fronts there 150 kilometres further west. No longer could Gehlen rely on a copious supply of PoWs and captured documents. No longer was he getting useful reports from a Luftwaffe that was severely depleted in its surveillance capabilities.

Chapter 14

SOVIET COUNTERINTELLIGENCE

'Enemy agents whose guilt has been established and who
cannot be used to further advantage are to be shot.'

Lavrentiy Beria,
23 May 1942[1]

Identification of German agents was an important part of the routine work of the OOs. In November 1941, OO leader Pavel Zelenin, warned that 'Enemy intelligence agents are trying to infiltrate our military units [masquerading as] Soviet soldiers who have escaped from German PoW camps'. He suggested suitable candidates from amongst these men should be recruited as double agents and sent behind the enemy's front line.[2] The OOs started rounding up Red Army soldiers on the feeblest of pretexts. A person could be shot for praising the German technical equipment or for using propaganda leaflets that had been dropped by the Luftwaffe to 'roll-up' their tobacco into makeshift cigarettes. Arrests of those found perpetrating these trivial 'crimes' became so excessive that the head of the Main Directorate of Military Tribunals was obliged to intervene and suggest that no arrest should be made unless 'the ill intention of the servicemen who possessed leaflets' had been established by supporting evidence'.[3]

Towards the end of 1942, OO officers acting under a *politicheskii rukovoditel* (political mentor) or *voennye komissary* (military commissar) began sending their own agents behind German lines to penetrate the enemy's intelligence organisations and collect information. Political commissars now became known as *zampolity* appointed by *Purkka* (the Political Directorate of the People's Commissariat for National Defence). At company level, every three days, a *zampolit* wrote a bulletin to his superior regarding the political morale of his company. Red Army commanders hated the *zampolity* and mocked them for their ignorance of military affairs but it was no laughing matter when, in trying to justify their privileged position and participation, *zampolity* 'ruined the lives of many good and courageous people, accusing them of defeatist thoughts or enemy propaganda … or making scapegoats of them for military failures.'[4]

The informants system employed by the Soviets was undoubtedly the most important component of their counterintelligence strategy. It had been honed to a very high level by the communists within the civilian population since before the Russian Revolution of 1917. People at all levels of society were coerced into spying on friends, neighbours, co-workers and even family. Every citizen was required by law to report suspicious activity. Informants were particularly important in areas where German agents would seek to penetrate for vital information such as railway stations and freight yards. The network was all-pervasive extending even into the NKVD itself and all the armed services. A United States Army study based on German documents suggest that as much as 10 per cent of the Red Army may have been informants working for Smersh.[5] The role of informants in the Red Army is illustrated by no less than 4,300 informant networks being created on the Stalingrad front during the months of October and November 1942.[6] In the civilian population of some 200 million, it is likely that the proportion of informants was equally high. Redundancy was built into the system but in a country like the Soviet Union that hardly mattered. It is doubtful if the Germans had any idea, especially at first, just how deeply embedded in the Soviet system the informant system was. In a society saturated with informants, the job of foreign agents was all but impossible.

There were various categories of informant. Secret agents would infiltrate dissident groups and report on activity. Residents were controllers of informant networks and then there were informers themselves who were recruited by Smersh agents. Once accepted to the role, an informant was required to write down a brief personal history, which was filed away, and they were then given a codename. In theory each informant was unaware of the identity of other informants and they were often called on to spy on each other. Overall, the system was extremely effective in keeping the population in check and severely restricted German agents' operations, but when the German advance of 1941 overran huge areas of the Soviet Union, millions of Soviet soldiers along with informants were taken captive, which meant that to control the many new armies raised a recruitment and training programme of new informants was inaugurated.

Alongside informants, Soviet rear area security controlled the movement of all Soviet citizens. Checkpoints were everywhere set up at random to examine documents to identify foreign agents and deserters and to interrogate anyone who looked suspicious. Regular soldiers would normally be required to carry up to ten different sets of documents from pay book to travel permits. Civilians had to carry photographic ID and work pass if moving from one place to another. Since great emphasis was placed on the scrutiny of documents, the Germans spent a great deal of resources creating false documentation, which they copied from a wide range of captured papers from Soviet PoWs. The Soviet State Security Document Technical Services, however, employed a variety of devices to confound the forgers by, for instance, marking official documents with apparently innocuous markings that the Germans might overlook or changing the format of travel passes at short notice or making tiny alterations to rubber stamps. Booklets were distributed to security forces at regular intervals to keep them up to date on what to look for when examining documents. It was not only documents. Clothing was closely examined and speech was tested to see if the accent corresponded to the region specified in their documents. Prohibited areas were set up in border areas to prevent infiltration and the civilian population, apart from essential workers, was evacuated from those parts closest to the front. Border guards would quickly surround certain areas and close in to sweep them to flush out suspected German agents who were handed over to the NKVD. Citizen's battalions were created to protect vital installations, such as power stations and to perform routine patrols.

As early as 1942, having just been catapulted into his post at FHO, Gehlen was bemoaning the fact that 'it was no easy task to see through Soviet deception measures [especially] on a strategic level'.[7] Much of the credit for this must be given to Soviet counterintelligence, which succeeded in confusing both the Abwehr and FHO with disinformation on a huge scale. Also by creating an intensely hostile environment for German agents behind their lines, the Soviets denied them even the faintest possibility of gaining intelligence about factory production of modern aircraft and the true scale of mobilisation and equipping of new armies.

The Soviet strategy of integrated offensive and defensive counterintelligence led to many apprehended German agents being returned to German lines as double agents either to spy or disseminate false information. Sometimes Soviet soldiers would be sent through the lines to give themselves up to the Germans masquerading as deserters or refugees. It was common for the Germans to use Soviet citizens as agents because of language and local knowledge, but it could easily backfire if the agent still had family in the Soviet zone and was caught, which the majority were. Such an agent caught by the Soviets might be coerced into returning as a double agent by threats aimed at their family. These agents already had credentials on the German side and might get the opportunity to become further integrated into German intelligence for instance as an interpreter or trainer of other agents. Others would give themselves up immediately to the Soviets once across the lines and offer their services.

It was a perilous and thankless task. No doubt the Germans suspected every agent that came back as having been 'turned' to some degree. Just how easy it was to determine an agents' affiliations is hard to gauge and how much credence to place on the intelligence they provided a matter of some judgement for their handlers. Much would have depended upon personal relationships. While the call to become an agent cannot have been all that welcome for most, the perks that came with the job, such as cigarettes, alcohol and maybe clothing, in a war that had stripped civilisation to its bare existential bones for civilians must have been a powerful motivator. There is no doubt that the low return rate for agents had much to do with the fact that many, once across the lines simply melted away into the countryside and left their German handlers to believe they had been caught or killed. On the other hand, there were probably more than a few who were quite adept at playing the role of either agent and double agent and enjoyed not only the material benefits, but also the thrill of deception.

Double agents returned to the German side could play a number of roles from liaising with partisans to infiltrating establishments, such as agent training camps like the one at Sulejowek. The few who managed to worm their way into one of the sixty training facilities would be very well placed to forewarn the Soviets of operations and pass along to them the identities of both German intelligence officers and their agents.

The practice of passing disinformation to the Germans was a mainstay of Soviet counterintelligence operations and radio became an essential component of that subterfuge during and after 1942. Soviet sources confirm that 'radio games' were a vital component of Soviet deception during the battles of Stalingrad, Kursk and Operation Bagration.[8] These were complex and carefully planned, requiring a high level of skill, security and coordination. To work effectively, radio communication between controller and agent had to be carefully monitored to ensure that messages were genuine and not 'planted' by the enemy. This involved prearranged codes known only to them. Omission of certain words would indicate that it was someone else and not the actual agent who was transmitting while other words or phrases would be a danger signal to say that the agent was transmitting under coercion. Often before going on a mission, characteristics of the agent's style and rate of keying (called fisting) was noted and periodically compared with that during transmissions from the field.

Prior to the Battle of Kursk, all German agents with radio equipment captured by the Soviets in and around that area were systematically used to transmit disinformation back to the controllers. All information they sent back supported the idea that the Soviets were digging into a defensive posture. Specifically, they reported that huge volumes of barbed wire were being brough in, anti-tank ditches were being dug and command bunkers being constructed. It was vitally important throughout any particular 'game' that misinformation was coordinated to produce a consistent narrative.

The dismal failure of the vast majority of German agent missions behind soviet lines strongly suggests that the Soviets had a source of intelligence in the Abwehr and SD who had access to detailed information about agent deployment. There have been a number of high-ranking suspects identifies a being Soviet agents, the most important of which was Martin Bormann. Reinhard Gehlen was convinced of Bormann's perfidy and claimed that he had fled to Moscow after the war, but there is ample evidence to show that he was either killed in Berlin on 9 April 1945 or fled to South America.[9] Baun's background and position as head of *Walli I* also put him in the frame especially considering the extremely high failure rate of his agents. OKH head until 1942, Franz Halder believed that 'nearly all the plans of OKH were revealed to the Soviets a soon as they were drawn up'.[10]

Chapter 15

OPERATION MONASTERY

'Operation Monastery was one of the most
successful deception games of the war.'
NKVD Lieutenant General
Pavel Anatolyevich Sudoplatov[1]

In November 1941, in one of the rooms of the Novodevichy Monastery, the poet Boris Sadovsky and his wife Nadezhda Ivanovna were entertaining a guest, Alexander Petrovich Demyanov, who worked as an engineer in the *Glavkinoprokat* company in Lithuania. The former leader of the Noble Assembly of Nizhny Novgorod, Prince Glebov, was also present. Sadovsky and Glebov were part of a circle of like-minded people hoping, in blithe disregard of all the evidence of German atrocities, to get German support for restoration of the Russian monarchy once the Red Army had been defeated. They hoped to enrol Demyanov, a man of aristocratic background, in their project.

Demyanov's family history might well have suggested to Sadovsky and his group that he was a likely candidate for recruitment to their cause but they were mistaken. It's true that his grandfather had been a Cossack and his father had served under the Tsar. His uncle had even been a member of the Russian White Army counterintelligence fighting against the Bolsheviks in the Russian Civil War and all this might well have drawn him into an anti-Bolshevik conspiracy, but he was forced to look the other way when he was expelled from St Petersburg Polytechnic Institute and arrested by the OGPU. The secret service wanted agents with exactly his sort of background to infiltrate and keep an eye on revanchist organisations for counterrevolutionary activity. They allowed him to give the impression that he was an anti-communist activist but threatened him with exposure as a spy if he would not cooperate and that would blight any legitimate career opportunities he may have had. He was forced by his handlers Viktor Ilyin and Mikhail Makliarski to perform small tasks for state security under the codename 'Heine' for most of the 1930s during which time he established himself as an electrical engineer in a Moscow film studio and became well known in the elite Moscow cultural, diplomatic and journalistic circles. These were exactly the areas that OGPU were worried about.

When the war started in 1939, he volunteered to join a cavalry unit, but retained his position as an intelligence agent with special responsibilities. He was sent to Berlin to make contact with White Russian émigré circles and casually make contact with German intelligence who had already dropped subtle hints in his direction. Returning to Moscow ahead of Barbarossa, Demyanov became involved in a plot to penetrate Abwehr operations in occupied territory by setting up a fictitious ragtag band of underground monarchy sympathizers, codename *Prestol* (Throne), awaiting the arrival of German troops in the Soviet capital. Through *Prestol*, he would offer his services to the German High Command hoping to get posts in a new anti-Communist organisation in occupied territories and then identify German agents in the Soviet Union and get information about the German spy network there. It was in his guise as a member of *Prestol* that he had befriended Glebov and got an invitation to the orphanage of the Novodevichy Monastery in military uniform telling Sadovsky that he had received a summons and was leaving on a secret mission to cross the front lines and make contact with German intelligence. Henceforth Demyanov's activities would become part of what the Soviets called Operation Monastery.

According to one account, in December 1941, he crossed the front line near Mozhiask some 100 kilometres west of Moscow and surrendered to the Germans pretending to be a deserter. Initially he was treated like an ordinary prisoner, but he insisted that he had important information and asked to be handed over to an Abwehr officer. He was taken to a concentration camp near Smolensk where he offered his services to the Abwehr as a double agent. Under brutal questioning he told his interlocutors that his mother and grandfather had been well known as White Russian sympathisers and he had many relatives in fascist Italy. This had little effect and he was hauled out and put against a wall in front of a firing squad who took aim and fired over his head. He still clung to his cover story but by this time, it had become known that Demyanov had already made contact with the Abwehr in 1939. After this he was accepted and placed in a private apartment where Abwehr agents trained him in the use of radio, primed him for missions in Moscow and gave him the codename 'Max'. His relationship with the

Sadovsky circle was of little interest to the Abwehr and instead he was instructed to go back to the Soviet Union and observe the transport of military equipment and forces to determine in which section of the front an offensive was being prepared.

On 15 March 1942, Demyanov was parachuted into the Soviet Union near Rybinsk in the Yaroslavl region with two other agents. They were arrested and beaten by local security forces, but Demyanov persuaded them to call the KNVD who quickly came to collect the three men and took them to Yaroslavl. Demyanov's two companions were arrested but he was sent to Moscow. He was now a highly-trained NKVD operative who the Abwehr thought was working for them.

Two weeks later he started transmissions under the guidance of Lieutenant General Pavel Sudoplatov, head of the NKVD's Administration for Special Tasks. The idea, of course, was to send misinformation but they had to be extra careful to make sure that there was enough truth in the reports so as not to contradict others that the Abwehr might be getting from other agents in the same area. False claims of accidents or war damage were backed up by press releases that were sure to be seen and reported on by other German agents. As an example of subterfuge. Trains were loaded with timber and covered with tarpaulins. Demyanov would then report them as carrying tanks which could not be disputed by other sources. His radio communications with the Abwehr were coordinated by Colonel Rudolph Abel, who, under the work name of William Fisher, was indicted for spying in the United States by the FBI and later exchanged for the U-2 pilot Gary Powers in 1960.

Two German couriers living in Moscow, Stankevich and Shakurov, were duped into visiting the offices of Demyanov's father-in-law, which had been set up as a meeting place for the mythical *Prestol* group. When they were taken, Stankevich agreed to cooperate as a double agent and join in the 'radio games' but Shakurov would not agree. Demyanyov signalled to the Abwehr that Shakurov 'drank too much, was lazy and afraid' and for the sake of security should be eliminated. Other couriers were given safe passage back to Germany to report that the 'Max' operation was running smoothly.[2]

Demyanov now told his Abwehr handlers that he had managed to get a position as a junior communications officer in the *Stavka*. This, he told them, gave him access to low-level information about troop movements around Rzhev. What he told the Abwehr supported other misinformation that was being played out suggesting that a major Soviet offensive was being planned in the area. There was a Soviet offensive at Rzhev but it turned out to be small-scale and only a diversion to take German attention away from Stalingrad. It may well have been Gehlen's oft stated opinion that the Soviets were incapable of mounting more than one major offensive at any one time that caused FHO to take their eyes off Stalingrad at a critical moment.

In what must be seen as an extremely high-risk enterprise, the reason for which is difficult to understand, Demyanov was twice allowed to cross over and meet with his Abwehr handlers, once in 1942 and again in 1943. Undoubtedly, such meetings would have boosted his credentials with the Germans, but could only have been authorised if Sudoplatov had almost total confidence that Demyanov would not be exposed. He would have to be sure that Demyanov would not inadvertently give something away that might compromise him and through him, the whole of Operation Monastery. This implies extreme faith in Demyanov's character and ability. The other implication is that Sudoplatov knew what the Abwehr knew about Demyanov and concluded that they had no suspicions whatsoever about his reliability. That of course means that the KNVD must have had a high-level source in German intelligence. Any clues as to who that might have been has remain locked up in intelligence files in Moscow. What it does say, unequivocally, is that Demyanov was a very cool character and a very accomplished double agent.

In the following year, Demyanov sent misleading reports concerning Soviet reserves behind the Kursk salient. They were, he said, cumbersome and incapable of rapid manoeuvre which Gehlen fed into his assessment before the attack which severely underestimated Soviet resources and capabilities on that front.

Two other instances of Demyanov's effectiveness stand out. He reported on a high-level meeting in the Kremlin between Stalin and his generals on 4 November 1942 in which it was agreed to bring forward all planned offensives in the regions of Grozny, Voronezh, Rzhev and Leningrad to 15 November. Later on 27 April 1944, he sent details of a meeting discussing plans for the summer offensives all of which were incorporated into FHO assessments. Unfortunately for Gehlen, Demyanov had predicted an attack against Army Group South when Operation Bagration was actually launched against Army Group Centre.

The Germans also had an intelligence source, *Luftmeldekpf Suedost*, in the form of Richard Kauder operating from Sofia which they also called 'Max'. The lack of clear evidence leaves only speculation to bring together the pieces that connect Demyanov and Kauder.

Richard Kauder was a man 'of middle height, with a round face, well fed and well dressed ... who spent his nights in restaurants and cafes dining well and dating women'.[3] Born in Vienna in 1900 into a Jewish family, Kauder's early career had seen him working as a sports journalist, first in Zurich then Paris and finally Berlin, as a sporting goods salesman and an estate agent. After the Nazis came to power he moved to Budapest where he honed his multifarious talents as a high-class pimp and procurer of documents, such as residence permits and travel visas and as an unofficial foreign exchange dealer. Organising the latter two, which were especially important to members of the Jewish community, brought him to the attention of the United States consul in Zagreb, John J. Meily, with whom Kauder developed a shady business relationship. Meily was an avid collector of antique weapons and Kauder was able not only to point him in the direction of dealers but arrange for illicit currency exchanges so that he could purchase them. In this way Kauder inveigled himself into Meily's confidence sufficiently to be given special access to the Zagreb embassy. Not one to look a gift horse in the mouth, Kauder took advantage of this privilege by raiding Meily's personal and diplomatic files. This inevitably found him making arrangements with other agencies who were active in Budapest, especially Rudolf Graf von Marogna-Redwitz, the Abwehr chief in Vienna, and the SD.[4] In return for agreeing to work for the Abwehr, Marogna-Redwitz promised to protect Kauder's mother from persecution in Vienna. Kauder's cover name in Abwehr files was Richard Klatt and the codename for the espionage network he was about to set up was 'Max'.

Canaris had given his personal approval to the recruitment of Kauder and would, obviously, have been acquainted with details of the Demyanov operation. Since both operations were set up at around the same time this suggests that the two were connected since both sources were given the same codename 'Max'. If this was so then it appears as if Kauder was recruited to act as a conduit for intelligence coming from Demyanov. For this to work, Kauder would need his own links to Moscow and Demyanov would have had to be recruited by the Abwehr before 1941. This is perfectly possible given that Demyanov spent much of 1939–1940 in Berlin mixing with Soviet émigrés when, under orders from the NKVD, he could have offered his services to the Germans and, at that time rather than later, been allocated the German codename 'Max'. There are conflicting narratives describing how Kauder created his network of spies.

One version has it that he was approached by an Austrian friend, Joseph Schultz in Vienna in 1941 who told him that he had a network of 'friends' in the Soviet Union who were willing to report on Soviet military movements. Kauder took the idea to Marogna-Redwitz who passed it up the line to Berlin. Canaris approved the scheme and set him up to operate independently of the main Abwehr station in Sofia run by Colonel Otto Wagner. Schultz then introduced Kauder to Ira Longin, an ex-White Russian ex-Cossack officer, later described by US interrogators as 'an intelligent [but habitual] liar' and a White Russian general Anton Turkul.[5] Between the four of them they established *Dienststelle I* or 'Klatt Bureau' in a villa in the central part of Sofia, Bulgaria in 1942. This is significant because Bulgaria was the only German ally that continued to have diplomatic relationships with the Soviet Union, a country that maintained a huge staff of the Soviet Embassy in Sofia including many political and military spies. Turkul claimed to control a fascist group of White Russian military émigrés in Europe and had his own intelligence network centred in Rome. Kauder took over Turkul's radio network of wireless agents in the Red Army signals staff and told the Abwehr that the reports he was getting were collated in the Soviet Union at one or more centres and then transmitted via intermediaries to Istanbul and Samsun, Turkey, when they were radioed to Sofia.[6]

Another version says that Kauder met up with Longin, someone he had known previously, in Budapest in June 1940. Knowing that Longin was involved with an émigré network, it was Kauder who made the approach to Longin about getting intelligence from inside the Soviet Union. Longin consulted Turkul, who was the leader of his group. Between them they persuaded Marogna-Redwitz to set them up as *Luftmeldekpf Suedost*, with the codename 'Max', under the administrative control of Wagner. Longin was allocated the cover name of Iliya Lang.[7]

Yet another narrative has Schultz introducing Kauder to Turkul in Vienna in 1941 and it was Turkul who told Kauder he had friends inside the Soviet Union who were in positions to supply military information. It was Schultz again who took the next step of introducing Kauder to Marogna-Redwitz after which *Luftmeldekpf Suedost* was established. Only now did Longin come into the picture, when Turkul introduced him as someone who had his own network of Soviet spies communicating through Istanbul.[8]

When Wagner discovered that Kauder's radio communications with 'Max' were tortuously routed through Spain and Turkey rather than directly with Moscow he challenged Kauder to explain. He was not impressed by Kauder' explanation that it was all subterfuge to avoid detection and decided to keep a close eye on him. He was not the only one. Kauder was in daily radio contact with Marogna-Redwitz, but his communications were intercepted in December 1941 by British intelligence whose clear-eyed analysis of their content led them to suspect that Kauder was playing a double game.

Gehlen had no such doubts, however. He considered the 'Max' reports from Kauder to have high value and used them liberally when presenting the OKH with his estimates of Soviet deployments. It was, perhaps, a measure of his inexperience in intelligence that he did so. Kauder came with excellent credentials and his apparent access to the Kremlin was probably too important to question for someone like Gehlen who had just been drafted in. At the time, Gehlen believed that Kauder's sources were a senior staff officer working at the front or army headquarters of the Red Army and a colonel in the Red Army signal troops. It was Wagner, finding himself in the shadow cast by Kauder's brilliance, who persisted with his scrutiny of the 'Max' set-up and went to Canaris and Marogna-Redwitz with his concerns.

Kauder's intelligence seemed to be comprehensive and usually tallied with other sources but on close examination they showed a lack of detail and tended to be cloaked in generalisations. How was it, Wagner asked, that Kauder's Kremlin source was able to transmit extended radio reports without being detected. Anyone spending such an amount of time sending illicit signals in German territory, for instance, would be discovered very quickly. It was a bit of a turf war between Wagner and Marogna-Redwitz who insisted that the Luftwaffe rated Kauder's intelligence as first class and vital to their operations and, they claimed, almost always proved to be accurate. It was a ringing endorsement and one that it was difficult to argue against, but a wary Canaris realised that although the 'Max' input was generally sound it added little to what was already known and, in fact, nothing much would be lost if it did not exist. He, himself, occasionally relied on 'Max' intelligence when briefing Hitler. Hedging his bets, he took Wagner aside after the meeting and advised him to carry on watching Kauder, but he was told definitely not to interfere with his work.

Wagner called on Sonderführer Kleinhampel of Abwehr IIIF to investigate Kauder. He reported that Kauder's explanations for the rerouting of radio communications through Samsun and Istanbul was, to say the least, suspect. Surveillance of Kauder's associates found them having meetings with a Soviet intelligence officer based at the bar of the Royal Theatre in Sofia. This same Soviet officer was also observed drinking with a female friend of Kauder at the same location and on one occasion, Longin was seen leaving the Soviet Legation.

Wagner decided to run a Hungarian attaché, Otto Hatz, as a double agent to see if he could find out where Kauder's information was coming from. The results were inconclusive but suggested that both Hatz and Kauder had been fed identical misinformation even though they operated completely independently of each other. George Romanoff was a member of Turkul's émigré organisation and stayed at Longin's apartment in Sofia during a three-week period in 1943. He later told United States Army investigators that there was simply not enough room in the apartment for Longin to hide all the radio equipment he would have needed to run his network. What he also observed was that Longin went every day to an apartment occupied by his girlfriend and came back with information he passed on to Kauder.

British intercepts of 'Max' communications found his intelligence to be up to date and well-arranged, but the overall impression was that it was considering unlikely that such a large spy ring could operate inside the Soviet Union over such a long period without detection and they suspected it was an elaborate double cross. British military intelligence, MI14, however, found the intelligence truly valuable in anticipating Soviet moves and concluded that there was practically nothing to support the theory of deliberate deception.

Meanwhile, Canaris and Gehlen had continued to show absolute faith in Kauder's intelligence much of which proved to be accurate and timely and refused to close 'Max' down. Neither man could accept that the Soviets were capable of running such a sophisticated deception involving two of their most productive sources on the Eastern Front. In 1944, even Guderian argued that to do so would be an act of 'criminal irresponsibility'.[9] However, it would be a characteristic of such a high-grade deception that the Soviets would build German confidence in the intelligence source by passing important and verifiable information in order to occasionally deceive at crucial moments. They could easily minimise the risks of passing accurate intelligence while maximising the benefits of misdirection. The Soviets were able to measure the effect of the deception on German operations through their 'Cambridge Spies' in MI6, Anthony Blunt, Kim Philby and John Cairncross, all of whom had access to German communications through their ULTRA intelligence. Without further evidence to the contrary, it is likely that both Demyanov and Kauder were both part of the same 'Max' operation although there is nothing to show that either was aware of the other.

Then, on 12 February 1945, two days before the Red Army took Budapest, Kauder's group relocated to Vienna at which point Austrian customs officers confiscated from him three boxes containing cash, an expensive stamp collection and jewellery. He was arrested by the SS, but, after two months in detention, he was released only to be taken prisoner by the Americans. Kauder, his Hungarian mistress Ivolia Kalman, Ira Longin and General Anton Turkul were interrogated at Oberursel detention centre, where the Germans had interrogated Allied air crews during the Second World War, while Smersh arrested other members of the Klatt Bureau, including Kauder's wife, Gerda Filitz. Filitz told the Soviets that the Klatt Bureau worked for Luftwaffe-1 Abwehr (Ast) in Vienna where Kauder had been first employed by the Abwehr in 1939. His contact there was Lieutenant Colonel Roland von Wahl-Welskirch, but he also had a direct line to Berlin through Schellenberg. It was Ira Longin's people, Filitz said, who supplied Kauder with the bulk of his intelligence about the Soviet Union. Kauder had no direct contact with them. Valentina Deutsch, one of Kauder's radio operators further claimed that Longin worked for Turkul.

The matter is further complicated by a report sent by Beria, to Stalin in 1944 in which he stated that an analysis of Kauder's radio traffic between Sofia and Budapest during the years 1941 to 1944 showed them to be 'pure fantasies'.[10] Furthermore, Smersh had no evidence of any illicit radio communications between Soviet territory and Sofia at this time. None of the Klatt members taken captive by the Soviets was executed and only one, Otto Hatz, is reported to have received a lengthy prison sentence and he was released after only four years. The balance of probabilities suggests that Kauder was a Soviet *maskirovka* agent but any real evidence of links with Demyanov remains locked in Kremlin vaults.

Chapter 16

SMERSH

'On 31 May 1919 a proclamation entitled "Beware of Spies"
was printed in Pravda. It started with the exclamation
"Death to Spies" and both Lenin's and Dzerzhinskiy's
signatures were appended to the article.'[1]

In September 1938, the Politburo had modified the structure of the NKVD according to the instructions of a man from Stalin's own home state of Georgia whom he had known for some time and had personally recommended for the first secretary position. Lavrentiy Beria, the first Communist Party secretary of Georgia, had arrived in Moscow in August 1938 and within a few days was appointed, on Stalin's recommendation, as first deputy commissar to Nikolay Yezhov head of the NKVD. Soon afterwards, Yezhov became a victim of Stalin's purges and was shot after which the odious paedophile Beria took his place. He supervised many of the arrests and executions that followed and administered the Gulag network of slave labour camps. In February 1941, he became a deputy prime minister of the Soviet Union.

At the same time, the Praesidium of the Supreme Soviet decided to cut the NKVD down to size because it threatened to become not only unwieldy but an entity in which too much authority was concentrated. It was broken down into a separate interior security (NKVD) and a department of state security (NKGB). While NKVD looked after border protection, civil defence and prison camps, the NKGB, under Beria's former deputy V.N. Merkulov, had amongst its portfolio, the departments for intelligence and counterintelligence. Military counterintelligence was transferred back to the NKVD in the form of the OO Directorate (UOO) under Viktor S. Abakumov, but its function remained essentially the same as before, to root out counter revolutionaries, saboteurs and traitors in the armed forces. Its power increased through a network covering the entire military establishment.

During this time, the NKVD oversaw of use of slave labour on road construction programmes carried out security operations using paramilitary and police formations. A 'Directive for the Senior Officers of the NKVD in towns liberated from the Enemy' (Order No. 2221) of May 1942 is clear evidence that already the Red Army was recovering lost ground. It called for the NKVD to hunt down 'enemy agents, traitors and other anti-Soviet elements [and] deal with spies and criminals, airborne agents and small enemy units ... left behind'. They set up security posts and checked the papers of all who passed through including Soviet soldiers.

Meanwhile, NKGB agents called *seksots* were recruited from a variety of social strata and embedded in all institutions throughout the Soviet Union. Often they would masquerade as tradesmen, such as chimney sweeps to gain access to the premises of suspects. Some agents would be recruited from reactionary groups to spy on meetings. When meetings were raided by security police, the agent would be arrested along with others but then released to take up a new assignment in a different region.

Utter catastrophe had loomed for Stalin after the German Panzer columns had surged across the border and smashed through Soviet defences in 1941. With the road to Moscow virtually undefended, on 17 July 1941, the OOs were placed back under NKVD control to stiffen resistance in the armed forces. Beyond the control of the military, under Abakumov, the Special Sections were authorised to arrest deserters and execute them on the spot in the 'struggle against espionage and treason', and in this regard they 'played a significant role in preserving the fighting capability of the Red Army, prevented its collapse and upheld its morale'.[2] According to Beria's files, the number of deserters and draft dodgers caught by the NKVD Rear Guard Troops reached 1,666,891 men; of these, 1,210,224 were deserters. It was Abakumov who, on Beria's authority, arrested and executed a number of military commanders. Artillery General V.S. Goncharov and General K.M. Kachanov paid the ultimate price of the Red Army failures.

For some eighteen months, the Soviets were on the defensive, but after Stalingrad all that changed. The Red Army went onto the offensive at the start of 1943 and started taking back territory lost to the German advance. While the OOs were still concerned with discipline and morale of the Soviet forces they were now given the task of 'cleansing' the liberated territories of German espionage networks, taking responsibility for the growing number of German prisoners

(170,000 at Stalingrad alone) and the processing of returning Soldiers who had been released from German PoW camps.

At this time, Soviet intelligence and counterintelligence knew little about the structure of the German intelligence and security services, and it was clear that military counterintelligence needed to concentrate on fighting the German enemy rather than focusing on internal subversion. To cope with the increased workload, Stalin, who had acquired new powers of control by being appointed a marshal of the Soviet Union, ordered the reorganisation of his security services. Under Merkulov's leadership, a group of intelligence officers came up with suggestions to realise Stalin's ambition that 'no spy, agent, or terrorist would escape the attention of the special departments'.[3] One proposal would see a new NKGB called *Smerinsh* (*Smert' Inostrannym Shpionam* or Death to Foreign Spies), which would include military counterintelligence. The name was subsequently shortened to Smersh (*Smert Shpionam* or Death to Spies). The other envisaged two separate organisations, the NKGB and Smersh, which would become a directorate within the NKO.

The decision was to break up the NKVD into two separate entities controlled by Beria with responsibility for the organisation of slave labour, police work and PoW camps and to revive the NKGB to handle foreign intelligence and counterintelligence within the Soviet Union, under Merkulov. Alongside this were created three new counterintelligence departments on 19 April 1943 all under a new entity which he named Smersh and formally made a part of the NKO. Essentially, Smersh was the UOO, renamed and made independent of the main body of secret services as a counterweight to the NKBD and NKGB and so reduce Beria's influence. Of all the Soviet security and intelligence services, Smersh has been generally the least understood and the least studied.[4]

The Red Army was much more integrated into the political structure than was the case with the Wehrmacht in Germany. Smersh, originally an OO section of the NKVD, assumed broad responsibilities for counterespionage in 1943 operating within Red Army units. It was divided into two sectors,

Headquarters

- A central administration.
- An agency attached to every theatre command.
- An agency attached to every army command (*c.*100 men) to handle prisoners, set up communications and run espionage agents across the front lines.

Field Organisation

- Supervision of personnel and maintenance of security.

A Smersh division would have an operational deputy assigned to each regiment and nine to each battalion. These would run two types of agents: mobile and resident each of whom would six to eight informers who in turn would be assigned to five or six suspected army men. Smersh agencies remained directly subordinate to the People's Commissariat for Defence unlike the GRU who were subordinate to the staffs of the unit where they operated.

Smersh was created as a 'vitally important instrument of political repression'[5], but official Soviet histories assert that Stalin constructed it so that 'in the decisive phase of the war the defence of the country be united [and] armed security assured'.[6] Abakumov was made deputy minister of defence and head of the new organisation retaining most of the UOO's personnel. Unlike the UOO, however, the chain of command led directly from Abakumov to Stalin. He reported directly to Stalin who had special plans for the organisation to establish political control over the territorial gains he expected the Red Army to make in Eastern Europe and Germany. Stalin was now *de facto* a dictator; General Secretary of the Communist Party, Chairman of the Council of Commissars, Chairman of the wartime GKO, Defence Commissar and Commander-in-Chief of the Armed Forces. Through its close link with Stalin, Smersh acquired immense authority. As a counterintelligence and security agency for the army, it was able to call on the resources of both the NKVD and NKGB without being accountable to either. From mid-1943 onwards, finding and arresting German agents was its primary task but it also took on the enormous task of arresting and vetting Soviet collaborators in German-occupied territories.

The order creating Smersh ascribed to it the following duties:

a) Combating spy, diversion, terrorist, and other subversive activity of foreign intelligence in the units and organizations of the Red Army.

b) Combating anti-Soviet elements that have penetrated into the units and organizations of the Red Army.

c) Taking the necessary agent-operational [i.e. through informers] and other (through commanding officers) measures for creating conditions at the fronts to prevent enemy agents from crossing the front line and to make the front line impenetrable to spies and anti-Soviet elements.

d) Combating traitors of the Motherland in the units and organizations of the Red Army (those who have gone over to the enemy side, who hide spies or provide any help to spies).

e) Combating desertion and self-mutilation at the fronts.
f) Investigating servicemen and other persons who have been taken prisoner of war or have been surrounded by the enemy.
g) Conducting special tasks for the People's Commissar of Defense.[7]

While on a practical level, he probably liaised and co-ordinated
extensively with Beria, operationally, Abakumov had been elevated to
equal him in status and was directly under Stalin's unremitting control
and leadership. He provided Stalin with daily reports. Running what
was effectively a state within a state, his officers had wide powers of
arrest, interrogation, judgement and execution. Soon the ruthlessness
of Smersh interrogators became legendary. The investigative officers,
known as *smershevtsy*, tortured and killed thousands of both real and
imagined 'enemies of the state' in areas of the Soviet Union previously
occupied by the Germans and in areas outside its borders that were
occupied by the Red Army. There was clearly going to be no shortage
of work for them. The scale of Russian collaboration with the Nazis that
Smersh encountered was quite staggering. The huge number of Soviet
volunteers to work for the Germans was so great that, in December
1942, to administer them Lieutenant General Heinz Hellmich had been
appointed 'General for Eastern Troops' and attached to the Second
Section of the OKH General Staff's Organisational Department headed
by Claus von Stauffenberg.

Structurally, Smersh closely resembled the OOs but at first Smersh
did not carry out active or offensive counterespionage operations and
concentrated more on general surveillance of Red Army troops. They
wore the uniform of the particular branch they were attached to with
no special insignia. Then as the Red Army forced the Wehrmacht
back, whole new classes of Smersh targets presented themselves, from
political activists to émigré and White Guard organisations that had
dispersed throughout Europe after the end of the Russian Civil War.
As an instrument of Stalin's power, Smersh became one of the most
important agencies involved with creating the conditions for the
reintroduction of Soviet political control and the subjugation of the
'liberated' areas. A key component of its strategy was the neutralisation
of German intelligence services. The Abwehr estimated that the number
of Soviet agents deployed against them over the course of the war was
in the region of 130,000. While no more than 10 per cent of them under
Smersh's direct control, it was noted that these agents were a cut above
the rest in terms of training and performance and certainly contributed
proportionately more to the Soviet counterespionage effort. This extra
capability allowed Smersh to employ more sophisticated methods

including 'turning' German agents who returned to German lines and infiltrated the German spy schools at Smolensk, Poltava and Königsberg. This tactic bore abundant fruit by identifying agents long before they ever set foot behind Soviet lines and laid the groundwork for successful double-agent operations.

A result of the Red Army enjoying a change to the offensive meant that there was opening up an ever-broadening strip of Soviet-occupied land that had recently been under German control. As the Wehrmacht had been pushed back, they left their agents behind equipped and trained by Baun's *Walli I* to set up spy networks and it was these that Smersh set out to destroy along with all other anti-Soviet elements and nationalist groups, such as the Ukrainian Insurgent Army that was proving to be a thorn in the Red Army's side. Smersh played a role alongside the NKVD when whole ethnic groups such as the Chechen, Caucasian Ingush, Karachay-Balkar and Crimean Tatars were deported to Kazakhstan and Siberia, losing at least one quarter and perhaps half of their population in transit.

As the Red Army inexorably rolled west, it was the *Arma Krajowa* (Polish Resistance – AK) who were next in Smersh's line of fire. Ten groups, under the command of Colonel Kozakevich, were allocated to assist KNVD forces to identify and arrest the AK leadership and agents of the Polish government in exile. It was not exactly classic Smersh territory, but valuable experience for developing its role. Those most passionately hunted down, however, were those who had aligned themselves with the former Soviet general Andrei Vlasov.

In December 1939, Vlasov had returned from a successful appointment in China to be appointed commander of the 99th Infantry Division in the western part of Ukraine and promoted to brigadier general. This new 'intelligent and energetic leader' raised the level of competence of his troops to such an 'extremely high level' that Timoshenko proclaimed it to be the best-trained division of the Red Army. Promotion to major general quickly followed and appointment to commander of the 4th Mechanized Corps on the Ukrainian-Polish border.

During summer 1941, now commander of the 37th Army, Vlasov was responsible for the defence of Kiev, and in November of that year was summoned by Stalin and given command of the 20th Army in the defence of Moscow. There he led one of the most significant counterattacks and he became a hero lauded in the Soviet press. Further promotion to lieutenant general followed. Stalin even considered appointing him commander of the Stalingrad front, an assignment that was eventually given to Timoshenko.

When Vlasov took over command in March 1942, his army was in a dire situation. It occupied an extended, narrow salient in German territory and only large-scale reinforcements, completely out of the question, or withdrawal to the Volchov river could avoid an encirclement. It was not until 20 May that Stalin ordered a withdrawal but Vlasov's army had become isolated. They took a terrible beating with 14,000 killed and 32,000 taken prisoner. Vlasov lost most of his staff officers during a sudden artillery barrage on his headquarters and spent days wandering through the woods of the Volchov river until, on 12 July, he was taken prisoner by the Germans and incarcerated in a camp for high-ranking PoWs. It was here that he wrote a letter to the German authorities, in which he proposed to exploit the anti-Stalinist sentiments among the Russian population and the PoWs and set up a Russian people's army.

As a result of his letter, Vlasov received a visit in the late summer 1942 from Oberleutnant Eugen Dürksen, an OKW propaganda officer who had been looking for some time for an anti-Stalinist Soviet general who was willing to sign pamphlets that tried to persuade Soviet soldiers to desert. Through Dürksen, Vlasov came into contact with Hauptmann Wilfried Strik-Strikfeldt, a Russian born-and-bred employee of Gehlen's FHO who convinced Vlasov to take charge of an anti-Stalinist liberation movement. In summer 1942, Vlasov's signature was on leaflets dropped over Soviet frontline troops inciting them to desert. The operation had a modicum of success with the result that a training camp was set up in Dabendorf for recruits to teach them the ideals of the liberation movement and the flaws of the Stalinist system.

The Germans had reached what would be the high point of Barbarossa with some 70 million Soviet citizens living under their occupation. Vlasov was an imposing presence and, with his powerful voice, went round preaching to large audiences urging them, in clear, simple and passionate language, to join in a movement to overthrow the Stalin regime and create a new, free democratic nation. The idea of raising a Soviet army fighting on the German side, however, was not one that found favour in Berlin where Hitler called it 'a delusion of the highest order'.[8] Of all the leading Nazis, it was Himmler who took most notice of Vlasov, perhaps seeing his followers as a new source of recruits for the SS where the Soviet Kaminsky-Brigade was already active. Himmler authorised the setting up of the *Komitet Osvobozhdeniya Narodov Rossi* (Committee for the Liberation of the Russian Peoples – KONR), and a military force *Russkaya Osvoboditel'Naya Armiya* (Russian liberation Army – ROA) under Vlasov's name. He indicated that the Germans would recognise the ROA not as mercenaries but as allies with equal status to the Wehrmacht. Soviet labourers and PoWs flocked to the cause but it was all too late. With the Red Army on Germany's borders, enthusiasm for the ROA dwindled, equipment was in short supply and there no longer seemed to be a role for Vlasov, who had never been fully trusted at the best of times.

In its death throes with nothing left to lose, a desperate OKH gave Vlasov supreme command over two divisions, a brigade and a small air force and, in April 1945, gave him the impossible task of retaking a Soviet bridgehead on the Oder. Instead Vlasov took his army to Czechoslovakia and, hoping to ingratiate himself with the Western Allies, conveniently changed sides by helping to liberate Prague and taking 10,000 German prisoners. Vlasov now sent emissaries to make contact with Unites States forces but was ignored. He was given a chance to escape to Spain where General Franco had offered him political asylum but he rejected it.

Vlasov was taken prisoner in the Americans zone of Prague on 12 May 1945. He was handed over to the Soviets, sent to Moscow and placed in Lubyanka Prison as Prisoner No. 31. After a trial presided over by Abakumov, he was found guilty of treason and hanged on 1 August 1946.

Smersh units were subordinate to the military groups in which they served but remained a strictly independent security force and military commanders had no operational control over them. They carried out defensive counterespionage surveillance to combat anti-Soviet activity, maintain morale and discipline and deter desertions. As part of their morale-boosting efforts, they also took it upon themselves to address troop's legitimate grievances and tried to improve their living conditions and nutrition. More attention was given to training of agents and building working relationships with the army commands where they were deployed. Amongst the first of Smersh's contributions was intelligence derived from its London *rezident* in May 1943 who had access to ULTRA decrypts predicting a German offensive at Kursk and even providing the German codename *Unternehmen Zitadelle*.

The primary focus of Smersh, however, remained countering German intelligence and counterintelligence and with its close links to Stalin, became the chief Soviet intelligence agency. The exposing and destruction of German agents and networks, described by the Soviets as 'fascist criminals' became a central facet of reestablishing political control of the liberated areas. It took over the organisation of agents and sabotage groups behind German lines from the OO special services.

Abakumov fully understood how Soviet politics worked and took steps to protect his position by undermining the NKVD and casting aspersions on Beria and Merkulov. Stalin assiduously maintained a balance of power between Smersh and the NKVD, however, by favouring one or the other at different times. German intelligence essentially failed to detect the existence of Smersh until early 1944 and even then only vaguely understood its structure or function. Even after the war, United States analysts struggled to unravel the complex web of Smersh bureaucracy.

It was not long before Smersh was uncovering evidence of atrocities committed by the German *Einsatzgruppen* often with the connivance of ex-Soviet soldiers in their ranks. During the first year of the German occupation, SK10a, a 120-man sub-unit of *Einsatzgruppe D* commanded by Otto Ohlendorf, exterminated the Jewish population in the towns of Berdyansk, Melitopol, Mariupol and Odessa, and then in the cities of Taganrog on the Sea of Azov and Rostov-on-Don.

Later under the command of SS-Obersturmbannführer Dr Kurt Christmann, the unit exterminated 7,000 inhabitants of Krasnodar, including patients in the municipal hospital, a convalescent home and a children's hospital. This crime was uncovered by the Soviets when the town was retaken in 1943 and eleven local inhabitants were put on public trial for having participated in the atrocity. Eight defendants were sentenced to death and publicly hanged while the rest were sentenced to twenty years in special hard labour camps.[9] This contrasts with the German response in 1972, which was to sentence four members of SK10a to four years imprisonment.

After Stalingrad Abakumov discovered new proof that the Germans had murdered 160,000 people in Kharkov and Smolensk many of whom were asphyxiated with carbon monoxide in specially equipped mobile 'murder vans'. Abakumov invoked a secret decree of the Presidium passed on 19 April 1943, which provided a legal basis for the punishment of German war criminals and collaborators. The first Soviet trial of German war criminals was held on 15 December when three Germans and one Russian were accused of war crimes along with six other high-ranking German military, intelligence, and military police officers who were not in court.

Chapter 17

OPERATION ZEPPELIN

'Three secret training schools for Zeppelin agents were
organized in the concentration camps at Buchenwald,
Sachsenhausen, and Auschwitz.'[1]

By the end of 1941, with Leningrad and Moscow still not in German
hands, it was clear that neither the Abwehr nor SD knew nearly enough
about the country they had invaded, and both attempted to correct
these deficiencies. Sturmbannführer Heinz Gräfe was head of *Amt VI
C* and responsible for the entire eastern intelligence in the Abwehr's
foreign intelligence service. And it was he who came up with the idea
of using particularly suitable PoWs as agents for reconnaissance in
the Soviet hinterland. He drafted a memorandum, 'The resilience of
the Soviet Union and the possibilities of its decomposition', in which
he emphasised the importance of attacking 'the moral potential of
the Soviets'. 'There is an opportunity to select suitable groups from
the enormous human reservoir of prisoners of war' he said, 'and use
them in the active fight against the Soviet Union in the political and
sometimes military field'. He went on to say that

> Specially selected agents should carry out national propaganda among
> the anti-Soviet peoples and try to do so in areas where the conditions
> appear to exist to organize local national revolts. Under certain
> circumstances, these groups can be used to organize assassinations
> against the Soviet rulers and to prepare acts of sabotage.[2]

Naturally, Gräfe, 'a man of considerable ability and enterprise'
recommended himself to lead the project.[3] The idea was enthusiastically
received and Gräfe was encouraged to submit a detailed study, which
became a 'Plan for an action for political attempts at subversion in

the Soviet Union'. In the second study, Gräfe once again described a necessary action to politically disintegrate the Soviet Union by strengthening and exploiting the existing anti-Bolshevik attitude, especially among national minorities. The plan envisaged different groups to realise four objectives:

- Intelligence groups – to collect and transmit political information from the Soviet Union.
- Propaganda groups – for the dissemination of national, social and religious propaganda.
- Rebel groups – to organise and conduct uprisings.
- Subversive groups for political subversion and terror.

Himmler had already ordered Schellenberg to set up an organisation to get more intelligence on the Soviet Union and he was quickly seduced by Gräfe's very attractive idea, which envisaged masses of SD-trained agents conducting guerilla warfare in the Soviet rear. Schellenberg doubted that an appeal to anti-Soviet sentiments would be sufficient motivation for the recruits to achieve all that would be required of them and suggested that they needed to be convinced that they were fighting for the restoration of independence for their homeland regions. He submitted the plan to Hitler who was not over excited by the idea but he authorised it in early 1942. It was an important step towards Himmler's goal of taking control of all German military intelligence services.

Soon the PoWs were sifted for volunteers to take part in special military operations against the Soviets, but there was a difference of opinion between the Abwehr and the SD over who should have access to these 'volunteers'. Gestapo chief Heinrich Müller took the initiative and had Gräfe and the whole of *Amt IV C* seconded to the Gestapo and, under a top-secret plan, the RSHA created a special reconnaissance and sabotage force called *Untenehmen Zeppelin* (Operation Zeppelin). It was understood that Zeppelin could only function administratively as part of the Wehrmacht, but operationally it was placed under the command of SD who already had their own *Einsatzgruppen* involved in the extermination of Bolsheviks, Jews and partisans in the Soviet Union.

Right from the start, Gräfe knew that the general quality of recruits would be low and when deployed behind Soviet lines a large proportion would simply give themselves up, which meant that very large numbers would be needed. Out of 15,000 volunteers, some 3,000 were considered suitable for secondment. These were sent to special training camps to be trained in sabotage, subversion, radio transmissions and all the other skills they would require. At the same time, they were indoctrinated with anti-Semitic propaganda and encouraged to believe that they would become part of a nationalist movement. As part of this deception, they would be called 'activists' rather than agents. The relatively small staff at Zeppelin headquarters were housed in the service building of the VI RSHA Directorate, in the Grunewald area, Berkaerst-Rasse, 32/35, and then in the Wannsee area at Potsdamer Strasse, 29. To support the operation, the *Havelinstitut* was created in Wannsee and staffed mostly with academics from various *Ostforschung* (research institutes). As a training centre, the institute also became the centre for handling all radio communications with activists in the field.

Only suitable healthy volunteers were recruited for the secret operations. Those who were not suitable for this, but had already passed the template, were usually sent to a police unit or were transferred to the military Zeppelin units, which also carried out guarding tasks for Zeppelin facilities. Recruits were sent to camps according to ethnicity. Russians went to Jablon in the Lublin District under the command of Hans Schindowski. The main camp for Turkish PoWs was briefly in Warsaw-Legionowo in 1942, then came to Breslau-Oswitz under the command of Hauptsturmführer Heinrich Fenner, while the main camp for Caucasians was located in Yevpatoria in the Crimea, under the direction of Hauptsturmführer Theodor Girgensohn. The main centre for advanced training was at *Sonderlage Sandeberge* where recruits underwent up to six months of training. Another camp at Sachsenhausen took the very best from Sandeberge for even more specialised instruction.

A small Zeppelin *Sonderkommando* group was attached to each SS *Einsatzgruppen* task force in the Soviet Union for the final training, control and coordination of Zeppelin operations in the front sector but remained under the Zeppelin staff of Group VI C of the RSHA. This sometimes led to significant problems in operational control, because the task force commanders viewed the Zeppelin commandos, who operated primarily as self-contained field units with a high degree of decentralisation from Berlin, as a disruptive factor. There were four Zeppelin commands engaged in the selection of PoWs for agent training, interrogation of PoWs about the political and military situation in the Soviet Union and the collection of Soviet uniforms, documents and artifacts for use by agents.

- Zeppelin command in the Einsatzgruppe A was established at Krasnogwardeisk-Gattchina under Hauptsturmführer Lothar Fendler and operated in the Leningrad region.
- Zeppelin command in the Einsatzgruppe B was established at Smolensk under Hauptsturmführer Karl-Wilhelm Bitz.

- Zeppelin command in the Einsatzgruppe C was established at Kiev under Brigadier Max Thomas.
- Zeppelin command in the Einsatzgruppe D was established at Eupatoria in the Crimea under Sturmbannführer Walter Kurreck.

Missions commenced in June 1942 when groups were given various tasks of espionage, diversion, sabotage, infiltration, dissemination of propaganda and instigation of resistance. Many groups were captured or wiped out soon after landing or agreed to cooperate with the Soviets. When intelligence was brought back *Amt VI* had no way of verifying its credibility against disinformation planted by Soviet security forces. In February 1943, Gräfe concluded that intelligence gathering was satisfactory, but that the subversion and sabotage activities had not brought any success and so he ordered that Zeppelin operations be restricted to intelligence gathering missions. The whole enterprise had been authorised because it had appealed to Himmler's fantasies rather than being subjected to scrutiny of its practicality and probability of success. Essentially all the resources allocated to Zeppelin had been squandered with nothing to show at this stage.

One band of activists was formed under the banner of the Battle Union of Russian Nationalists (BSRN) led by Vladimir Vladimirovich Gil (German codename I.G. Rodionov). Gil had been captured 16 July 1941 and sent to Suwalki PoW camp where he became commandant of the Soviet prisoners. Conditions were catastrophically bad. An outbreak of typhus almost wiped out the whole camp leaving only 2,000 of the original 60,000 inmates by April 1942. By then, however, Gil had been moved to Sachsenhausen where he created the anti-Soviet Russian National People's Party with twenty-five other Red Army Officers and this became the BSRN on 20 April 1942. Zeppelin officers Hans Schindowski and Emil Haussmann encountered the BSRN while looking for volunteers and recruited them whole group which was then numbered around 130. Under SD supervision the men were moved to Parczew and Lublin in eastern Poland for special training. By the end of the summer they had merged with a similar group from Stalag 319 to reach brigade strength and, with Himmler's approval, became known as *SS Druzchina* and split into *Druzchina I* under Gil and *Druzchina II* under Andrej Blazhevich.

To test the morale of these men, *Druzchina* was deployed against partisans in Belarus in October 1942 before they were used for a possible Zeppelin mission. It was a sobering experience for the Germans because a month later sixty-three of them defected to the partisans. Sturmbannführer Otto Kraus decided to screen for further pro-Soviet sentiment by deploying *Druxzchina* as part of an *Einsatzgruppen* civilian extermination operation in Luzhki on 11 February 1943. This saw a further a further thirty-six desertions and a near mutiny. The Germans responded by shooting the ringleaders.

It was obviously necessary to impose some rigorous control and it was planned to merge incorporate the remaining *Druzchina* into a special Abwehr unit *Graukopf* under the ex-Soviet general Sergei Ivanov and restructured into a brigade of Andrei Vlasov's Russian Liberation Army, but there was strong resistance throughout the group and Gil objected to the move.

In summer 1943, *Druzhina* were deployed against Soviet partisans led by Ivan Filippovich Titkov in Dokshysty. Messages were exchanged between Gil and Titkov after which the whole Druzhina Brigade defected on 16 August 1943. All ninety German officers on Gil's staff were hanged. The defectors went on to form the 1st Anti-Fascist Brigade that fought the Germans and was destroyed in April 1944 during the anti-partisan Operation *Frühlingsfest*.[4] Some versions of the *Druzhina* narrative claim that Gil was a Soviet agent all along.

Whilst few, in any, Zeppelin sabotage operations were successful, the organisation proved better at gathering intelligence. One three-member team managed to infiltrate the Soviet People's Commissariat of Transport and was able to send reports on Red Army movements. Other lone agents wormed his way onto the staff of Marshal Rokossovsky, the man responsible for the preparation of Operation Bagration. While as many as fifteen teals were active behind Soviet lines in late 1944, most intelligence from simple interrogations of Soviet PoWs.

The Russian People's Party of Reformists (RMPR) was formed in a concentration camp at Weimar by ex-Soviet major general Ivan Bessanov. This was reformed as the Political Centre for the Fight Against Bolshevism (PCB) and incorporated into Zeppelin in late 1942. This group of 200 activists and some 60 radio operators was trained in the Leibus Monastery near Breslau and planned to launch a resistance movement in Siberia, but only 3 small parties were ever despatched. They were soon swept up by the NKVD and all members executed. The PCB fell apart and Bessanov was incarcerated again this time in Sachsenhausen. Operation Ulm was led by 'Hitler's favourite commando', Otto Skorzeny. His plan was to drop agents in the Urals to sabotage steel making facilities but the lack of available aircraft saw all these plans shelved.

Perhaps the best known of all Zeppelin operations was the plot to kill Stalin. Once again we find a number of different narratives spun around its leader, the Zeppelin-trained Major Pyotr Ivanovich

Tavrin-Šilo also known as Politov. Tavrin was trained in sabotage and assassination techniques in Riga along with his wife Lidia Yakovlevna Shilova whose speciality was radio. Both were extensively coached to take on the cover of Smersh officers. Tavrin carried papers identifying him as a member of the 39th Army of the 3rd Belorussian Front travelling to Moscow on business. He had undergone plastic surgery to simulate wounds that excepted him from military duty. He also carried medals and documents relating to their award. While he was being fitted out with a Soviet-style overcoat, the tailor, who happened to be a Soviet agent, realised that Tavrin was going to be spirited into the Soviet Union and duly reported it to his handler who arranged for Tavrin to be put under surveillance.

The KNVD used three Zeppelin agents who had been picked up near Smolensk to feed information back. The three had been a scouting party to identify a suitable landing site for the Arado Ar232B transport aircraft that was to take Tavrin and his wife along with a Soviet M-72 motorcycle with sidecar. In the early hours of 6 September 1944 the aircraft descended towards the landing site, but was hit by anti-aircraft fire and forced to abort. The damage was such that it crash landed, however, many miles away. Tavrin and his wife were able to speed off on the motorcycle, but the five-man crew remained to be rounded up by Soviet security. Soon, the two spies were stopped in a road block where guards noticed that Tavrin had his medals pinned on the wrong side of his coat. A search uncovered seven pistols, a radio set, hand grenades and a large amount of Soviet currency. Tavrin and his wife were arrested and executed. There remains too little documentary evidence to indicate what overall measure of success was enjoyed by Zeppelin, but such as there is suggests that it was low and fell far short of expectations given the time and expense invested.

The Battle of Kursk was the last great German offensive on the Eastern Front. During the five months following that, the Soviets launched a general offensive on all fronts forcing the Germans to fall back in search of a good defensible line, an 'Eastern Wall', such as the Dnepr river east of Minsk. OKH fully understood the military necessity for such a move but Hitler was opposed to giving up any ground while the Soviets hoped to deny the Germans sufficient time to establish such defences and engaged in a race to beat them to Dnepr where they hoped to establish bridgeheads on the west bank thereby denying sanctuary to the German forces. The result of the political constraints placed on OKH by Hitler's intransigence meant that such defences as were created on the Dnepr could not be started until it was too late for anything, but hasty, makeshift measures.

In their drive to the Dnepr, the Soviets employed *maskirovka* with mixed success. It was clearly much more difficult for the Germans to collect intelligence about Soviet troop movements in such a dynamic battleground especially as the Germans were constantly being forced to fall back. Regrouping of Soviet forces was done in secrecy from both enemy air and ground observation and generally under radio silence. Almost uninterrupted rain hampered troop movements but also played a definite positive role in suppressing Luftwaffe reconnaissance. FHO had to rely to a very great extent on the intuition of its analysts, their experience and understanding of Soviet mentality.

Commander of the Soviet Western Front, General V.D. Sokolovsky, created a false concentration of forces with false artillery and anti-tank fortifications to divert attention away from the planned attack east of Kirov. Intensive reconnaissance was carried out in sectors where no assault was planned to cause the German to reinforce the sectors and lay minefields but this did not prevent the Germans from detecting Soviet groupings in several of the main attack sectors. Despite this, German intelligence did, in fact, correctly identify where the main attack would come, but they did not manage to detect all the Soviet forces that would take part. It cannot be said that *maskirovka* was particularly successful. General N.N. Voronov recorded that 'The enemy, without a doubt, knew about our offensive preparations and implemented a series of measures to counter it.'[5]

The Soviets managed to set up a number of small bridgeheads, but in general the Germans were able to consolidate their position on the Dnepr. Only at Lyutezh, north of Kiev, did the Soviets see a chance to break through. Voronov arranged for diversionary activity in the direction of Smolensk at Dukhovshchina while the Soviet 49th and 10th armies simulated attack preparations along the Warsaw to Moscow road. German intelligence identified the Soviet rifle forces facing them but assessed the Soviet point of main effort south of where it actually was at the same time as completely failing to detect three Soviet mobile corps.

The objective was to create the impression that the offensive would continue on its present direction to encircle Dukhovshchina from the left, when in fact the main attack prepared to encircle and seize the city from the right flank. Army smoke generating units helped to simulate troop movements from the army right to the left flank and then, on the day before the Soviet offensive, their aircraft struck German defensive concentrations opposite the false Soviet concentration areas. Initially, Soviet *maskirovka* within the Western and Kalinin fronts failed, and the Germans transferred enough forces to halt Soviet attacks after only minimal gains. Subsequently, however, the broad front Soviet attack achieved *maskirovka* success in a number of sectors, primarily because the Germans were unable to detect the real location of the Soviet main attack.

At this time, FHO had a fairly comprehensive picture of the Soviet order of battle and Gehlen's reports gave quite an accurate picture of Soviet intentions. On 11 October 1943, he wrote that the Soviets were preparing for

> a new and greater attack operation ... to exploit the opportunity to enlarge the successes achieved so far. [They would] form some large operationally usable bridgeheads on the Dnepr ... using two operating groups of forces, one from the Pereyaslav area, the other from the north of Kiev.[6]

In late October, in a large-scale *maskirovka* operation, the Soviets, indeed, had rapidly moved 3rd Guards Tank Army into position, but complete deception was not achieved. Army Group South was well aware that Kiev was the target although the lines of attack would depend very much on the deployment of armour units to the east and north-east of the city. On 9 November, Gehlen, relying on intelligence sources that were daily becoming less reliable, said that 'the main effort of the enemy overall operations ... is undoubtedly directed against the southern half of the eastern front', but based on their superiority in forces, the Soviets would

> almost certainly build another main effort in the areas of Army Group Centre and North [to] pursue far-reaching objectives ... It is [the area around Kiev] one looks for the main effort of enemy operations [with the intention of] opening a larger gap between Army Group South and Centre ... A breakdown of the Ost Front seems to be inevitable if we are unable to block ... their initial deployment.[7]

On 3 November, the 4th Panzer Army was on the receiving end of a massive Soviet artillery bombardment and Kiev fell to the Soviets three days later.

The Soviet priority now was to maintain the strategic initiative and avoid falling into a war of position, which might see a recurrence of First World War trench warfare bleeding both armies in a stalemate. There still existed large German forces of Soviet soil at Leningrad, Belorussia, the Ukraine and in the Crimea that would take a huge Soviet effort to dislodge. Their strategy evolved to create groups of forces more powerful than the Germans and employ them using shock tactics with an increased role for tanks, artillery and aviation. This would require sizeable masses of reserve formations and large units to create a decisive superiority of forces in selected areas but such forces would have to be moved secretly from one sector to another. The Soviets planned to mask to as great a degree as possible the direction of the main strategic thrusts to achieve surprise and keep German forces off balance. The efficient use of strategic, operational and tactical *maskirovka* was crucial to concentrate forces secretly in key sectors and to divert German attention from the real offensive sectors.

The Soviet plans in autumn 1943 called on the Leningrad and Volkhov armies to destroy the German Eighteenth Army, relieve Leningrad, and prepare to drive the Germans out of the Baltics. Success would depend largely on their ability to concentrate forces secretly in key sectors and to divert German attention from the real offensive sectors. General L.A. Govorov's Leningrad front planned two attacks to create a continuous front south of Leningrad both of which required diversionary activity and false attack preparations one of which was a simulated attack out of the western portion of the Oranienbaum, which included the firing of a false artillery preparation and false radio nets. To further confuse German intelligence the Soviets conducted reconnaissance throughout the entire front sector, particularly in simulated attack areas. The German Eighteenth Army obliged by stripping the real attack sector of two SS divisions, which were sent to reinforce existing German forces opposite the false Soviet attack sector. They Soviets organised radio and telephone disinformation, simulated false assembly areas and carried out intensive offensive field training. Tanks and artillery were mocked up. Fake tanks and artillery were mocked up while vehicles deliberately employing poor light discipline and exaggerated engine sounds to create a false impression of new concentration areas. The army staff deliberately passed orders over telephone lines, which they knew were monitored by the Germans. Commander of the Soviet Ukrainian Front, Marshal I.S. Konev, called for the creation of false assembly areas in forests west of Kirovograd. In total, there were seventeen false concentration areas for tanks and artillery and emplaced, and seventeen dummy fuel and ammunition warehouses. Vehicles moved back and forth using poor *maskirovka*, and troops lit bonfires to animate the area. Tractors simulated the noise of assembling tanks, and communications personnel established radio nets complete with false messages to simulate the radio nets of a normal tank army. Artillery simulated occupation of offensive firing positions. All these false offensive preparations peaked five to six days before the real offensive.

By November, German intelligence knew that the real Soviet build-up was in the Oranienbaum bridgehead, but, on 10 January 1944, Colonel General Georg Lindemann, commander of the German Eighteenth Army, categorised it as 'modest, at least in terms of reserves' and predicted that it would 'most likely be stopped'.[8] Overall, German intelligence detected only a fraction of the Soviet strength and failed to observe Soviet offensive preparations.

Chapter 18

OPERATION BEREZINO

On 18 August 1944, a radio message was received at German intelligence headquarters in Berlin addressed to 'Saturn'.

> In a place called Berezino west of Mogilev, a large German unit, a regiment or more, is hiding in the forests. Alexander [Demyanov] talked to a captured Ober-Efreyatore of this unit, who informed him that the group intended to break through to the west, but because of the large number of wounded and lack of weapons ammunition and food and further advancement is impossible.[1]

Berlin replied a week later,

> Saturn to Alexander. We ask Alexander to contact this unit. We intend to drop various cargoes for them and could send a radio operator. To do this we must know the exact location of the part, the password will be Hanover.[2]

It was an elaborate trap laid by the Soviets, however, and one authorised at the highest level. Stalin had ordered an expansion of Operation Monastery in an attempt to make the Germans believe that a large number of their soldiers were still active behind Soviet lines. German Army Group Centre had been overwhelmed and overrun with large numbers of Wehrmacht troops lost presumed killed or captured. If the Germans could be convinced that they still had substantial operationally viable forces in the Soviet rear they might well be persuaded to divert scarce resources to supporting them.

Two NKVD officers, Mikhail Maklyarsky and Victor Ilyin, tasked with making a detailed plan for Operation Berzino, as it was called, based it on Operation Monastery with 'radio games' at its heart. The man chosen to put the plans into operation was Lieutenant General Pavol Sudoplatov. The essential feature was described by Stalin as a methodical physical destruction of German special forces and their intelligence capability by persuading the Germans to send in agents on rescue missions and lead them into traps.

Lieutenant Colonel Heinrich Gerhard Scherhorn's 36th Security Regiment of the 286th Security Division had been destroyed and he was captured by the Soviets on 9 July 1944 near Minsk. He had been one of a group of 1,800 Germans surrounded near the Berezino river. The Germans were aware that such a group had been isolated in that region and had some intelligence to suggest that it was still holding out. Soviet counterintelligence knew about this situation from radio intercepts and started passing misinformation through the *Prestol* network to create a fiction. The besieged Germans were determined to make it back to their own lines, the story went, but they were running short of ammunition and had many wounded who required immediate medical aid. What the Germans did not know, and did not find out, was that all but 200 had been killed and the rest, including Scherhorn, taken captive.

Scherhorn had been selected because the plan required a leader of sufficiently high rank who actually existed and whose ability to rally people around himself and lead them along the enemy's rear for a long time would not be doubted. He would also be someone who could be coerced into participating in the deception. Sudoplatov searched PoW camps for a suitable candidate and found Scherhorn who had commanded a rearguard regiment, but was now a broken man convinced that Germany would be defeated. He agreed to cooperate and was given the codename 'Shubin'. A group of sixteen men under the command of Major G.B. Borisov flew to Glukhoe near Minsk to act as bait.

Colonel Worgitzky, Chief of Intelligence for Army Group Centre, after much deliberation decided that there was a high probability that the information was reliable and that steps should be taken to relieve Scherhorn's group by dropping supplies and sending in radio operators to establish communications. The man chosen to make contact with Scherhorn's fictitious force was Otto Skorzeny who described what happened in his memoirs. A plan, codename *Freischütz* (magic shooter), had four groups, each of five men, with wireless transmitting set, parachute rations for four weeks, tents, etc., and Russian machine pistols, all disguised as Red Army soldiers. Meticulous preparations included the men being given the vile Russian *machorka* cigarettes and having their heads shaved. Some would be dropped near Borisov and Cervenj, east of Minsk, while others were to be dropped near Djerzinsk and Viteika and make a concentric approach to Minsk.

On the night of 15 September 1944, three German radio operators landed at specified coordinates, but were quickly captured and coerced into taking part in the 'radio games' by sending back false information. On 27 October, two more parachutists, one doctor Jeschki and Harry Vivor followed, but, like the previous men, they were immediately taken captive. When, under Soviet control, they reported back, the correct password was given and also the secret codeword indicating that the speaker was not being held by the Soviets. Scherhorn, himself, was forced to take part in the subterfuge by speaking a few words personally. The group now numbered some 2,500 men, Scherhorn said, with several hundred wounded.

Despite regular communications with Scherhorn's men, Army Group Centre was still not entirely convinced, but could not risk abandoning forces that appeared to be a thorn in the Soviet flesh. Radio messages continued pleading for help. They continued to drop supplies, men and equipment at designated site and even sent an engineer to scout for a suitable landing zone so that evacuation of wounded could begin, but Scherhorn was becoming ever more distant from a constantly retreating German army and fuel was in desperately short supply. Skorzeny was no fool and suspected foul play so he sent other agents not connected to *Freischütz* to try and verify the existence of Scherhorn's group. Unfortunately for him, all eight men were caught and forced to become part of the subterfuge.

All this time, Scerhorn was reporting that his men were moving westward engaged the rear units of the Red Army, conducted sabotage, taking prisoners and collected intelligence. All this was reinforced by an intricate web of other misinformation, such as newspaper reports and fake agent messages.

On 23 March, Hitler announced that members of Scherhorn's officer corps, who were actually far from Berezino in Soviet captivity, were to be promoted. Scherhorn himself was awarded the Knight's Cross and promoted to colonel. It was Hitler's way of abandoning the men because very soon afterwards all contact was broken off.

Between September 1944 and May 1945, the Germans flew thirty-nine missions in support of Scherhorn and lost a total of twenty-two agents. Besides that they dropped several tons of cargoes with medicines and warm clothes along with 2,258,330 roubles. On 1 May, a final message went out to Scherhorn from Berlin, that would have drawn wry smiles from the Soviet listeners.

The air fleet equipment ready for shipment cannot be delivered. It is with a heavy heart that we are forced to discontinue our assistance to you. Based on the current situation, we can no longer maintain radio contact with you. No matter what the future brings, our thoughts will always be with you, who at this difficult time have been forced to give up their hopes.[3]

Chapter 19

OPERATION BAGRATION

'This system of operational deceptive measures proved its
worth. History has shown that the enemy was profoundly
misled concerning our real intentions.'

General Shtemenko,
Deputy Chief of the Soviet General Staff.[1]

The fall of Canaris had been slow but inexorable ever since the Allied
landings in North Africa (Operation Torch) for which he had given no
warning. Himmler was forever circling for a chance to strike and take
the Abwehr into his own domain of control and there was no shortage
of ammunition he could aim in Canaris's direction. The Abwehr had
become a byword for financial corruption and political disaffection
with the Nazi regime. Canaris had filled the Abwehr with idle and
corrupt staff to the point where it was 'a loose and irresponsible
collection of worthless characters whom he refused to control or
dismiss'.[2] All efforts to reform the Abwehr by OKW, after Stalingrad
when intelligence about enemy intentions became acute, were blocked
by Canaris.

The close connection to the Franco regime in Spain and the
importance of that relationship for the Nazis had, for years, been a
factor in Canaris's ability to protect his position, but when Spain altered
its stance from non-belligerence to neutrality on 1 October 1943 that
lifeline was snapped. This was at a time when there was a significant
power shift as Hitler reacted to an almost tangible inclination within
OKW, which was showing clear signs of doubting a final victory, for
compromise. The Nazis, on the other hand, had stiffened their resolve
to hold out until the very end and it was the SS that became the party's
instrument of enforcement and took measures to increase its control of
the military. As Himmler's authority over the OKW grew, so did that

of Schellenberg's Amt IV of the RSHA at the expense of the Abwehr. No longer did Amt IV restrict itself to political intelligence, now it stretched its claws to take in economic and operational intelligence also. Schellenberg had a direct line to Himmler and through him to Hitler which gave him enormous power.

In mid-March 1943, Canaris, together with Piekenbrock, Lahousen and von Bentivegni had visited von Kluge's Army Group Centre headquarters near Smolensk. There they held a meeting with General Henning von Tresckow, chief of Kluge's General Staff, and came to a mutual understanding that 'Only Hitler's death will put an end to this mad slaughter of people in the concentration camps and in the armies fighting this criminal war.' Days later Fabian von Schlabrendorff smuggled a time bomb, disguised as bottles of cognac, onto Hitler's aircraft but it failed to detonate because of the extreme cold in the aircraft's cargo space.[3]

Keitel had, for some time, been unimpressed by the performance of Abwehr I, II and III and had Piekenbrock, Lahousen and von Bentivegni transferred to the front. Colonel Georg Hansen came in to lead Abwehr I, while Colonel Wessel Freiherr von Freytag-Loringhoven took over Abwehr II. Both had also been complicit in the Hitler bomb plot. With Himmler looking over his shoulder, Hansen, in particular, posed a serious threat to Canaris by trying to purge his department of 'dead wood' and bring it more into line with OKH standards but corruption was so ingrained in the fabric of the Abwehr that he was unable to make any progress. Then, on 12 February 1944, Hitler fired Canaris ostensibly for 'professional and personal failures', which had 'risen to an intolerable level' and replaced him with Hansen. Canaris would end his life in the most brutal fashion hanging from the end of a 'piano wire' on 9 April 1945 at Flosssenbürg concentration camp.

A battle now ensued for control of the Abwehr between Himmler and OKW although it was assumed that it would, in fact, be Hitler who would be effectively in control. Notwithstanding that, Himmler chaired a meeting at Salzburg on 10 May between Hansen, acting for the Abwehr and Schellenberg and Sandberger for the RSHA where he said the title of Abwehr was 'un-German' and would be changed. The essential structure would remain, however. Abwehr I and II would merge to become the *Militarisches Amt* (Mil Amt) with Hansen in charge but crucially now under the authority of the RSHA. Arrangements would be made, he said, for a few 'privileged' Abwehr personnel to join the new organisation.

This arrangement was hardly in place before Hansen and many other Abwehr General Staff officers were implicated in the 22 July

1944 Stauffenberg *Walküre* attempted putsch and failed assassination attempt on Hitler. Hansen was executed in Plötenzee prison six weeks later and Schellenberg took full control of the Abwehr. Although a skilful political manipulator Schellenberg was, however, a sorry specimen of an intelligence officer and Gehlen urged Keitel to fight for some degree of FHO independence from SS control but Keitel was not willing to confront Himmler. Instead Gehlen worked on Schellenberg and managed to convince him to leave the field work to FHO and improvised an ad hoc relationship with both Baun and Schmalschläger to try and ward off any future moves by Schellenberg.

After the Soviet taking of Kiev, German forces were pushed back to the Bug river then at the beginning of March 1944, the Red Army carried out a renewed offensive in the Ukraine and by the end of March the front had been pushed all the way to Bessarabia and Czechoslovakia. In the north, the Red Army lifted the siege of Leningrad, after almost 880 days, and the Red Army advanced to the border with the Baltic countries.

In May 1944, the Eastern Front had stabilised along the line Pleskau-Vitebsk-Shlobin-Kowel-Stanislau-Jasi-Odesa. Field Marshal Ernst Busch's Army Group Centre held an arc into Belarus between Polozk and Pinsk, while the Red Army correspondingly held an arc south in Ukraine. The Germans were no longer capable of launching a large-scale offensive, something that would certainly not be remedied after the Allied D-Day landings on 6 June 1944. All they could do was prepare their defences for an impending Soviet attack and hope to grind out a stalemate. Concerned not least because of the high percentage of non-German and, therefore, less reliable, divisions in his sector, Busch requested permission to withdraw in order to shorten his line and relieve the danger of a pincer movement against the salient, but his request was denied. Hitler was determined to hold fortified regions around large cities close to the front line in order to allow time for counterattacks that only he thought possible. He gave Busch a dressing down saying that he, like all his other generals, spent too much time looking over his shoulder instead of taking decisive action.[4] It would be the last time that Busch would challenge Hitler's decisions.

Stavka considered a number of strategic options and concluded that their main effort should be a simultaneous offensive along the lines Polotsk-Svencionys, Orsha-Minsk, Mogilev-Minsk and Bobruisk-Slutsk with the aim of encirclement and destruction of the German Army Group Centre. The 'Max' spy network reported on a meeting at the Kremlin on 27 April 1944 at which two summer offensives were discussed. In what was probably Demyanov's most important misdirection, he reported that Stalin had approved a plan for a Ukraine offensive over the alternative of a thrust towards Brest-Litovsk. What had actually been decided was for five successive and interdependent operations with Operation Bagration as the centre. An opening diversionary offensive on the Finnish borders would begin on 10 June and the main offensive would target Army Group Centre on 19 June. Once the Germans had committed their strategic reserves, two more attacks would follow at L'vov-Sandomierz and Lublin-Brest. Finally, would come the Jassy-Kishinev Offensive toward the Balkans. During the course of the war, the Red Army would acquire some 400,000 US-built 2.5-ton 'Studery' Studebaker US6 trucks and military jeeps 'Willis', many of which had already arrived which gave them an edge in terms of mobility over the Germans who were to a very large extent still reliant on horse-drawn transport apart from their Panzer units. This might have favoured the open spaces of Ukraine as the main centre of a Soviet attack and that is what the Germans expected but it was Belarus with large forests, lakes, swamps and generally poor infrastructure where the Soviets chose to strike.

It fell to group intelligence and FHO to predict where the centre of gravity of the Soviet offensive would be and they failed in the most spectacular fashion. As early as May 1944, the Wehrmacht leadership, led by Hitler, supported by the FHO, concluded that the Soviet summer offensive would start from eastern Galicia, in Ukraine, and go in one of two possible directions, either towards Romania and the Balkans, or towards the Baltic coast. Only limited operations were expected in Belarus. This almost total agreement amongst German commanders was essentially because that is what they, themselves, would have chosen to do if faced with a similar situation. With a keen understanding of Wehrmacht mentality, the Soviets would do everything they could to convince the Germans that this is exactly what they had decided to do.

Soviet strategic *maskirovka* began with a directive from Zhukov and General Aleksei Antonov, Chief of the Operations Directorate of the Red Army General Staff, on 29 May, outlining the movement of forces. The bulk of these were to be kept at least 50 kilometres from the front until five to seven days before the offensive and they could not move into their attack positions until one or two nights before the assault was to begin. To support their attack, the Soviets needed overwhelming artillery support to achieve rapid penetrations on the flanks of the fortified regions, but this had to be concealed from the Germans. Newly arrived formations were banned from conducting ground reconnaissance and their commanders were authorised to wear the uniforms of private soldiers to misdirect German surveillance.

All orders were handwritten and hand delivered eliminating almost all radio traffic. Individuals with knowledge of the plan were kept to an absolute minimum. Daily ground and air inspections of deception efforts were carried out and reported on. In the words of Marshal Vasilevsky, 'All that colossal work had to be conducted in conditions of strict secrecy in order to hide from the enemy the huge complex of preparatory work for the forthcoming summer offensive.'[5]

A key component of plan was denying the Germans knowledge of the location of the Soviet tank armies. These were below strength having been unable to fully recover from Kursk but radio traffic was deliberately designed to hide this fact from the Germans. German intelligence summaries in late May had put all six Soviet tank army headquarters in Ukraine, but, in reality, they had few tanks there. FHO had failed to detect the movement of smaller tank corps, mechanised corps and cavalry corps units moving north. It had been a deliberate tactic to reveal their location before withdrawing them beyond the scope of German reconnaissance so that when they appeared much further north it came as a complete surprise.

There was an enormous amount of rail traffic prior to the offensive to move three armies, twenty-nine rifle divisions, nine tank or mechanised corps and two cavalry corps. In addition, the rail network also carried 5,718,916 tons of supplies in 126,589 freight cars in the weeks before the attack. It was no surprise that this movement of men and supplies fell behind schedule, but rather than allow movement by day and reveal the deception Stalin postponed the offensive from 14 to 23 June.

On 10 May, FHO had warned of an imminent attack from the area south of the Pripyat marshes in the direction of Army Group Ukraine North, along Army Group Centre's southern flank in Belarus but by early June Gehlen was warning that 'A new estimate of the enemy situation should be considered in the face of the increasing strength of Soviet air forces opposite army Group Centre.'[6]

Artillery, which was difficult to camouflage and cumbersome to relocate, needed to be put in place well ahead of an attack and there was strong evidence of it massing in the centre also. FHO situation maps for May had shown little change in the strength of Soviet infantry in the centre, but things were changing. FHO reports on 3 June had noted increased activity, but dismissed it as Soviet deception and predicted that any diversionary attack in the centre could be defended with available reserves. Because of the lack of Luftwaffe reconnaissance and extreme radio *maskirovka*, little could be discerned beyond a narrow strip immediately behind the Soviet front line and this is where the mass of Soviet preparations was taking place. Only on the Ukraine front had FHO been able to identify and locate strong reserves. In particular, the air component in the south was considerably stronger than elsewhere on the front. This was all part of the Soviet deception, of course.

On 19 June, Keitel backed up Gehlen's assessment and expressed his confidence that no major offensive in the centre was to be expected. While FHO had accurately assessed the forces directly in front of Army Group Centre, Gehlen was not aware of the Soviet forces massed in reserve. He had been blinded by strict *maskirovka* discipline, radio silence and the lack of Luftwaffe reconnaissance. His report, 'Comprehensive Estimate of the Overall Enemy Situation before the German East Front and Presumed Enemy Intentions', presented to OKH on 13 June stated that all available evidence showed the main Soviet offensive would be launched between 15–20 June in Ukraine. There was now little dispute within all German army groups across the whole front that enemy activity presages an imminent Soviet attack but only the 9th Army command expected the main effort to be in the centre. Dozens of German agents had been rounded up in the vicinity of Vibetsk, Orsha, Mogliev and Minsk and 'turned' to transmit false information, which supported other *maskirovka* operations that persuaded Gehlen's FHO that the attack would come furthers south. It would prove to be another of its systematic underestimations of Soviet capabilities. Soviet *maskirovka* had driven Hitler and OKH to rely on 'their cognitive biases and mental models', which increased 'the disparity between their perceived and that of the actual operational reality.'[7] By manipulating FHO intelligence, the Soviets caused the Germans to relocate the potent 56th Panzer Corps on 30 May from Busch's Army Group Centre and sent it south leaving Busch with hardly any mobile forces and so creating a critical imbalance. On 17 June, the message was the same,

> the point of main effort of future Russian offensive operations can be expected to be unchanged and directed against Army Group North Ukraine … The preparations for an attack before the front of [Army Group Centre] obviously serves to tie down the reserves.[8]

There was no denying, however, that the Soviets were executing troop deployments in preparation for an offensive against Army Group Centre and all intelligence estimates registered that. However hard FHO peered into the mist of Soviet deception it could not locate the Soviet mobile reserve. This was the crucial piece of the intelligence jigsaw that was missing and until it was found Gehlen stuck to his guns. This assessment would remain essentially unchanged until 25 June when the FHO daily intelligence briefing began ominously with words that must have been an acute embarrassment for Gehlen, 'Contrary to previous intelligence…'.

Overall, the Soviets had amassed a 2.5:1 advantage in men, a 2.9:1 advantage in artillery and mortars, a 4.3:1 advantage in tanks and assault guns, and a 4.5:1 advantage in aircraft. In crucial attack zones near Rogachev and south of Svetlogorsk the advantage was a massive 10:1 ratio of forces.

Partisan action played a crucial role preceding the Soviet attack. The landscape of the western Soviet Union had made railways the single most important means of transport across the vast spaces. They were the essential avenues of strategic operations. Immediately before the Battle of Kursk, building on the experience of an increasingly effective partisan campaign over the previous year, tens of thousands of Soviet partisans had initiated 'Operation Rail War' to slow German reinforcements and logistical supplies. In July 1943 alone, the Germans reported at least 1,100 separate railway attack and then, during the nights of 3 and 4 August, Army Group Centre reported 4,100 railway demolitions. 'Operation Concert' was a similar operation launched after Kursk in support of operations in the direction of Smolensk. During September and October 1943, 1,061 trains, and 72 railway bridges were damaged or destroyed. Now all the experience gained through these two operations would be employed in Operation Bagration.

Belorussia was the site of the most vigorous partisan movement in the Soviet Union. It had as many as 270,000 men and women organised in 157 brigades and smaller detachments. They played a significant role throughout the operation, planting around 10,000 demolition charges and destroying more than 11,000 railway cars and 34 armoured trains. Consequently, they made the German resupply, retreat and lateral troop movements almost impossible and forced Marshal Busch to commit 15 per cent of his forces to combat partisans in a counterguerrilla warfare.[9]

Preceding Operation Bagration, the partisans had struck during the night of 19 June setting off more than 9,500 demolition charges on German rail lines, and the main lines from Mogilev to Vitebsk and from Minsk to Orsha were knocked out of action for several critical days. As the Red Army advanced, partisans prepared river and stream crossing points for Russian tank and infantry units. They took and held bridgeheads ahead of the advance and cut off German lines of retreat.

When the strength of the Soviet forces was becoming apparent on 27 June, FHO concluded that it was because the Soviets were bringing up new forces to exploit an unexpected development and was still in denial about the real situation. In the space of the two months between 22 June and 19 August 1944, Operation Bagration saw the deployment of more than 2 million Red Army soldiers, almost 6,000 tanks, 6,000 aircraft and 32,000 guns, which decimated the German Army Group Centre, and isolated its Army Group North. The Soviets obliterated thirty German divisions and opened a path more than 300 kilometres wide through, which they poured on the way to Berlin. Operation Bagration would prove to be arguably the single largest German intelligence failure of the war and Hitler's worst military setback.

It has not, however, been accorded the same importance as Stalingrad or Kursk, but in terms of the sheer number of soldiers and tanks that Stalin deployed for the offensive and the significantly improved Soviet performance it should. Bagration successfully employed *maskirovka*, partisans, vastly improved combined infantry-armour tactics and superior weaponry, such as the Shturmovik ground-attack aircraft and the formidable T-34 medium tank to dramatically turn the tide of war against the Third Reich. Hitler lost 350,000 men, of whom 160,000 were taken prisoner, and 31 generals. In Moscow, 57,000 of the prisoners were paraded through the streets as a display of Soviet dominance on the battlefield.

POSTSCRIPT

The poor performance of FHO in evaluating the capabilities and the strength of the Red Army in connection with the planning of Barbarossa is beyond dispute.[1] Germany lost the intelligence war. It failed at every crucial moment both in the west and in the east, from the gross underestimation of Soviet forces in 1941, to the catastrophe of Stalingrad and the D-Day landings. The German approach to intelligence was characterised by a failure to assign sufficient importance to it. The atmosphere within OKW prior to the launch of Barbarossa was permeated with extreme hubris and inflexibility, which opened a rift between its perceptions and reality. The General Staff had a deep loathing and contempt for communism, which threatened their traditions and hierarchical dominance of German life. There was undoubtedly a fundamental sense of racial superiority over the Slavic races of the east, a feeling that was nurtured and compounded by the mass of Nazi propaganda. When Hitler turned his eyes towards the Soviet Union, he did so without the benefit of even a rudimentary investigation of its military and industrial power. The received wisdom of the day was that, as Hitler put it, 'Russia is ripe for collapse'.[2]

After its failure to defeat Finland in the Winter War of 1939–1940, Hitler called the Red Army 'a joke'. OKW studies concluded that it would take between nine and seventeen weeks to destroy the forces of the Soviet Union. This widespread sense of superiority blinded the Germans to the need for intelligence about their enemy which, in any case, was extremely difficult to collect. This blindness to Soviet potential and capabilities was a deliberate act to forestall any threat to morale that might have crept in if the true nature of the enemy was known. The intelligence services were in no way incentivised to step up and give advice where it was not wanted.

The OKW despised the intelligence services outside army control. Intelligence was very much *infra dig* for the Junkers elite who valued 'honourable ignorance' over 'useful knowledge gained by devious means'.[3] The role of intelligence began to change fundamentally for the Wehrmacht, however, when its attack lost momentum towards the end of 1941. Even up to autumn 1942, intelligence had been conducted in support of a Wehrmacht that, despite setbacks, was in the ascendant and arrogantly ascribed little of its success to the Abwehr and FHO. After Stalingrad, the German army was forced onto the defensive. With the initiative now with the enemy, it became vitally important to anticipate their actions and accurately assess the level of force to be expected, its focus and the timing of its application. Deception, such a successful component of German operations in 1942 became a devastating part of Soviet tactics and strategy. German intelligence so long dismissed as irrelevant had little time to prepare for its propulsion into the limelight. Kinzel was quickly dispensed with and Halder's man Gehlen was brought in to galvanise the FHO. When he took over, he diligently amassed a huge quantity of intelligence about almost every aspect of the Red Army and steadily improved his evaluations of the Soviet order of battle, but, faced with a failing agent network, reduced aerial reconnaissance and only radio intelligence to rely on, he could not provide OKW with a clear picture of Soviet strength and intentions. This was very much down to Soviet *maskirovka* and misinformation but was also a consequence of German radio intelligence failure to crack key Soviet codes in the same way that the British and Polish intelligence had broken Enigma. The higher levels of Red Army command remained immune to infiltration as did all the major Soviet intelligence agencies.

One of the fundamentally difficult problems faced by Gehlen and other intelligence agencies was the lack of debate over military strategy. Increasingly throughout the war decisions were made by Hitler alone and where intelligence urged caution or tactical withdrawal from threatening situations it was swept aside as 'defeatist' and contrary to a 'fighting spirit' that defined Hitler's military philosophy. It was universally accepted that 'when the Führer has made a decision, we must no longer disturb his intuition.[4]

It must not be assumed, however, that had Hitler taken more notice of Gehlen, the outcome of the war might have been different. It is impossible to say how things might have turned out had different decisions been made because Gehlen was far from perfect in his analysis and recommendations. Along with OKW, he had underestimated the strength of Soviet forces and overestimated the ability of German forces to resist. His failures stand out as contributing, but far from defining, contributions to the German defeat on the Eastern Front.

Hitler and Stalin were alike in many ways not least in the way they committed grievous errors due to their unwillingness to listen to unwelcome news. Their dictatorial powers allowed them to do this and the whole trajectory of the Second World War was influenced in no small degree by the failure of these two men to give sufficient attention to intelligence.

The Soviets showed that they understood the enemy's military mindset in ways that the Germans did not and they exploited German weaknesses and prejudices. Much of their *maskirovka* combat intelligence was designed to reinforce German preconceptions and encourage them to take certain actions for which they had a natural instinct and then strike in ways that such action had not prepared them for. Other aspects of Soviet intelligence were more mixed in terms of effectiveness. Terror had long been a device employed by the Soviet state to create and hold an iron grip on the Soviet people and it was an extension of this instrument through Smersh that made the Soviet Union, such an extremely hostile environment for German agents. Twenty-five years of brutal oppression was also the agency that drove so many Red Army personnel to desert or surrender and make themselves available to German intelligence. The contribution made by terror tactics to both preservation of the Soviet state and the eradication of enemy agents cannot be overestimated.

As the defeated nation in 1945, Germany faced retribution. Some Nazi leaders were dealt with at the Nuremberg War Trials and lesser criminals through numerous individual acts of extrajudicial execution. The fate of German intelligence personnel was mixed. Smersh captured von Bentivengi on 15 May 1945 and Bruno Streckenbach, Heydrich's former deputy in the RSHA and the Einsatzgruppen supervisor on 22 May.

In February 1946, Soviet prosecutors tried Piekenbrock, von Bentivegni and Streckenbach and sentenced them to twenty-five years in labour camps later changed to imprisonment. Then, after spending several years in Vladimir Prison, in October 1955, the three were released and returned to Germany. Gehlen surrendered to the Americans and took with him all the Walli I and FHO files. Wessel, Baun and Herre were taken by the Americans also and with Gehlen became the founding fathers of the post-war West German intelligence agency.

Appendix 1

SOVIET INTELLIGENCE AND SECURITY SERVICES

From	To	Service	Chief
20 December 1917	6 February 1922	VCheKa	Felix Dzerzhinsky
6 February 1922	15 November 1923	GPU	Felix Dzerzhinsky
15 November 1923	20 July 1926	OGPU	Felix Dzerzhinsky
20 July 1926	10 May 1934	OGPU	Vyacheslav Menzhinskiy
10 May 1934	25 September 1936	GUGB/NKVD	Genrikh Yagoda
25 September 1936	8 December 1938	GUGB/NKVD	Nikolai Yezhov
8 December 1938	3 February 1941	GUGB/NKVD	Lavrenty Beria
3 February 1941	20 July 1941	NKGB/NKVD	V.N. Merkulov

20 July 1941	14 April 1943	NKVD/GUGB	Lavrenty Beria V.N. Merkulov
14 April 1943	19 March 1946	NKGB	V.N. Merkulov

VCheKa	*Vserossijskaya Chrezvychajnaya Komissiya* (All-Russian Extraordinary Commission for Combating Counter-Revolution, Sabotage and Speculation)
GPU	*Gosudarstvennoe Politicheskoe Upravlenie* (State Political Administration)
OGPU	*Ob'edinennoe Gosudarstvennoe Politicheskoe Upravlenie* (Joint State Political Directorate)
NKVD	*Naródny Komissariát Vnútrennih del* (People's Commissariat for Internal Affairs)
GUGB	*Glavnoe Upravlenie Gosudarstvennoi Bezopastnosti* (NKVD's Chief Directorate for State Security)
NKGB	*Naródny Komissariát Gosudarstvennoi Bezopasnosti* (People's Commissariat for State Security)

Appendix 2

SOVIET MILITARY COUNTERINTELLIGENCE ORGANISATIONS

Created	Military Counterintelligence Unit Name	Leader
10 July 1934	*Osobyi otdel*	M.I.Gai (10 July 1934 – 28 November 1936)
25 December 1936	5 *otdel*	I.M. Leplevsky (28 Nov 1936 – 14 June 1937) N.G. Nikolaev-Zhurid (14 June 1937 – 28 Mar 1938)
28 March 1938	2 *upravlenie*	L.M. Zakovsky (28 March 1938 – 20 April 1938) N.N. Fedorov (20 April 1938 – 29 September 1938)

29 September 1938	4 *otdel*	N.N. Fedorov (29 September 1938 – 20 November 1938) V.M. Bochkov (28 December 1938 – 23 August 1940) A.N. Mikheev (23 August 1940 – 3 February 1941)
3 February 1941	3 *Upravlenie*	A.N. Mikheev (3 February 1941 – 19 July 1941)
3 February 1941	3 *Upravlenie*	A.I. Petrov (3 February 1941 – 10 January 1942)
3 February 1941	3 *otdel*	A.M. Belyanov (3 February 1941 – 19 July 1941)
17 July 1941	*Upravlenie osobykh otdelov*	V.S. Abakumov (19 April 1941 – 14 April 1943)
19 April 1943	*Glannoe upravlenie kontrrazvedki*	V.S. Abakumov (19 April 1943 – 27 April 1946)
19 April 1943	*Upravlenie kontrrazvedki*	P.A. Gladkov (19 April 1943 – Jul 1944)
19 April 1943	*Otdel kontrrazvedki*	S.P. Yukhimovich (19 Aprril 1943 – 19 July 1944) V.I.Smirnov (July 1944 – 19 March 1946)

Osobyi otdel	OO GUGB / NKVD (Special Department of the Main State Security Directorate)
5 *otdel*	GUGB / NKVD (5th GUGB Department)
2 *upravlenie*	UOO / NKVD (*Upravlenie Osobykh Otdelov*) (2nd Directorate)
4 *otdel*	GUGB / NKVD (4th GUGB Department)

3 *Upravlenie* (Mikheev)	3rd NKO Directorate
3 *Upravlenie* (Petrov)	3rd NKVFM Directorate
3 *otdel*	3rd NKVD Department
Upravlenie osobykh otdelov	UOO/NKVD (Special Departments Directorate)
Glannoe upravlenie kontrrazvedki	GUKR/SMERSH/NKO (Main Counterintelligence Directorate SMERSH)
Upravlenie kontrrazvedki	UKR/SMERSH/NKVFM (Counterintelligence Directorate SMERSH)
Otdel kontrrazvedki	OKR/SMERSH/NKVD/MVD (Counterintelligence Department SMERSH)

STRUCTURE OF SOVIET INTELLIGENCE

Appendix 3–5. The following charts are approximations since the structures changed throughout the war, but they give a good guide.

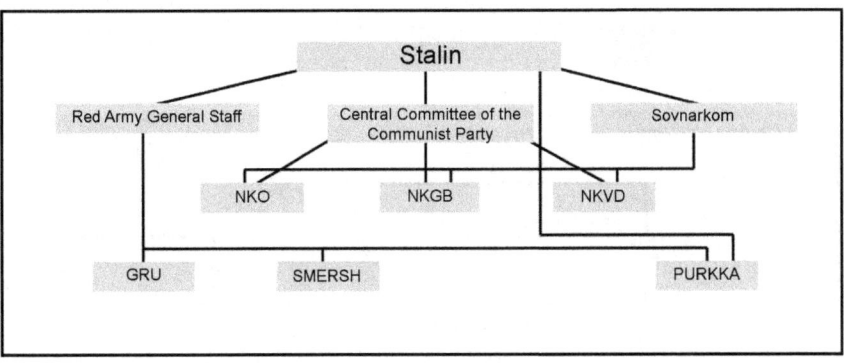

Sovnarkom	Council of People's Commissars
NKO	People's Commissariat for Defence
NKGB	People's Commissariat for State Security
NKVD	People's Commissariat for Internal Affairs
GRU	Armed Services Intelligence
SMERSH	Directorate for Counterespionage
PURKKA	Political Directorate of the People's Commissariat for National Defence

Appendix 4

ABWEHR COMMAND AND OPERATIONS STRUCTURE

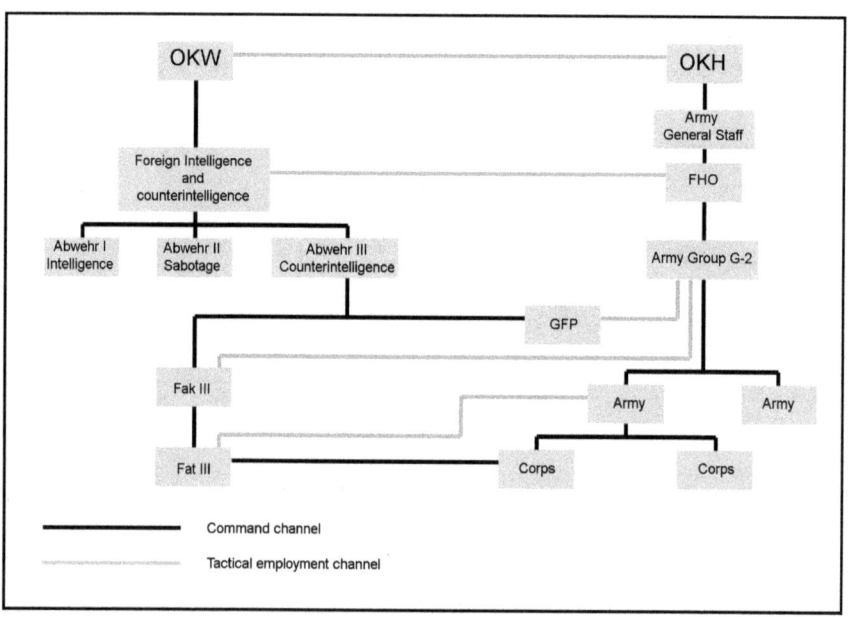

OKW   *Oberkommando der Wehrmacht* (German Armed Forces High Command

OKH   *Oberkommando des Heeres* (German Army High Command)

FHO   *Fremde Heere Ost* (Foreign Armies east)

Army Group G-2	German General Staff Intelligence (the army group commander of the G-2 provided assistance for the army group Abwehr officer in FAK III, with additional help from the GFP)
GFP	Geheime Feldpolizei (Secret Field Police)
Fak III	Frontaufklrungscommando III
Fat III	Frontaufkldrungstrupp III

Appendix 5

MOBILE ABWEHR UNITS ON THE EASTERN FRONT

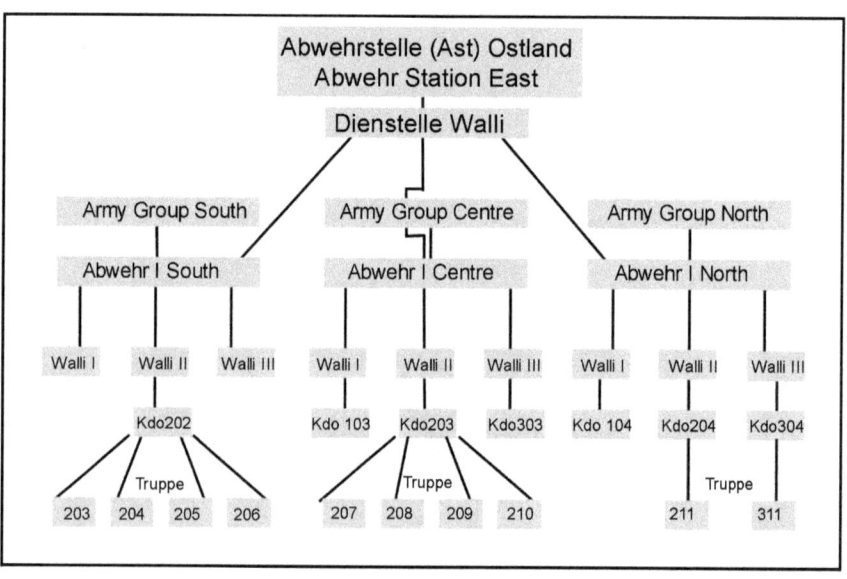

NOTES

Chapter 1: Intelligence and Counterintelligence

1   Yarhi-Milo, Karen, *Knowing the Adversary* (Princeton University Press, 2014), p.1

2   Stephan, Robert W., *Stalin's Secret War* (University Press of Kansas, 2004), p.45

3   Ridley, Norman, *The Role of Intelligence in the Battle of Britain* (Pen & Sword Books, 2022), p.viii

4   Overy, Richard, *Strategic Intelligence and the Outbreak of the Second World War* (War in History, Volume 5, Number 4, 1998), p.453

5   Imperial War Museum, FO Box 156 Göring interrogation, p.3

6   Stephan, *Stalin's Secret War*, p.55

Chapter 2: The Early Years of Soviet Intelligence

1   https://spartacus-educational.com/RUSDzerzhinsky.htm

2   Carr, E.H., *The Origin and Status of the VCheKa* (Soviet Studies 10),

3   Berstein, Vadim, *Smersh: Stalin's Secret Weapon* (Backbite Publishing, Kindle edition), p.30

4   Colonna, Antonella, *The Establishment of the Russian Intelligence* (Centro Studi University, Rome, 2018)

5   ibid

6   Pringle, Robert W., *Guide to Soviet and Russian Intelligence Services* (Journal of US Intelligence Studies, 2011), p.51

Chapter 3: The Abwehr

1   Paine, Lauran, *German Military Intelligence in World War II, The Abwehr* (Military Heritage Press, 1984), p.31

2   Winks, Robin W., *Cloak & Gown: Scholars in the Secret War, 1939–1961* (Yale University Press, 1996), p.281

3   Trevor-Roper, Hugh, *The Last Days of Hitler* (University of Chicago Press, 1992), p.75

4   Davies, Norman, *No Simple Victory: World War II in Europe, 1939–1945* (Viking, 2008), p.251

5   Trevor-Roper, p.75

6   Pahl, Magnus, *Fremde Heere Ost: Hitlers militärische Feindaufklärung* (Ch. Links Verlag, 2012), p.57

7   Paine, p.35

8   Stephan, *Stalin's Secret War*, p.122

9   ibid, p.35

Chapter 4: Secret German-Soviet Cooperation

1   Gatzke, Heinz W., *Russo-German Military Collaboration During the Weimar Republic* (The American Historical Review Volume LXIII, Number 3, 1958), p.588

2   Ridley, Norman, *The Road to Barbarossa* (Pen & Sword Books, 2023), p.9

3   ibid, p.10

4   ibid, p.100

5   Stephan, *Stalin's Secret War*, p.125

6   Roberts, Geoffrey, *The Soviet Union and the Origins of the Second World War: Russo-German Relations and the Road to War 1933–1941* (Palgrave, 1995), p.15

7   Ridley, Norman, *The Road to Barbarossa*, Pen and Sword, 2023 p.170

Chapter 5: Soviet Intelligence Before Barbarossa

1   Murphy, David E., *What Stalin Knew, The Enigma of Barbarossa* (Yale University Press, 2005), p.57

2   Kuromiya, Hiroaki, *Stalin's Great Terror and Espionage* (Indiana University, 2009), p.10

3   Czak, Steven, *Soviet Intelligence on the Eve of War 1939–1941* (University of Calgary, 2014), p.51

4   ibid, p.44

5   Murphy, p.11

6   ibid, p.16

7   '*Izvestia*' of CPSU Central Committee, No. 1 (1990), pp.193–208

8   '*Iz svodki 5 upravleniia RKKA po sobytiiam na zapade*, 13 June 1940', in Gavrilov 2008, 434–435,

9 Ellis, Frank, *Barbarossa 1941: Reframing Hitler's Invasion of Stalin's Soviet Empire* (Modern War Studies, University Press of Kansas, Kindle edition), p.173

10 *'Iz svodki 5 upravleniia* RKKA *o polozhenii v Germanii,* 21 June 1940', in Gavrilov 2008, 438–439

11 *'Soobshchenie "Meteora" iz Berlina o perebroske nemetskikh chastei na vostok,* 9 July 1940', in Gavrilov 2008, 440.101

12 *'Agenturnoe soobshchenie "Ramzaia" iz Tokio o napravlennosti trekhstoronnego pakta,* 8 October 1940,' in Gavrilov 2008, 477

13 Ellis, p.179

14 ibid, p.190

15 ibid, p.193

16 *'Spetssoobshchenie razvedyvatel'nogo upravleniia general nogo shtaba Krasnoi Armii "O mobilizatsionnykh meropriiatiiakh v sopredel'nykh s SSSR kapitalisticheskikh stranakh",* 14 February 1941', in Gavrilov 2008, 532–535

17 Czak, p.68

18 Brower, Daniel R., *The Soviet Union and the German Invasion of 1941: A New Soviet View* (The Journal of Modern History, Volume 41, Number 3, 1969), p.332

19 Ellis, p.124

20 Czak, p.73

21 Erickson, John, *The Soviet High Command* (Macmillan, 1962), p.577

22 Kokoshin, Andrei A., *The German Blitzkrieg against the USSR, 1941* (Belfer Center, 2016), p.44

23 Suvorov, Viktor, *Who Was Planning to Attack Whom in June 1941, Hitler or Stalin* (Military History, Volume 130, Issue 2, 2008), p.50

24 Ellis, p.444

25 Brower, p.332

26 Gilbert, Martin, *Golden Eggs: The Secret War, 1940–1945, Part II – Intelligence and the Eastern Front* (International Churchill Society, 2013)

27 ENIGMA decrypt CX/MSS/59/T10

28 'Personal', Kremlin, Moscow, 7 November 1942: Churchill papers, 20/82

29 Erickson, The Soviet High Command, p.569

30 Czak, p.90

31 Murphy, p.180

32 Erickson, The Soviet High Command, p.579

33 Kuromiya, p.2

Chapter 6: German Intelligence before Barbarossa

1   Paine, p.50

2   Stephan, *Stalin's Secret War*, p.124

3   ibid, p.50

4   ibid, p.50

5   ibid, p.569

6   ibid, p.225

7   Pahl, *Fremde Heere Ost*, p.64

8   Pahl, Magnus, '*My strength is My Mistrust*': Hitler and His Military *Intelligence on the Eastern Front*, (German Historical Institute, London, 2020), p.108

9   Kahn, David, *Hitler's Spies, German Military Intelligence in World War II* (Macmillan, 1978), p.115

10 Wadman, David, *Aufklärer Luftwaffe Reconnaissance Aircraft and Units 1935–1941* (Midland, 2007), p.15

11 Neilson, Andreas L., *The German Air Force General Staff* (USAF Historical Studies, No, 173, 1959), p.35

12 Wadman, p.15

13 Kahn, p.428

14 Pahl, *Fremde Heere Ost*, p.76

15 ibid, p.77

16 Erickson, *The Soviet High Command*, p.574

17 Kahn, p.254

Chapter 7: Operation Barbarossa

1   Kravchenko, Viktor, *I Chose Freedom: The Personal and Political Life of a Soviet Official* (Scribbners, 1946), p.374

2   Boog, Horst, Forster, Jurgen and Hoffman, Joachim, *Militargeschichtliches Forschungsamt, Germany and the Second World War: Volume 4* (Oxford University Press, 2015), p.323

3   Fugate, Bryan, *Operation Barbarossa: Strategy and Tactics on the Eastern Front, 1941*, (Presidio Press, 1984)

4   Erickson, *The Soviet High Command*, p.566

5   ibid, p.575

6   Ellis, p.256

7   Kahn, p.460

Chapter 8: German Field Intelligence

1   Kahn, p.249

2   Höhne, Heinze and Zolling, Hermann, *The General Was a Spy* (Pan Books, 1972), p.16

3   Stephan, *Stalin's Secret War*, p.225

4   Pahl, *'My Strength is My Mistrust'*, p.119

5   *Espionage – Sabotage – Conspiracy: German and Russian Operations 1940–1945*, (Office of Naval Intelligence, 1947), p.29

6   ibid, p.51

7   ibid

Chapter 9: Operation Kremlin

1   Stephan, *Stalin's Secret War*, p.29

2   Donohue, Alan P., *Operation Kreml: German Strategic Deception on the eastern Front in 1942, Chapter 5 Weaving the Tangled Web* (Army University Press, Fort Leavenworth, Kansas, 2018), p.94

Chapter 10: Stalingrad

1   Gehlen, Reinhard, *The Service* (World Publishing, 1972), p.59

2   King, Curtis S., *Operation Bagration: Maskirovka at its Height, Summer 1944, Chapter 7 Weaving the Tangled Web* (Army University Press, Fort Leavenworth, Kansas, 2018), p.115

3   Svenson, Nils Charlie Gunnar, *Sovjetisk maskirovka under Operation Bagration set gennem NATOs principper for vildledning* (Institut for Strategi og Krigsstudier, 2022)

4   Glantz, David M., *Soviet Military Deception in the Second World War* (American Intelligence Journal, Volume 12, Number 1, 1991), p.90

5   Pahl, *'My Strength is My Mistrust'*, p.109

6   Gehlen, p.21

7   Höhne, Heinze and Zolling, Hermann, p.11

8   Pahl, *'My strength is My Mistrust'*, p.114

9   Glantz, *Soviet Military Deception in the Second World War*, p.135

10 Thomas, David, *Foreign Armies East and German Military Intelligence in Russia 1941–45* (Journal of Contemporary History, Volume 22, Number 2, 1987), 282

11 Glantz, *Soviet Military Deception in the Second World War*, p.157

12 Glantz, David M., *The Fundamentals of Soviet Razvedka* (Soviet Army Studies Office, Fort Leavenworth, Kansas, 1989), p.7

13   Kurlat, F.L. and Studnikov, L.A., *Brigada osobogo naznacheniia* (Voprosy istorii No 9, 1982), p.95

14   Ridley, Norman, *Reinhard Gehlen: Hitler's Spymaster*, (Pen & Sword Books, 2023)

15   Thomas, p.285

Chapter 11: German Signals Intelligence

1   Critical Analysis of German Operational Intelligence Part II, (nsa.gov)

2   Ridley, *Reinhard Gehlen: Hitler's Spymaster*

3   Kokoshin, p.38

4   Praun, Albert, *German Radio Intelligence* (Historical Division Headquarters, European Command, Department of the Army, 1953), p.94

Chapter 12: Soviet Partisans

1   Howell, Edgar M., *The Soviet Partisan Movement 1941-1944*, (Department of the Army, Washington DC, 1956), p.211

2   ibid, p.43

3   OKW, WFSt/L (1 Op.), Ergaenzung zur Weisung 33, 23.7.41, NMT C-52/GB-485 file

4   *Befh. d. Rueckw. H. Geb. Mitte, Ia, Zufuehrung weiterer Sicherungskraefte*, 14.12.41, *H. Geb.* 14684/file

5   Howell, p.51

6   ibid, p.64

7   ibid, p.354

8   ibid, p.117

9   ibid, p.157

10   ibid, p.164

11   ibid, p.185

12   Stephan, *Stalin's Secret War*, p.211

Chapter 13: Operation Citadel

1   Erickson, John, *The Road to Berlin* (Westview, 1984), p.122

2   Tittenhofer, Mark A., *The Rote Drei: Getting Behind the Lucy Myth* (CIA Historical Review Program, 1993)

3   Mulligan, Timothy P., *Spies, Ciphers and 'Zitadelle': Intelligence and the Battle of Kursk, 1943*, (Journal of Contemporary History, Volume 22, Number 2, 1987), p.237

4   ibid, p.239

5   ibid, p.243

6   Kahn, p.436

7   ibid, p.418

8   Zamulin, V.N., *The Red Army's Plans in Documents of German Intelligence Agencies Prior to Operation Citadel* (Southwest State University Kursk, 2022, p.742

9   ibid, p.745

10   ibid, p.746

11   ibid, p.743

12   Gehlen, p.67

13   ibid, p.68

14   Glantz, *Soviet Military Deception in the Second World War*, p.199

15   ibid, p.202

16   Stephan, *Stalin's Secret War*, p.123

Chapter 14: Soviet Counterintelligence

1   Stephan, *Stalin's Secret War*, p.73

2   OO Directive No. 003260, Southern Front, dated November 18, 1941, in Organy gosudarstvennoi bezopasnosti, 3 (2), 316–8

3   Berstein, Vadim, *Smersh; Stalin's Secret Weapon* (Backbite Publishing, Kindle edition), p.168

4   Arbatov, Georgii, *Nastupali po gogolevskim mestam* (Novaya gazeta, No. 86, 2006)

5   Stephan, *Stalin's Secret War*, p.58

6   ibid, p.61

7   ibid, p.88

8   ibid, p.104

9   Ridley, Norman, *Hitler's Gold*, (Pen & Sword Books, 2023), p.150

10   Stephan, *Stalin's Secret War*, p.110

Chapter 15: Operation Monastery

1   Stephan, *Stalin's Secret War*, p.155

2   ibid, p.160

3   Kahn, p.314

4   ibid, p.312

5   Stephan, *Stalin's Secret War*, p.165

6   Kahn, p.312

7   Stephan, *Stalin's Secret War*, p.168

8   ibid

9   ibid, p.172

10   Berstein, p.227

Chapter 16: Smersh

1   Stephan, Robert W., *Smersh: Soviet Military Counter-Intelligence During the Second World War* (Journal of Contemporary History, Volume 22, Number 4), p.591

2   Litera, Bohuslav, *Smersh: The Activities of the Soviet Military Counterintelligence During the Second World War* (Acta Universitatis Carolinae, 2001), p.40

3   Berstein, p.252

4   Pringle, p.122

5   Stephan, Smersh: *Soviet Military Counter-Intelligence During the Second World War*, p.591

6   Litera, p.45

7   Berstein, p.39

8   Shapiro, Julia, *Nazi Conspirator, Russian Patriot: Judging General Andrei Vlasov* (College of Liberal Arts and Sciences, University of Florida, 2022)

9   Berstein, p.341

Chapter 17: Operation Zeppelin

1   Chuev, S.G., *Spetssluzhby III Reikha. Kniga 1 and II* (St Petersburg, Neva, 2003), p.192

2   Zeppelin Company, wikidata.de/Unternehmen Zeppelin

3   CIA Situation Report No 8. SF/52/4/22/10, 1946

4   Zhukov, Dmitry Alexandrovish, *1-я русская бригада СС 'Дружина'* [1st Russian SS brigade 'Druzhina']. Veche (Kovtun, I.I. 2010), p.175

5   Glantz, *Soviet Military Deception in the Second World War*, p.245

6   Nes, H. van, *Bagration: Study of the Destruction of Army Group Centre during the Summer of 1944 as Seen From the Point of View of Military Intelligence*, (1985 Art of War Symposium, From the Dnepr to the Vistula: Soviet Offensive Operations, November 1943, p.57

7   ibid, p.58

8   Glantz, *Soviet Military Deception in the Second World War*, p.367

Chapter 18: Operation Berezino

1   www.deviantart.com/crassor/art/Operation-Berezino-
     Intelligence-18-1043689213

2   ibid

3   ibid

Chapter 19: Operation Bagration

1   Stephan, *Stalin's Secret War*, p.148

2   CIA file ASGF. 52/20, The German Intelligence Service and the War, cia.
     gov

3   Berstein, p.428

4   King, p.121

5   ibid, p.123

6   Nes, p.264

7   Merhi, Wassim, *Through the Lens of Systems Thinking: Operation Bagration
     and the Insights on Contemporary Operational Art* (School of Advanced
     Military Studies, US Army Command and General Staff College Fort
     Leavenworth, 2019), p.32

8   Nes, p.274

9   Glanz, David M. and House, Jonathan M., *When Titans Clashed: How the
     Red Army Stopped Hitler* (University Press of Kansas, 2015), p.267

Postscript

1   Thomas, p.288

2   Kahn, p.447

3   ibid, p.532

4   ibid p.539

SOURCES AND BIBLIOGRAPHY

Arbatov, Georgii, *Nastupali po gogolevskim mestam* (Novaya gazeta, No. 86, 2006)

Berstein, Vadim, *Smersh; Stalin's Secret Weapon* (Backbite Publishing, Kindle edition)

Biddiscomb, Perry, *Unternehmen Zeppelin: The Deployment of SS Saboteurs and Spies in the Soviet Union, 1942–1945*, (Europe-Asia Studies Volume 52, Number 6, 2000)

Boog, Horst, Forster, Jurgen and Hoffman, Joachim, *Militargeschichtliches Forschungsamt, Germany and the Second World War: Volume 4*, (Oxford University Press, 2015)

Brower, Daniel R., *The Soviet Union and the German Invasion of 1941: A New Soviet View* (The Journal of Modern History, Volume 41, Number 3, 1969)

Burden, Anthony, *An Analysis of Why Stalin is to Blame for the German Invasion* (University of Alberta, undated)

Campbell, Kenneth, *Walter Schellenberg: SD Chief* (American Intelligence Journal, Volume 25, 2007)

Carr, E.H., *The Origin and Status of the VCheKa* (Soviet Studies 10)

Chuev, S.G., *Spetssluzhby III Reikha. Kniga 1 and II* (St Petersburg, Neva, 2003)

Colonna, Antonella, The Establishment of the Russian Intelligence, (Centro Studi University, Rome, 2018)

Czak, Steven, *Soviet Intelligence on the Eve of War 1939–1941*, (University of Calgary, 2014)

Davies, Norman, *No Simple Victory: World War II in Europe, 1939–1945* (Viking, 2008)

Donohue, Alan P., *Operation Kreml: German Strategic Deception on the Eastern Front in 1942, Chapter 5 Weaving the Tangled Web*, (Army University Press, Fort Leavenworth, Kansas, 2018)

Ellis, Frank, *Barbarossa 1941: Reframing Hitler's Invasion of Stalin's Soviet Empire*, (Modern War Studies, University Press of Kansas, Kindle edition)

Erickson, John, *The Road to Berlin*, (Westview, 1984)

Erickson, John, *The Soviet High Command*, (Macmillan, 1962)

Farmer, Rachel, *Shocking but not Surprising, British and Soviet Intelligence Surrounding Operation Barbarossa* (Tsinghua Review, Volume 2 Number 1, 2022)

Ferris, John Robert, *Intelligence and Strategy* (Routledge, 2005)

Fugate, Bryan, *Operation Barbarossa: Strategy and Tactics on the Eastern Front, 1941* (Presidio Press, 1984)

Gatzke, Heinz W., *Russo-German Military Collaboration During the Weimar Republic* (The American Historical Review Volume LXIII, Number 3, 1958)

Gehlen, Reinhard, *The Service* (World Publishing, 1972)

Gilbert, Martin, *Golden Eggs: The Secret War, 1940–1945, Part II – Intelligence and the Eastern Front* (International Churchill Society, 2013)

Glantz, David M., *Soviet Military Deception in the Second World War* (American Intelligence Journal, Volume 12, Number 1, 1991)

Glantz, David M., *The Fundamentals of Soviet Razvedka* (Soviet Army Studies Office, Fort Leavenworth, Kansas, 1989)

Glantz, David M., *Soviet Operational Intelligence in the Kursk Operation* (Soviet Army Studies Office, Fort Leavenworth, Kansas, 1988)

Glantz, David M., *Soviet Military Deception in the Second World War* (Frank Cass, 1989)

Glanz, David M. and House, Jonathan M., *When Titans Clashed: How the Red Army Stopped Hitler*, (University Press of Kansas, 2015)

Hamilton, David L., *Deception in Soviet Military Doctrine and Operations* (Naval Postgraduate School Monterey, 1986)

Höhne, Heinze and Zolling, Hermann, *The General was a Spy* (Pan Books, 1972)

Holcomb, James F., *Soviet Special Operations: the Legacy of the Great Patriotic War* (Soviet Army Studies Office, US Army Combined Arms Center, Fort Leavenworth, Kansas, 1987)

Howell, Edgar M., *The Soviet Partisan Movement 1941–1944*, (Department of the Army, Washington DC, 1956)

Hubbard-Hall, C. and O'Sullivan, A., *Landscapes of intelligence in the Third Reich: visualising Abwehr Operations During the Second World War* (Journal of Intelligence History, 2020)

Johnson, Ian Ona, *Faustain Bargain, The Soviet-German Partnership and and the Origins of the Second World War* (Oxford University Press, Kindle edition, 2021)

Jordan, Jonathan W., *Operation Bagration* (World War II Magazine, July/August, 2006)

Jordan, Jonathan W., *Soviet Offensive of 1944* (World War II Magazine, July/August, 2006)

Kahn, David, *Hitler's Spies, German Military Intelligence in World War II* (Macmillan, 1978)

King, Curtis S., *Operation Bagration: Maskirovka at its Height, Summer 1944, Chapter 7 Weaving the Tangled Web* (Army University Press, Fort Leavenworth, Kansas, 2018)

Kokoshin, Andrei A., *The German Blitzkrieg Against the USSR, 1941* (Belfer Center, 2016)

Kravchenko, Viktor, *I Chose Freedom: The Personal and Political Life of a Soviet Official*, (Scribbners, 1946)

Kurlat, F.L. and Studnikov, L.A., *Brigada Osobogo Naznacheniia* (Voprosy istorii No. 9, 1982)

Kuromiya, Hiroaki, *Stalin's Great Terror and Espionage* (Indiana University, 2009)

Litera, Bohuslav, *Smersh: The Activities of the Soviet Military Counterintelligence During the Second World War* (Acta Universitatis Carolinae, 2001)

McTaggart, Pat, *Soviet Partisans: The Rag-Tag Scourge Along WWII's Eastern Front* (warfarehistorynetwork.com/article/soviet-partisans-the-rag-tag-scourge-along-wwiis-eastern-front/, 2006)

Merhi, Wassim, *Through the Lens of Systems Thinking: Operation Bagration and the Insights on Contemporary Operational Art* (School of Advanced Military Studies, US Army Command and General Staff College Fort Leavenworth, 2019)

Mihalka, Michael, *German Strategic Deception in the 1930s*, (Office of the Secretary of Defence, 1980)

Moullec, Gaël-Georges, *Soviet Intelligence on the Eve of the Great Patriotic War*, (Volume 3, Issue 1, 2020)

Mueller, Michael, *Canaris, The Life and Death of Hitler's Spymaster* (Frontline Books, 2007)

Müller, Rolf-Dieter, *Reinhard Gehlen, Geheimdienstchef im Hintergrund der Bonner Republik, Die Biografie, 1902–1979* (Christoph Links Verlag GmbH, 2018)

Mulligan, Timothy P., *Spies, Ciphers and 'Zitadelle': Intelligence and the Battle of Kursk, 1943* (Journal of Contemporary History Volume 22, Number 2, 1987)

Murphy, David E., *What Stalin Knew, The Enigma of Barbarossa* (Yale University Press, 2005)

Neilson, Andreas L., *The German Air Force General Staff* (USAF Historical Studies No. 173, 1959)

Nes, H. van, *Bagration: Study of the Destruction of Army Group Centre During the Summer of 1944 as Seen From the Point of View of Military Intelligence* (1985 Art of War Symposium, From the Dnepr to the Vistula: Soviet Offensive Operations, November 1943 – August 1944, A Transcript of Proceedings, (Carlisle Barracks, PA, US Army War College, 1985)

Okami, Jun, *Von Seeckt 1920–1926: A Study of Military Management* (University of Surrey, 1998)

Overy, Richard, *Strategic Intelligence and the Outbreak of the Second World War* (War in History, Volume 5, Number 4, 1998)

Paehler, Katrin, *The Third Reich's Intelligence Services, The Career of Walter Schellenberg* (Cambridge University Press, 2017)

Pahl, Magnus, *'My strength is My Mistrust': Hitler and His Military Intelligence on the Eastern Front* (German Historical Institute, London, 2020)

Pahl, Magnus, *Fremde Heere Ost: Hitler's Militärische Feindaufklärung* (Ch. Links Verlag, 2012)

Paine, Lauran, *German Military Intelligence in World War II, The Abwehr*, (Military Heritage Press, 1984)

Praun, Albert, *German Radio Intelligence* (Historical Division Headquarters, European Command, Department of the Army, 1953)

Pringle, Robert W., *Guide to Soviet and Russian Intelligence Services* (Journal of US Intelligence Studies, 2011)

Pringle, Robert W., *Military Counterintelligence and Stalin's Control of the USSR* (International Journal of Intelligence and Counterintelligence No. 21)

Radomska, Sofiya, *Soviet-German Relations in the Inter-War Period* (Södertörns högskola University College, Stockholm, 2006)

Reese, Mary Ellen, *General Reinhard Gehlen: The CIA Connection* (George Mason University Press, 1990)

Ridley, Norman, *The Role of Intelligence in the Battle of Britain* (Pen & Sword Books, 2022)

Ridley, Norman, *Hitler's Gold*, (Pen & Sword Books, 2023)

Ridley, Norman, *The Road to Barbarossa* (Pen & Sword Books, 2023)

Roberts, Geoffrey, *The Soviet Union and the Origins of the Second World War: Russo-German Relations and the Road to War 1933–1941*, (Palgrave, 1995)

Rotundo, Louis, *Stalin and the Outbreak of War in 1941* (Journal of Contemporary History, Volume 24, Number 2, 1989)

Sella, Amnon, *Barbarossa: Surprise Attack and Communication*, (Journal of Contemporary History, Volume 13, Number 3, 1978)

Shapiro, Julia, *Nazi Conspirator, Russian Patriot: Judging General Andrei Vlasov* (College of Liberal Arts and Sciences, University of Florida, 2022)

Skorzeny, Otto, *My Command Operations: The Memoirs of Hitler's Most Daring Commando* (Schiffer Publishing Limited, 1998)

Smith, Robert C., *The State of Strategic Intelligence, June 1941: The War With Russia – Operation Barbarossa* (Merriam Press, 2020)

Snyder, Timothy, *Bloodlands, Europe Between Hitler and Stalin* (Vintage, Kindle edition)

Stephan, Robert W., *Smersh: Soviet Military Counter-Intelligence During the Second World War* (*Journal of Contemporary History*, Volume 22, Number 4)

Stephan, Robert W., *Stalin's Secret War* (University Press of Kansas, 2004)

Steven, Czak, *Soviet Intelligence on the Eve of War,1939–1941* (University of Calgary, 2014)

Stewart, Kermit G., *Russian Methods of Interrogating Captured Personnel in WWII* (Department of the Army, 1951)

Stolfi, Russel H.S., Ratley, Lonnie O., O'Neill. John F., *German Disruption of Soviet Command, Control and Communications in Operation Barbarossa, 1941* (Naval Postgraduate School Monterey, 1983)

Suvorov, Viktor, *Who Was planning to Attack Whom in June 1941, Hitler or Stalin*, (Military History, Volume 130, Issue 2, 2008)

Svenson, Nils Charlie Gunnar, *Sovjetisk Maskirovka Under Operation Bagration Set Gennem NATOs Principper for Vildledning* (Institut for Strategi og Krigsstudier, 2022)

Thomas, David, *Foreign Armies East and German Military Intelligence in Russia 1941–45* (Journal of Contemporary History, Volume 22, Number 2, 1987)

Tittenhofer, Mark A., *The Rote Drei: Getting Behind the Lucy Myth* (CIA Historical Review Program, 1993)

Trevor-Roper, Hugh, *The Last Days of Hitler* (University of Chicago Press, 1992)

Valenta, Jiri, *Deception in Soviet Military Doctrine and Operations* (Naval Postgarduate School, Monterey, 1986)

Vautrinot, Kyle B., *Red Star Resurgent: Soviet Deception Operations at Stalingrad, 1942–1943, Chapter 6 Weaving the Tangled Web* (Army University Press, Fort Leavenworth, Kansas, 2018)

Vilasi, Antonella Colonna, *The Establishment of the Russian Intelligence* (Sociilogy Mind, 2018)

Wadman, David, *Aufklärer Luftwaffe Reconnaissance Aircraft and Units 1935–1941*, (Midland, 2007)

Wheeler, Douglas L., *Intelligence Between The World Wars 1919–1939* (Journal of US Intelligence Studies, 2013)

Winks, Robin W., *Cloak & Gown: Scholars in the Secret War, 1939–1961*, (Yale University Press, 1996)

Yarhi-Milo, Karen, *Knowing the Adversary* (Princeton University Press, 2014)

Zamulin, V.N., *The Red Army's Plans in Documents of German Intelligence Agencies Prior to Operation Citadel* (Southwest State University Kursk, 2022)

Critical Analysis of German Operational Intelligence Part II (nsa.gov)

The German Intelligence Service and the War (cia.gov, 2014)

Study of Intelligence and Counterintelligence Activities on the Eastern Front and in Adjascent Areas During WWII, (cia.gov, 1964)

German Counterintelligence Operations in Occupied Russia 1941–1944 (Office of the Chief of Military History, Department of the Army, 1953)

The Great German Campaign in Russia – Planning and Operations 1940–1942, (Department of the Army, 1955)

The Vlasov Case: History of a Betrayal (The Russian State Archive of Social and Political History, Volume 2, 2020)

German Radio Intelligence (Department of the Army Office of the Chief of Military History, 1950)

Experiences of Ic and Abwehr Personnel (cia.gov, 2001)

INDEX